GUIDE TO FINANCIAL MARKETS

OTHER ECONOMIST BOOKS

Guide to Analysing Companies
Guide to Business Modelling
Guide to Business Planning
Guide to Cash Management
Guide to Commodities
Guide to Decision Making
Guide to Economic Indicators
Guide to Emerging Markets
Guide to the European Union
Guide to Financial Management
Guide to Hedge Funds
Guide to Investment Strategy
Guide to Management Ideas and Gurus
Guide to Managing Growth
Guide to Organisation Design
Guide to Project Management
Guide to Supply Chain Management
Numbers Guide
Style Guide

Book of Business Quotations
Book of Isms
Book of Obituaries
Brands and Branding
Business Consulting
Business Strategy
Buying Professional Services
Doing Business in China
Economics
Managing Talent
Managing Uncertainty
Marketing
Marketing for Growth
Megachange – the world in 2050
Modern Warfare, Intelligence and Deterrence
Organisation Culture
Successful Strategy Execution
The World of Business

Directors: an A–Z Guide
Economics: an A–Z Guide
Investment: an A–Z Guide
Negotiation: an A–Z Guide

Pocket World in Figures

GUIDE TO FINANCIAL MARKETS

Why they exist and how they work

Sixth edition

Marc Levinson

THE ECONOMIST IN ASSOCIATION WITH
PROFILE BOOKS LTD

Published by Profile Books Ltd
3a Exmouth House
Pine Street
London EC1R 0JH
www.profilebooks.com

Typeset in EcoType by MacGuru Ltd
info@macguru.org.uk

Printed in Great Britain by Clays, Bungay, Suffolk

A CIP catalogue record for this book is available from the British Library

Hardback ISBN: 978 1 78125 106 5
Paperback ISBN: 978 1 78125 107 2
e-book ISBN: 978 1 84765 953 8

The paper this book is printed on is certified by the
© 1996 Forest Stewardship Council A.C. (FSC).
It is ancient-forest friendly. The printer holds FSC chain of custody SGS-COC-2061

FSC
www.fsc.org
MIX
Paper from
responsible sources
FSC® C018072

Contents

1 Why markets matter   1
2 Foreign-exchange markets   17
3 Money markets   44
4 Bond markets   70
5 Securitisation   111
6 International fixed-income markets   137
7 Equity markets   154
8 Futures and options markets   197
9 Derivatives markets   253

Index   275

1 Why markets matter

THE EURO IS SLIGHTLY HIGHER against the yen. The Dow Jones Industrial Average is off 18 points in active trading. A Chinese airline loses millions of dollars with derivatives. Following the Bank of England's decision to lower its base rate, monthly mortgage payments are set to fall.

All these events are examples of financial markets at work. That markets exercise enormous influence over modern life comes as no news. But although people around the world speak glibly of "Wall Street", "the bond market" and "the currency markets", the meanings they attach to these time-worn phrases are often vague and usually out of date. This book explains the purposes different financial markets serve and clarifies the way they work. It cannot tell you whether your investment portfolio is likely to rise or to fall in value. But it may help you understand how its value is determined, and how the different securities in it are created and traded.

In the beginning

The word "market" usually conjures up an image of the bustling, paper-strewn floor of the New York Stock Exchange or of traders motioning frantically in the futures pits of Chicago. These images themselves are out of date, as almost all of the dealing once done face to face is now handled computer to computer, often with minimal human intervention. And formal exchanges such as these are only one aspect of the financial markets, and far from the most important one. There were financial markets long before there were exchanges and, in fact, long before there was organised trading of any sort.

Financial markets have been around ever since mankind settled down to growing crops and trading them with others. After a bad harvest, those early farmers would have needed to obtain seed for the next season's planting, and perhaps to get food to see their families through. Both of these transactions would have required them to obtain credit from others with seed or food to spare. After a good harvest, the farmers would have had to decide whether to trade away their surplus immediately or to store it, a choice that any 21st-century commodities trader would find familiar. The amount of fish those early farmers could obtain for a basket of cassava would have varied day by day, depending upon the catch, the harvest and the weather; in short, their exchange rates were volatile.

The independent decisions of all of those farmers constituted a basic financial market, and that market fulfilled many of the same purposes as financial markets do today.

What do markets do?

Financial markets take many different forms and operate in diverse ways. But all of them, whether highly organised, like the London Stock Exchange, or highly informal, like the money changers on the street corners of some African cities, serve the same basic functions.

- **Price setting.** The value of an ounce of gold or a share of stock is no more, and no less, than what someone is willing to pay to own it. Markets provide price discovery, a way to determine the relative values of different items, based upon the prices at which individuals are willing to buy and sell them.

- **Asset valuation.** Market prices offer the best way to determine the value of a firm or of the firm's assets, or property. This is important not only to those buying and selling businesses, but also to regulators. An insurer, for example, may appear strong if it values the securities it owns at the prices it paid for them years ago, but the relevant question for judging its solvency is what prices those securities could be sold for if it needed cash to pay claims today.

■ **Arbitrage.** In countries with poorly developed financial markets, commodities and currencies may trade at very different prices in different locations. As traders in financial markets attempt to profit from these divergences, prices move towards a uniform level, making the entire economy more efficient.

■ **Raising capital.** Firms often require funds to build new facilities, replace machinery or expand their business in other ways. Shares, bonds and other types of financial instruments make this possible. The financial markets are also an important source of capital for individuals who wish to buy homes or cars, or even to make credit-card purchases.

■ **Commercial transactions.** As well as long-term capital, the financial markets provide the grease that makes many commercial transactions possible. This includes such things as arranging payment for the sale of a product abroad, and providing working capital so that a firm can pay employees if payments from customers run late.

■ **Investing.** The stock, bond and money markets provide an opportunity to earn a return on funds that are not needed immediately, and to accumulate assets that will provide an income in future.

■ **Risk management.** Futures, options and other derivatives contracts can provide protection against many types of risk, such as the possibility that a foreign currency will lose value against the domestic currency before an export payment is received. They also enable the markets to attach a price to risk, allowing firms and individuals to trade risks so they can reduce their exposure to some while retaining exposure to others.

The size of the markets

Estimating the overall size of the financial markets is difficult. It is hard in the first place to decide exactly what transactions should be included under the rubric "financial markets", and there is no way to compile complete data on each of the millions of sales and purchases occurring each year. Total capital market financing was approximately

$6.5 trillion worldwide in 2011, excluding purely domestic loans that were not resold in the form of securities (see Table 1.1).

TABLE 1.1 **Amounts raised in financial markets**
Net of repayments, $bn

	2000	2004	2006	2008	2011
International bank loans	714	1,343	2,816	−1,279	185
International bonds and notes	1,148	1,560	2,617	2,436	1,212
International money-market instruments	87	61	168	82	−6
Domestic bonds and notes	865	2,461	2,322	2,282	2,566
Domestic money-market instruments	377	774	983	1,462	−611
International equity issues	318	214	371	392	485
Domestic equity issues	901	593	717	999	617
Total excluding domestic loans	4,410	7,006	9,994	6,374	4,448

Sources: Bank for International Settlements; World Federation of Exchanges; Thomson Reuters

The figure of $4.5 trillion for 2011, sizeable as it is, represents only a single year's activity. Another way to look at the markets is to estimate the value of all the financial instruments they trade. When measured in this way, the financial markets accounted for $180 trillion of capital in 2011 (see Table 1.2). This figure excludes many important financial activities, such as insurance underwriting, bank lending to individuals and small businesses, and trading in financial instruments such as futures and derivatives that are not means of raising capital. If all of these other financial activities were to be included, the total size of the markets would be much larger.

Cross-border measure

Another way of measuring the growth of finance is to examine the value of cross-border financing. Cross-border finance is by no means new, and at various times in the past (in the late 19th century, for example) it has been quite large relative to the size of the world economy. The period since 1990 has been marked by a huge increase

TABLE 1.2 **The world's financial markets**
Year end, $trn

	2000	2004	2006	2008	2011
International bonds and notes	6.1	13.2	18.4	23.9	28.5
International money-market instruments	0.3	0.7	0.9	1.1	1.0
Domestic bonds and notes	23.8	35.9	49.7	59.7	69.6
Domestic money-market instruments	6.0	8.2	10.1	12.8	11.5
International bank loans	8.3	13.9	18.9	22.5	22.3
Equities	31.1	37.2	50.7	32.6	47.4
Total value outstanding	75.6	109.1	148.7	152.6	180.3

Sources: Bank for International Settlements; World Federation of Exchanges

in the amount of international financing broken by financial crises in Asia and Russia in 1998, the recession in the United States in 2001, and the financial meltdowns of 2008–09 in the United States and 2008–13 in Europe. The total stock of cross-border finance in 2013, including international bank loans and debt issues, was more than $52 trillion, according to the Bank for International Settlements.

Looking strictly at securities provides an even more dramatic picture of the growth of the financial markets. A quarter of a century ago, cross-border purchases and sales of securities amounted to only a tiny fraction of most countries' economic output. Today, annual cross-border share and bond transactions are several times larger than GDP in a number of advanced economies – Japan being a notable exception.

International breakdown

The ways in which firms and governments raise funds in international markets have changed substantially. In 1993, bonds accounted for 59% of international financing. By 1997, before the financial crises in Asia and Russia shook the markets, only 47% of the funds raised on international markets were obtained through bond issues. Equities became an important source of cross-border financing in 2000, when share prices were high, but bonds and loans regained importance in the low-interest-rate environment of 2002–05. In 2008, syndicated lending fell off as lack of capital forced banks to restrain their lending activities. Issuance of international bonds was relatively flat in the years following 2008, as non-financial companies increased their bond issuance even while banks reduced their outstanding bond indebtedness. Table 1.3 lists the amounts of capital raised by the main instruments used in international markets.

TABLE 1.3 **Financing on international capital markets**
Type of instrument, $bn

	2000	**2004**	**2008**	**2012**
Bonds and money-market instruments	1,241	1,621	2,416	705
Equities	317	214	392	630
Syndicated loans	1,485	1,807	1,682	1,841
Total	3,043	3,642	4,490	3,176

Source: Bank for International Settlements

Turn-of-the-century slowdown

By all these measures, financial markets grew rapidly during the 1990s. At the start of the decade, active trading in financial instruments was confined to a small number of countries, and involved mainly the same types of securities, bonds and equities that had dominated trading for two centuries. By the first years of the 21st century, financial markets were thriving in dozens of countries, and new instruments accounted for a large proportion of market dealings.

The expansion of financial-market activity paused in 1998 in response to banking and exchange-rate crises in a number of countries. The crises passed quickly, however, and in 1999 financial-market activity reached record levels following the inauguration of the single European currency, interest-rate decreases in Canada, the UK and Continental Europe, and a generally positive economic picture, marred by only small rises in interest rates, in the United States. Equity-market activity slowed sharply in 2000 and 2001, as share prices fell in many countries, but bond-market activity was robust.

Trading in foreign-exchange markets fell markedly at the turn of the century. Credit and equity markets around the world were buoyant in 2006–07, but then contracted abruptly as financial crisis led to the failures of several major financial institutions and a dramatic reduction in lending. Although credit markets began to recover in 2009, their expansion was subdued because of the prolonged financial crisis affecting the euro zone, recession or sluggish growth in a number of major economies, and new regulatory requirements that constrained bank lending and discouraged use of certain financing methods, notably securitisation. By making large-scale purchases of bonds in 2010–13, the major central banks played a significant role in supporting credit-market expansion to meet the needs of businesses and households.

The long-run trends of increased financial-market activity can be traced to four main factors:

■ **Lower inflation.** Inflation rates around the world have fallen markedly since the 1980s. Inflation erodes the value of financial assets and increases the value of physical assets, such as houses and machines, which will cost far more to replace than they are worth today. When inflation is high, as was the case in the United States, Canada and much of Europe during the 1970s and throughout Latin America in the 1980s, firms avoid raising long-term capital because investors require a high return on investment, knowing that price increases will render much of that return illusory. In a low-inflation environment, however, financial-market investors require less of an inflation premium, as they do not expect general increases in prices to devalue their assets.

■ **Pensions.** A significant change in pension policies occurred in many countries starting in the 1990s. Since the 1930s, and even earlier in some countries, governments have operated pay-as-you-go schemes to provide income to the elderly. These schemes, such as the old age pension in the UK and the social security programme in the United States, tax current workers to pay current pensioners and therefore involve no saving or investment. Changes in demography and working patterns have made pay-as-you-go schemes increasingly costly to support, as there are fewer young workers relative to the number of pensioners. This has stimulated interest in pre-funded individual pensions, whereby each worker has an account in which money must be saved, and therefore invested, until retirement. Although these personal investment accounts have to some extent supplanted firms' private pension plans, they have also led to a huge increase in financial assets in countries where private pension schemes were previously uncommon.

- **Stock and bond market performance.** Many countries' stock and bond markets performed well during most of the 1990s and in the period before 2008, with the global bond-market boom continuing until interest rates began to rise in 2013. Stockmarkets, after several difficult years, rose steeply in many countries in 2012 and 2013. A rapid increase in financial wealth feeds on itself: investors whose portfolios have appreciated are willing to reinvest some of their profits in the financial markets. And the appreciation in the value of their financial assets gives investors the collateral to borrow additional money, which can then be invested.

- **Risk management.** Innovation has generated many new financial products, such as derivatives and asset-backed securities, whose basic purpose is to redistribute risk. This led to enormous growth in the use of financial markets for risk-management purposes. To an extent previously unimaginable, firms and investors could choose which risks they wished to bear and use financial instruments to shed the risks they did not want, or, alternatively, to take on additional risks in the expectation of earning higher returns. The risk that the euro will trade above $1.40 during the next six months, or that the interest rate on long-term US Treasury bonds will rise to 6%, is now priced precisely in the markets, and financial instruments to protect against these contingencies are readily available. The risk management revolution thus resulted in an enormous expansion of financial-market activity. The credit crisis that began in 2007, however, revealed that the pricing of many of these risk-management products did not properly reflect the risks involved.

As a result, these products have become more costly, and are being used more sparingly, than in earlier years.

The investors

The driving force behind financial markets is the desire of investors to earn a return on their assets. This return has two distinct components:

- **Yield** is the income the investor receives while owning an investment.

- **Capital gains** are increases in the value of the investment itself, and are often not available to the owner until the investment is sold.

Investors' preferences vary as to which type of return they prefer, and these preferences, in turn, will affect their investment decisions. Some financial-market products are deliberately designed to offer only capital gains and no yield, or vice versa, to satisfy these preferences. Investors can be divided broadly into two categories:

- **Individuals.** Collectively, individuals own a small proportion of financial assets. Most households in the wealthier countries own some financial assets, often in the form of retirement savings or of shares in the employer of a household member. Most such holdings, however, are quite small, and their composition varies greatly from one country to another. In 2010, equities accounted for 9% of households' financial assets in Germany but 34% in Finland. The great majority of individual investment is controlled by a comparatively small number of wealthy households. Nonetheless, individual investing has become increasingly popular. In the United States, bank certificates of deposit accounted for more than 10% of households' financial assets in 1989 but only 3.9% in 2010, as families shifted their money into securities held in retirement accounts. The 2008–09 stockmarket crash caused households to hold a smaller proportion of their assets in equities, but the extremely low interest rates available on bond investments and bank deposits drove individual investors back towards equities in 2013.

■ **Institutional investors.** Insurance companies and other institutional investors (see below), including high-frequency traders, are responsible for most of the trading in financial markets. The assets of institutional investors based in the 34 member countries of the OECD totalled more than $62 trillion in 2011. The size of institutional investors varies greatly from country to country, depending on the development of collective investment vehicles. Investment practices vary considerably as well. At the end of 2011, after a significant decrease in share prices, for example, US institutional investors kept roughly identical proportions of their assets in the form of shares and in bonds. Until recently, British institutional investors tended to hold a greater proportion of assets in shares, whereas institutional investors in Japan have tended to favour bonds and loans over shares.

Mutual funds

The fastest-growing institutional investors are investment companies, which combine the investments of a number of individuals with the aim of achieving particular financial goals in an efficient way. Mutual funds and unit trusts are investment companies that typically accept an unlimited number of individual investments. The fund declares the strategy it will pursue, and as additional money is invested the fund managers purchase financial instruments appropriate to that strategy. Investment trusts, some of which are known in the United States as closed-end funds, issue a limited number of shares to investors at the time they are established and use the proceeds to purchase financial instruments in accordance with their strategy. In some cases, the trust acquires securities at its inception and never sells them; in other cases, the fund changes its portfolio from time to time. Investors wishing to enter or leave the unit trust must buy or sell the trust's shares from stockbrokers. Worldwide, mutual funds had net assets of $27 trillion at the end of 2012.

TABLE 1.4 **Financial assets of institutional investors, 2011**
$bn

	Investment funds	Insurance companies and pension funds
Australia	255	1,336
Canada	768	1,572
France	1,513	2,381
Germany	1,567	2,381
Italy	205	707
Japan	3,745	6,058
Mexico[a]	93	144
Netherlands	475	1,634
Sweden	238	513
Switzerland	475	1,154
Turkey	161	143
UK	1,065	4,288
US	11,927	17,172

a 2010.
Source: OECD, average exchange rates from US Internal Revenue Service

Hedge funds

A third type of investment company, a hedge fund, can accept investments from only a small number of wealthy individuals or big institutions. In return it is freed from most types of regulation meant to protect consumers. Hedge funds are able to employ aggressive investment strategies, such as using borrowed money to increase the amount invested and focusing investment on one or another type of asset rather than diversifying. If successful, such strategies can lead to very large returns; if unsuccessful, they can result in sizeable losses and the closure of the fund.

All investment companies earn a profit by charging investors a fee for their services. Some, notably hedge funds, may also take a portion of any gain in the value of the fund. Hedge funds have come under particular criticism because their fee structures may give managers an undesirable incentive to take large risks with investors' money, as fund managers may share in their fund's gains but not its losses.

Insurance companies

Insurance companies are the most important type of institutional investor, owning one-third of all the financial assets owned by institutions. In the past, most of these holdings were needed to back life insurance policies. In recent years, a growing share of insurers' business has consisted of annuities, which guarantee policy holders a sum of money each year as long as they live, rather than merely paying their heirs upon death. The growth of pre-funded individual pensions has benefited insurance companies, because on retirement many workers use the money in their accounts to purchase annuities.

Pension funds

Pension funds aggregate the retirement savings of a large number of workers. Typically, pension funds are sponsored by an employer, a group of employers or a labour union. Unlike individual pension accounts, pension funds do not give individuals control over how their savings are invested, but they do typically offer a guaranteed benefit once the individual reaches retirement age. Pension-fund assets came to about $16 trillion in the OECD countries at the end of 2009. Three countries, the United States, the UK and Japan, account for the overwhelming majority of this amount. Pension funds, although huge, are slowly diminishing in importance as individual pension accounts gain favour.

Algorithmic traders

Algorithmic trading, also known as high-frequency trading, has expanded dramatically in recent years as a result of increased computing power and the availability of low-cost, high-speed communications. Investors specialising in this type of trading program computers to enter buy and sell orders automatically in an effort to exploit tiny price differences in securities and currency markets. They typically have no interest in fundamental factors, such as a company's prospects or a country's economic outlook, and own the asset for only a brief period before reselling it. Algorithmic trading firms control only a tiny proportion of the world's financial assets, but they account for a large proportion of the trading in some markets.

Other institutions

Other types of institutions, such as banks, foundations and university endowment funds, are also substantial players in the markets.

The rise of the formal markets

Every country has financial markets of one sort or another. In countries as diverse as China, Peru and Zimbabwe, investors can purchase shares and bonds issued by local companies. Even in places whose governments loudly reject capitalist ideas, traders, often labelled disparagingly as speculators, make markets in foreign currencies and in commodities such as oil. The formal financial markets have expanded rapidly in recent years, as governments in countries marked by shadowy, semi-legal markets have sought to organise institutions. The motivation was in part self-interest: informal markets generate no tax revenue, but officially recognised markets do. Governments have also recognised that if businesses are to thrive they must be able to raise capital, and formal means of doing this, such as selling shares on a stock exchange, are much more efficient than informal means such as borrowing from moneylenders.

Investors have many reasons to prefer formal financial markets to street-corner trading. Yet not all formal markets prosper, as investors gravitate to certain markets and leave others underutilised. The busier ones, generally, have important attributes that smaller markets often lack:

■ **Liquidity**, the ease with which trading can be conducted. In an illiquid market an investor may have difficulty finding another party ready to make the desired trade, and the difference, or "spread", between the price at which a security can be bought and the price for which it can be sold, may be high. Trading is easier and spreads are narrower in more liquid markets. Because liquidity benefits almost everyone, trading usually concentrates in markets that are already busy.

■ **Transparency**, the availability of prompt and complete information about trades and prices. Generally, the less transparent the market, the less willing people are to trade there.

■ **Reliability**, particularly when it comes to ensuring that trades are completed quickly according to the terms agreed.

■ **Legal procedures** adequate to settle disputes and enforce contracts.

■ **Suitable investor protection and regulation.** Excessive regulation can stifle a market. However, trading will also be deterred if investors lack confidence in the available information about the securities they may wish to trade, the procedures for trading, the ability of trading partners and intermediaries to meet their commitments, and the treatment they will receive as owners of a security or commodity once a trade has been completed.

■ **Low transaction costs.** Many financial-market transactions are not tied to a specific geographic location, and the participants will strive to complete them in places where trading costs, regulatory costs and taxes are reasonable.

The forces of change

Today's financial markets would be almost unrecognisable to someone who traded there only two or three decades ago. The speed of change has been accelerating as market participants struggle to adjust to increased competition and constant innovation.

Technology

Almost everything about the markets has been reshaped by the forces of technology. Abundant computing power and cheap telecommunications have encouraged the growth of entirely new types of financial instruments and have dramatically changed the cost structure of every part of the financial industry.

Deregulation

The trend towards deregulation has been worldwide. It is not long since authorities everywhere kept tight controls on financial markets in the name of protecting consumers and preserving financial stability. But since 1975, when the United States prohibited stockbrokers from setting uniform commissions for share trading, the restraints have been loosened in one country after another. Although there are great differences, most national regulators agree on the principles that individual investors need substantial protection, but that dealings involving institutional investors require little regulation.

Liberalisation

Deregulation has been accompanied by a general liberalisation of rules governing participation in the markets. Many of the barriers that once separated banks, investment banks, insurers, investment companies and other financial institutions have been lowered, allowing such firms to enter each others' businesses. The big market economies, most recently Japan and South Korea, have also allowed foreign firms to enter financial sectors that were formerly reserved for domestic companies.

Consolidation

Liberalisation has led to consolidation, as firms merge to take advantage of economies of scale or to enter other areas of finance. Almost all the UK's leading investment banks and brokerage houses, for example, have been acquired by foreigners seeking a bigger presence in London, and many of the medium-sized investment banks in the United States were bought by commercial banks wishing to use new powers to expand in share dealing and corporate finance. Financial crisis led to further consolidation, as the insolvency of many major banks and investment banks led to forced mergers in 2008.

Globalisation

Consolidation has gone hand in hand with globalisation. Most of the important financial firms are now highly international, with operations in all the major financial centres. Many companies and governments take advantage of these global networks to issue shares and bonds outside their home countries. Investors increasingly take a global approach as well, putting their money wherever they expect the greatest return for the risk involved, without worrying about geography.

This book

The following chapters examine the most widely used financial instruments and discuss the way the markets for each type of instrument are organised. Chapter 2 establishes the background by explaining the currency markets, where exchange rates are determined. The money markets, where commercial paper and other instruments are used for short-term financing, are discussed in Chapter 3. The bond markets, the most important source of financing for companies and governments, are the subject of Chapter 4. Asset-backed securities, complicated but increasingly important instruments that have some characteristics in common with bonds but also some important differences, receive special attention in Chapter 5. Chapter 6 deals with offshore markets, including the market for euro-notes. Chapter 7 discusses the area that may be most familiar to many readers – shares and equity markets. Chapter 8 covers exchange-traded futures and options, and Chapter 9 discusses other sorts of derivatives. The markets for syndicated loans and other kinds of bank credit are beyond the scope of this book, as are insurance products of all sorts.

2 Foreign-exchange markets

IN EVERY COUNTRY prices are expressed in units of currency, either that issued by the country's central bank or a different one in which individuals prefer to denominate their transactions. The value of the currency itself, however, can be judged only against an external reference. This reference, the exchange rate, thus becomes the fundamental price in any economy. Most often, the references against which a currency's value is measured are other currencies. Determining the relative values of different currencies is the role of the foreign-exchange markets.

The foreign-exchange markets underpin all other financial markets. They directly influence each country's foreign-trade patterns, guide the flow of international investment and affect domestic interest and inflation rates. They operate in every corner of the world, in every single currency. Collectively, they form the largest financial market by far. Hundreds of thousands of foreign-exchange transactions occur every day, with an average turnover totalling $5.3 trillion a day in 2013.

Foreign-exchange trading dates back to ancient times, and has flourished or diminished depending on the extent of international commerce and the monetary arrangements of the day. In medieval times, coins minted from gold or silver circulated freely across the borders of Europe's duchies and kingdoms, and foreign-exchange traders provided one form of coinage in trade for another to comfort people worried that unfamiliar coins might contain less precious metal than claimed. By the late 14th century bankers in Italy were dealing in paper debits or credits issued in assorted currencies, discounted according to the bankers' judgment of the currencies' relative values.

This allowed international trade to expand far more than would have been possible if trading partners had to barter one shipload of goods for another or to physically exchange each shipment of goods for trunks of precious metal.

Yet foreign-exchange trading remained a minor part of finance. When paper money came into widespread use in the 18th century, its value too was determined mainly by the amount of silver or gold that the government promised to pay the bearer. As this amount changed infrequently, businesses and investors faced little risk that exchange-rate movements would greatly affect their profits. There was little need to trade foreign currencies except in connection with a specific transaction, such as an export sale or the purchase of a company abroad.

Even after the main economies stopped linking their currencies to gold in the 1920s and 1930s, they tried to keep their exchange rates steady. The new monetary arrangements created at the end of the second world war, known as the Bretton Woods system after the US resort where they were agreed, were also based on fixed rates. These arrangements began to break down in the late 1960s, and in 1972 the governments of the largest economies decided to let market forces determine exchange rates. The resulting uncertainty about the level of exchange rates led to dramatic growth in currency trading.

The amount of trading decreased in the late 1990s for two principal reasons. First, the introduction of the euro as the currency of many European countries eliminated all exchange-market activity among those currencies. Second, consolidation in the banking industry worldwide greatly reduced the number of firms with a significant presence in the market. Currency trading rebounded in 2003–04 as institutional investors, especially hedge funds, speculated in foreign-exchange markets in hopes of generating greater yields than were available on stagnant stockmarkets. The development of "high-frequency" trading, in which computers place buy and sell orders as dictated by mathematical algorithms and may resell an asset within a few moments of purchasing it, has supported the continued growth of foreign-exchange trading since 2007.

How currencies are traded

The foreign-exchange markets comprise four different markets, which function separately yet are closely interlinked.

The spot market

Currencies for immediate delivery are traded on the spot market. A tourist's purchase of foreign currency is a spot-market transaction, as is a firm's decision immediately to convert the receipts from an export sale into its home currency. Most large spot transactions among financial institutions, currency dealers and large firms are arranged electronically, although telephone broking services remain important. The actual exchange of the two currencies is usually handled through the banking system and generally occurs two days after the trade is agreed, although some trades, such as exchanges of US dollars for Canadian dollars, are settled more quickly. As online trading has lowered trading costs, individual investors have become more active in the currency spot market. However, small spot transactions often occur face to face, as when a moneychanger converts individuals' local currency into dollars or euros.

The futures market

The futures markets allow participants to lock in an exchange rate at certain future dates by purchasing or selling a futures contract. For example, a US firm expecting to receive SFr10m might purchase Swiss franc futures contracts on the Chicago Mercantile Exchange. This would effectively guarantee that the francs the firm receives can be converted into dollars at an agreed rate, protecting the firm from the risk that the Swiss franc will lose value against the dollar before it receives the payment. The most widely traded currency futures contracts, however, expire only once each quarter. Unless the user receives its foreign-currency payment on the precise day that a contract expires, it will face the risk of exchange-rate changes between the date it receives the foreign currency and the date its contracts expire. (Futures markets are discussed in Chapter 8.)

The options market

A comparatively small amount of currency trading occurs in options markets. Currency options, which were first traded on exchanges in 1982, give the holder the right, but not the obligation, to acquire or sell foreign currency or foreign-currency futures contracts at a specified price during a certain period of time. (Options contracts are discussed in Chapter 8.)

The derivatives market

Most foreign-exchange trading now occurs in the derivatives market. Technically, the term derivatives describes a large number of financial instruments, including options and futures. In common usage, however, it refers to instruments that have different characteristics from exchange-traded options and futures contracts. Widely used currency derivatives include the following:

- **Forward contracts** are agreements similar to futures contracts, providing for the sale of a given amount of currency at a specified exchange rate on an agreed date. Unlike futures contracts, however, currency forwards are arranged directly between a dealer and its customer. Forwards are more flexible, in that they can be arranged for precisely the amount and length of time the customer desires.

- **Foreign-exchange swaps** involve the sale or purchase of a currency on one date and the offsetting purchase or sale of the same amount on a future date, with both dates agreed when the transaction is initiated. Swaps accounted for about 47% of all foreign-exchange trading in 2010, the lowest share in many years, as spot-market transactions gained in importance. Normally, swaps are short-term deals, lasting a week or less.

- **Forward rate agreements** allow two parties to exchange interest-payment obligations, and if the obligations are in different currencies there is an exchange-rate component to the agreement.

- **Barrier options and collars** are derivatives that allow a user to limit its exchange-rate risk.

FIG 2.1 **Foreign-exchange markets**
Average daily turnover, $bn

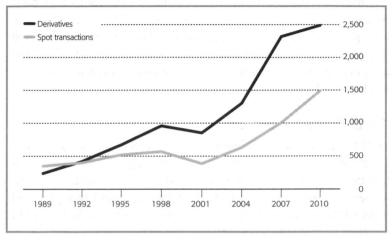

Source: Bank for International Settlements

Although large-scale derivatives trading is a recent development, derivatives such as foreign-exchange swaps have supplanted the spot market as the most important method of foreign-exchange trading, as shown in Figure 2.1. (Derivatives are discussed further in Chapter 9.)

Currency markets and related markets

In most cases, foreign-exchange trading is closely linked with the trading of securities, particularly bonds and money-market instruments. An investor who believes that a particular currency will appreciate will not want to hold that currency in cash form, because it will earn no return. Instead, the investor will buy the desired currency, invest it in highly liquid interest-bearing assets, and then sell those assets to obtain cash at the time the investor wishes to sell the currency itself.

Gearing up

Investors often wish to increase their exposure to a particular currency without putting up additional money. This is done by increasing leverage, also known as gearing. The simplest way for a currency-market investor to gain leverage is to borrow money to purchase additional foreign currency. Levering spot-market transactions is usually not worthwhile, as the interest that must be paid on the borrowed money can easily exceed the investor's gain from exchange-rate changes. Futures and options contracts allow investors to take larger bets on exchange-rate movements relative to the amount of cash that is required upfront. Large firms and institutional investors may take highly leveraged positions in the derivatives market, making large gains if the exchange rate between two currencies moves as anticipated but conversely suffering large losses if the exchange rate moves in the opposite direction.

The players

Participants in the foreign-exchange markets can be grouped into four categories.

Exporters and importers

Firms that operate internationally must pay suppliers and workers in the local currency of each country in which they operate, and may receive payments from customers in many different countries. They will eventually convert their foreign-currency earnings into their home currency. Historically, supporting international trade and travel has been the main purpose of currency trading. In modern times, however, the volume of currency dealing has swamped the volume of trade in goods and services.

Investors

Many businesses own facilities, hold property or buy companies in other countries. All these activities, known as foreign direct investment, require the investor to obtain the currency of the foreign country. Much larger sums are committed to international portfolio investment – the purchase of bonds, shares or other securities denominated in a foreign currency. The investor must enter the foreign-exchange markets to obtain the currency to make a purchase, to convert the earnings from its foreign investments into its home currency, and again when it terminates an investment and repatriates its capital.

Speculators

Speculators buy and sell currencies solely to profit from anticipated changes in exchange rates, without engaging in other sorts of business dealings for which foreign currency is essential. Currency speculation is often combined with speculation in short-term financial instruments, such as treasury bills. The biggest speculators include leading banks and investment banks, almost all of which engage in proprietary trading using their own (as opposed to their customers') money, as well as hedge funds and other investment funds. High-frequency traders in currencies are speculators as well.

Governments

National treasuries or central banks may trade currencies for the purpose of affecting exchange rates. A government's deliberate attempt to alter the exchange rate between two currencies by buying one and selling the other is called intervention. The amount of currency intervention varies greatly from country to country and time to time, and depends mainly on how the government has decided to manage its foreign-exchange arrangements. Additionally, many governments have created state-owned investment funds, called sovereign wealth funds, for the purpose of investing foreign currency received as a result of a trade surplus or the sale of natural resources. Their size and international focus can make sovereign wealth funds important participants in the currency markets.

The main trading locations

The currency markets have no single physical location. Most trading occurs in the interbank markets, among financial institutions which are present in many different countries. Trading formerly occurred mainly in telephone conversations between dealers, but almost all trading is now conducted over electronic systems. These systems work in different ways. Some systems allow a party seeking to exchange, say, €10m for yen to enter the request into a computer and wait for interested banks to respond with offers of the exchange rates at which they propose to transact the trade. Other systems match buy and sell orders automatically or link a large investor to a single bank.

As electronic systems have become more sophisticated, the spread between buy and sell offers has narrowed significantly, indicating that trading has become less costly for market participants.

Despite the legal and technological ability to trade currencies from anywhere, most banks conduct their spot-market currency trading in the same centres where other financial markets are located. London has emerged as the dominant location, with New York a considerable distance behind. Tokyo, which once challenged London and New York as a centre for currency trading, now lags far behind. A handful of huge international banks is responsible for most currency dealing worldwide. In London, nine banks handled 75% of turnover on the foreign-exchange market in 2010.

Table 2.1 shows the growth in trading of various types of foreign-exchange instruments. The amount of average daily trading in April 2013, as reported in Table 2.1, was 250% higher than the amount reported in 1998. The vigorous trading in 2013 was at least partly due to concerns about the stability of some emerging-market currencies, such as the Turkish lira and the Indian rupee.

TABLE 2.1 **Global foreign-exchange market turnover**
Daily averages in April, $bn

	1998	2004	2007	2010	2013
Spot transactions	568	631	1,005	1,488	2,046
Forward transactions	128	209	362	475	680
Foreign exchange swaps	734	954	1,714	1,759	2,228
Currency swaps	10	21	31	43	54
Options and other	87	119	212	207	337
Total	1,527	1,934	3,324	3,971	5,345

Source: Bank for International Settlements

The pattern of currency futures trading is quite different. Exchange-rate futures were invented at the Chicago Mercantile Exchange, and for many years it and the Brazilian exchange in São Paulo were the main exchanges on which currency futures were traded. In recent years, the National Stock Exchange of India and the Russian exchange have become important trading sites as their countries have become more prominent in international trade and investment. In terms of the face value of contracts traded, however, the Chicago Mercantile Exchange remains the leader, as shown in Table 2.2. No exchange-rate futures contracts are traded on the main exchanges in the European Union or Japan. A number of smaller exchanges, such as those in Bogotá and Tel Aviv, do trade currency futures contracts, usually based on the exchange rate between the local currency and the dollar, the euro or the yen. However, trading volume in most of these contracts is tiny.

TABLE 2.2 **Largest exchanges for currency-futures contracts**
2012

Exchange	No. of contracts traded	Notional value of contracts traded, $bn
National Stock Exchange of India	631,266,655	$597
MICeZ/RTS, Russia	410,545,200	$425
CME Group, US	203,302,545	$25,203
Bolsa de Mercadorias & Futuros, Brazil	85,120,548	$4,272
Korea Exchange	54,506,045	$551
Johannesberg SE	13,038,541	$15
MexDer	9,841,497	$99
ICE Futures	7,400,132	$510

Source: World Federation of Exchanges

Worldwide trading in currency futures peaked at 99.6m contracts in 1995. It then declined substantially as investors favoured derivatives that are not traded on exchanges, including forward contracts and swaps. Currency futures have regained popularity since 2004; total worldwide volume in 2012 was 1.4 billion contracts, more than ten times the figure for 2004.

Currency options contracts have been popular mainly in the United States, Brazil and India, and are looked upon with suspicion in some other countries. The leading exchanges for currency options are the Chicago Mercantile Exchange, the Bolsa de Mercadorias & Futuros and the National Stock Exchange of India. Currency options are also traded on several other exchanges, notably the former Philadelphia Stock Exchange, now known as NASDAQ OMX PHLX. In most cases, contracts are based on the exchange rate between a currency and the dollar, although some contracts use the yen, the euro or the pound sterling. After a period of rapid growth, total trading volume worldwide reached 272m contracts in 2012. It is not clear that exchange-traded options will retain their importance, however, as financial regulators are pushing for exchange-rate derivatives, which can be designed to suit a particular investor's needs more precisely than traditional options, to be traded on exchanges rather than in private deals between banks and their customers.

Many options trade over the counter, usually between financial institutions, rather than on exchanges. In over-the-counter transactions, the parties are directly dependent on one another for payment, as an exchange does not stand in as an intermediary. This means that if one of the parties fails while the option is outstanding, the other party may be unable to collect any amounts it is owed. Financial institutions typically manage this risk by maintaining a large number of option contracts that may partially cancel one another out; thus if Bank A fails and is unable to make a payment due to Bank B under a currency option contract, Bank B may be excused from making a payment due to Bank A under a similar contract. This process, called netting, is also applied to currency swaps and other types of derivative contracts.

Trading in over-the-counter currency options has rebounded after lagging in the late 1990s and early 2000s. The market value of over-the-counter currency options outstanding was $1.2 trillion in December 2012. The UK is by far the most important location for this business and has gained market share in recent years, followed at a considerable distance by the United States and Singapore.

Favourite currencies

The most widely traded currency is the US dollar, which has accounted for 40–45% of all trading since the first comprehensive survey in 1989.

Table 2.3 lists the most widely traded currencies, by share of total trading in April 2013, when a survey of currency-trading activity was conducted by central banks. The most popular currency trade, the exchange of US dollars and euros, accounted for 24% of currency-market activity, with dollar/yen trades accounting for 18%. Trades involving the euro and currencies other than the dollar accounted for 9% of all turnover in the foreign-exchange market. Only about 4% of all trades involved neither US dollars nor euros.

TABLE 2.3 **Global foreign-exchange trading**
Average daily turnover, %

	2001	2004	2007	2010	2013
US dollar	45.0	44.0	42.8	42.5	43.5
Euro	19.0	18.7	18.5	19.5	16.7
Japanese yen	11.8	10.4	8.6	9.5	11.5
Pound sterling	6.5	8.3	7.5	6.5	5.9
Australian dollar	2.2	3.0	3.3	3.8	4.3
Swiss franc	3.0	3.0	3.4	3.2	2.6
Canadian dollar	2.2	2.1	2.2	2.7	2.3
Mexican peso	0.4	0.5	0.6	0.6	1.2
Chinese yuan	0.0	0.0	0.2	0.4	1.1

Note: Published figures double-count transactions; figures in this table represent half of official totals.
Source: Bank for International Settlements

London is unusual among currency-trading centres in that its own currency, the pound sterling, has a comparatively minor role in the market. The most commonly traded currency pair in the London market is the US dollar and the euro, accounting for one-third of all trading. Only 15% of London trading in April 2013 involved sterling, whereas over 80% of trades had one side denominated in US dollars. The main trades handled in the London market are listed in Table 2.4.

The location and composition of currency trading were altered significantly by the launch of the single European currency, the euro, in January 1999. The volume of trading in many European centres,

TABLE 2.4 **Development of the London market**
% share of turnover by currency pair

Trade	2006	2009	2012
Dollar/euro	33	33	32
Sterling/dollar	15	13	13
Dollar/yen	13	12	11
Dollar/Swiss franc	4	4	5
Dollar/Australian dollar	3	5	7
Dollar/Canadian dollar	3	3	4
Sterling/euro	3	4	3
Euro/yen	2	2	2

Note: Data are for October of each year.
Source: Bank of England

including Paris, Brussels and Rome, has fallen dramatically since the euro's introduction. The creation of the euro also initially reduced the amount of trading in US dollars because many exchanges between smaller European currencies were formerly arranged by swapping into and then out of dollars; now, dealings between businesses in the euro-zone countries require no such complicated arrangements. Meanwhile, trading in some less prominent currencies, including those of Canada, Australia and the Scandinavian countries, has increased.

Trading in emerging-market currencies amounts to a tiny share of total daily trading. Almost all of this trading involves exchanges between the dollar and currencies from eastern Europe, Asia and Latin America. Trading in smaller currencies may fall further if more east European countries seek to adopt the euro, as Latvia agreed to do in 2013. However, rapid economic growth in some Asian and African countries may lead to increased trading of their currencies.

Settlement

Once two parties have agreed upon a currency trade, they must make arrangements for the actual exchange of currencies, known as settlement. At the retail level, settlement is simple and immediate: one party pushes Mexican banknotes through the window at a foreign-exchange office and receives US $20 bills in return. Trades on options and futures exchanges are settled by the exchange's own clearing house, so market participants face no risk that the other party will fail to comply with its obligations.

Large trades in the spot and derivatives markets, however, are another matter. When two parties have agreed a trade, they turn to banks to arrange the movement of whatever sums are involved. Each large bank is a member of one or more clearing organisations. These ventures, some government-owned and others owned co-operatively by groups of banks, have rules meant to assure that each bank lives up to its obligations. This cannot be guaranteed, however. The total amount of a large bank's pending currency trades at any moment – its gross position – may be many times its capital. Its net position, which subtracts the amount the bank is expecting to receive from the amount it is expecting to pay, is always far smaller. But if for some reason not all of those trades are settled promptly, the bank could suddenly find itself in serious difficulty.

Herstatt risk

The greatest risk arises from the fact that trading often occurs across many time zones. If a bank in Tokyo agrees a big currency trade with one in London, the London bank's payment will reach the Tokyo bank during Japanese business hours, but the Japanese bank's payment cannot be transferred to the London bank until the British clearing organisation opens hours later. If the Japanese bank should fail after it has received a huge payment from the UK but before it has made the reciprocal payment, the British bank could suffer crippling losses, and its failure could in turn endanger other banks unconnected with the original trade. This is known as Herstatt risk, after a German bank that failed in 1974 with $620m of partially completed trades. Reducing Herstatt risk by speeding up the settlement process has become a major preoccupation of bank regulators around the world, but it has proved difficult to eliminate the risk altogether.

Why exchange rates change

In the very short run exchange rates may be highly volatile, moving in response to the latest news. Investors naturally gravitate to the currencies of strong, healthy economies and avoid those of weak, troubled economies. The defeat of proposed legislation, the election of a particular politician or the release of an unexpected bit of economic data may all cause a currency to strengthen or weaken against the currencies of other countries.

Real interest rates

In the longer run, however, exchange rates are determined almost entirely by expectations of real interest rates. A country's real interest rate is the rate of interest an investor expects to receive after subtracting inflation. This is not a single number, as different investors have different expectations of future inflation. If, for example, an investor were able to lock in a 5% interest rate for the coming year and anticipated a 2% rise in prices, it would expect to earn a real interest rate of 3%.

Covered interest arbitrage

The mechanism whereby real interest rates affect exchange rates is called covered interest arbitrage. To understand covered interest arbitrage, assume that an investor in the UK wishes to invest £100 risk-free for one year, and can do so with no transaction costs. One possibility is for the investor to buy a one-year British government bond. Alternatively, the investor could exchange the £100 into a foreign currency, invest the foreign currency in a one-year government bond, and at the end of the year reconvert the proceeds into sterling. Which choice would leave the investor better off? That depends on the spot exchange rate; interest rates in sterling and in the foreign currency; inflation expectations; and the forward exchange rate for a date 12 months hence.

Suppose, to take a simple example, that the British interest rate is 5%, the US interest rate is 7%, the spot exchange rate is £1 = $1.60 and the one-year forward exchange rate is £1 = $1.61. Suppose further, for the sake of clarity, that the investor expects no inflation in either country. It would face the following choice:

Investment in the UK	Investment in the United States
Initial capital = £100	Initial capital = £100 × ($1.60/£1) = $160.00
Sterling interest rate = 5%	Dollar interest rate = 7%
Capital after 1 year =	Capital after 1 year = $171.20
£105.00	$171.20 × (£1/$1.61) = £106.34

With this combination of exchange rates, expected inflation rates and interest rates, the investor is guaranteed to earn a higher profit on US bonds than on British ones. The risk of buying US bonds is no higher than the risk of buying British bonds, as the investor can buy a forward contract entitling it to convert $171.20 into pounds at a rate of £1 = $1.61 in precisely one year, eliminating any need to worry about exchange-rate movements in the interim.

Covered interest parity

This guaranteed profit, however, will be fleeting. Many investors, whose computers are constantly scanning the markets for price anomalies, will spot this unusual opportunity. As they all seek to sell pounds for dollars in the spot market and dollars for pounds in the forward market in order to invest in the United States rather than in the UK, the pound will fall in the spot market and rise on the forward market. Eventually, market forces might lower the spot sterling/dollar rate to £1 = $1.59, and push the one-year forward rate to just above $1.62 = £1. At these exchange rates investors would no longer rush to exchange sterling for dollars to invest in the United States, because the one-year return from either investment would be the same. The two currencies will then have reached covered interest parity.

In the real world, of course, market interest rates and inflation expectations in all countries change by at least a small amount every day. For traders with hundreds of millions of dollars to invest, even the tiniest changes can create profitable opportunities for interest arbitrage for periods as brief as one day. Their efforts to obtain the highest possible return inevitably drive exchange rates in the direction of covered interest parity.

Managing exchange rates

Governments' decisions about exchange-rate management continue to be the single most important factor shaping the currency markets. Many different exchange-rate regimes have been tried. All fall into one of three basic categories: fixed, semi-fixed or floating. Each has its advantages, but all have disadvantages as well, as exchange-rate management is intimately related to the management of a country's domestic economy.

Fixed-rate systems

There are various types of fixed-rate systems.

■ **Gold standard.** The oldest type of fixed-rate regime is a metallic standard. The most famous example is the gold standard, introduced by the UK in 1840 and adopted by most other countries by the 1870s. Under a gold standard a country's money supply is directly linked to the gold reserves owned by its central bank, and notes and coins can be exchanged for gold at any time. If several countries adopt the gold standard, the exchange rates among them will be stable. In the late 19th and early 20th centuries, for example, the British standard set £100 equal to about 22oz troy of gold and the US standard set $100 equal to 4.5oz, so £1 could be exchanged for $4.86.

This system was thought to be self-correcting. If a country ran a current-account deficit because, for example, it imported more than it exported, foreigners acquired more of its currency than they wanted to hold. The central bank could not eliminate the current-account deficit by devaluation, reducing the amount of gold that a unit of currency bought and thereby making exports cheaper and imports dearer, as the gold standard precluded devaluation. Instead, as foreigners exchanged currency for gold the central bank's gold stores dwindled, forcing it to reduce the amount of money in circulation. The shrinkage of the money supply would throw the economy into recession, bringing the current account into balance by reducing demand for imports. This proved to be a painful method of correcting current-account imbalances, and the era of the gold standard was marked by prolonged depressions, or panics, in a number of countries. A true gold standard has not been used since the end of the first world war.

■ **Bretton Woods.** An alternative type of fixed-rate regime is that established at Bretton Woods, which was based on foreign currencies as well as gold. The Bretton Woods system tried to solve the problems of the gold standard by allowing countries with persistent balance-of-payments deficits to devalue under certain conditions. A new organisation, the International Monetary Fund (IMF), could lend members gold or foreign currencies to help them deal with short-term balance-of-payments crises and avert devaluation. In 1969 the IMF even created its own currency, special drawing rights (SDRs), which countries can use to settle their debts with one another. SDRs are distributed to central banks to increase their reserves. As of 2013, the value of SDR1 was arbitrarily set equal to 66 US cents plus €0.423 plus ¥12.1 plus 11.1 UK pence, so its value against any single currency fluctuates. The fixed-rate regime collapsed in the late 1960s and early 1970s for many of the same reasons as the gold standard.

■ **Pegs.** Another form of fixed exchange rates is a pegged rate. This means that a country decides to hold the value of its currency constant in terms of another currency, usually that of an important trading partner. Denmark, for example, pegs to the euro, as it trades overwhelmingly with the 18 euro-zone countries. A peg is always subject to change, and the knowledge that this could happen can itself destabilise the currency.

A currency board is a particular type of peg designed to avoid destabilisation. The board, which takes the place of a central bank, issues currency only to the extent that each unit of currency is backed by an equivalent amount of foreign-currency reserves. This assures that any person wishing to exchange domestic currency for foreign currency at the official rate will be able to do so. If investors sell domestic currency, the currency board's reserves fall and it automatically reduces the domestic money supply by an equal amount, forcing interest rates higher and quickly slowing the economy. A currency board is able to stabilise the currency only to the extent that the government can resist the objections of those hurt when interest rates rise. The main difference between a currency board and a simple peg, aside from the mandatory reserves, is that changing the exchange rate under a currency board requires passing a law. Hong Kong has a currency board that pegs its currency to the US dollar. Estonia had a currency board that pegged its currency, the kroon, to the euro until 2011, when it discontinued the kroon and adopted the euro as its currency.

Fixed-rate shortcomings

Despite their differences, all fixed-rate systems have the same shortcomings. As long as people are free to move money into and out of a country, interest rates must rise high enough for investors to want to hold its currency because they can earn an attractive return. The country's central bank is therefore forced to use its monetary powers solely for the purpose of keeping the exchange rate stable. This means that the central bank cannot pursue other goals, such as fighting inflation or lowering interest rates to revive a depressed economy.

Argentina's fixed peg to the US dollar, backed by a currency board, collapsed in January 2002. Again, the system's inflexibility was at fault. Argentina's government, having surrendered control of monetary policy in the interest of a fixed exchange rate, was unable to lower interest rates to combat a depression. High and rising unemployment and falling economic output led to a political backlash that forced the resignation of the government and the abandonment of the one-to-one exchange rate between the peso and the dollar. Many Argentinian businesses that had contracted debts in dollars were forced to default on their obligations, because their income in devalued pesos was insufficient to service their dollar-denominated obligations.

A fixed exchange rate also creates a riskless opportunity for investors to borrow in a foreign currency that has lower interest rates than their own, and this can lead to financial crises. To see why, assume that country A, where the one-year interest rate is 10%, pegs its currency to that of country B, where the one-year rate is 5%. An investor from country A can borrow at 5% in country B, exchange the foreign currency for its domestic currency, invest the money domestically at a 10% return, and after one year obtain the foreign currency to repay the loan at the same exchange rate. Earning this riskless profit is sensible from the point of view of an individual borrower, but if many firms follow the same strategy, country A's central bank may lack the foreign-currency reserves to meet the demand for country B's currency at the fixed rate. It may have to abandon the fixed rate, making it more costly for borrowers to buy the foreign currency to repay their loans and forcing some of them into default. This was the cause of crises in Indonesia, South Korea, Thailand and other East Asian countries in 1997.

Semi-fixed systems

The practical problems with fixed-rate regimes have led to hybrid systems meant to provide exchange-rate stability, leaving the government more flexibility to pursue other economic goals. Because all these systems leave room for currency fluctuations, they lead to much more trading in foreign-exchange markets than fixed-rate systems. Most of these systems involve a managed float, in which a government allows the currency's value to change as market forces determine, but actively seeks to guide the market. Variations include the following:

■ **Bands.** The European Exchange Rate Mechanism, to which most EU countries adhered before adopting a single currency in 1999, involved agreement that exchange rates against the German mark would stay within certain bands. So long as a currency remained within its band, it was allowed to float. If, however, a currency lost or gained considerable value against the mark and reached the top or bottom of its band, the country's central bank was obliged to adjust interest rates to keep the exchange rate within the band. Unfortunately, this system of managed floating did not prove as stable as its designers had hoped. In 1992 and 1993 the mark appreciated strongly against the pound sterling, the Italian lira, the Swedish krona and several other currencies in the system, requiring these countries to raise interest rates sharply in order to keep their exchange rates within their bands. The UK eventually withdrew from the system and allowed its currency to float freely. Several other countries stayed within the system only after accepting large devaluations and setting new bands for their currencies.

- **Target zones.** These are similar to bands except that governments' commitments are non-binding. A government might proclaim its desire for its currency to trade within a certain range against another currency, but might not commit itself to acting to keep the exchange rate within that range. As with bands, one government might unilaterally set a target zone for its currency against another currency, or target zones might be agreed multilaterally by a group of countries.

- **Pegs and baskets.** A third variant of managed float is for a country to peg to a basket of foreign currencies, rather than to just one. If a country pegs to a single currency and that currency then rises relative to a third currency, imports from the third country will become cheaper and exports to that country harder to sell. This can lead to a balance-of-payments crisis. Setting the peg as the average exchange rate against several currencies, rather than just one, insulates the country from such problems to some extent. The government can manage the currency simply by changing the weights assigned to each of the foreign-exchange currencies in the basket. Singapore and Kuwait are among the countries that manage their currencies against baskets of foreign currencies. In both cases, the composition of the basket is secret and is thought to change from time to time. China announced in 2005 that it would value its currency against a basket of currencies rather than the US dollar alone, and it disclosed the currencies in the basket but not their weights.

- **The crawling peg.** This is a mechanism for adjusting an exchange rate, usually in a pre-announced way. A central bank might, for example, announce that it will allow its currency's exchange rate with the dollar to depreciate by 1% per month over the coming year. This is less rigid than a fixed exchange rate, but it entails the same basic commitment: the central bank must use its monetary policy to keep the currency depreciating at the desired rate, rather than for other ends. If investors judge that the exchange rate is depreciating too slowly, they may exchange their domestic currency for foreign currency en masse, causing the central bank to run short of foreign reserves and forcing a devaluation, just as occurs with a fixed rate. In the wake of such a crisis in 1994–95, Mexico abandoned its crawling peg against the US dollar and allowed its peso to float.

Floating rates

In a floating-rate system, exchange rates are not the target of monetary policy. Governments and central banks use their policies to achieve other goals, such as stabilising domestic prices or stimulating economic growth, and allow exchange rates to move with market forces. The world's main currencies now float freely against one another, creating a large demand for currency trading. Several important countries, including Mexico, Brazil and South Korea, adopted floating rates after crises made managed exchange rates impossible to sustain. It would be incorrect, however, to say that exchange rates float completely freely. From time to time, one or more governments act, often without disclosing their intentions, to nudge a particular exchange rate in a certain direction. This usually occurs only when a currency is far cheaper or more expensive than economic fundamentals would seem to indicate.

The majority of countries manage exchange rates in one way or another. The lion's share of the world's economic activity, however, occurs in countries with floating rates.

Comparing currency valuations

How can markets and policymakers judge whether a currency is overvalued or undervalued? This is not a simple question. Some would answer never, arguing that the current market price is the only good indicator of a currency's value. There is, however, considerable empirical evidence that foreign-exchange markets frequently overshoot. This means that when political or economic news causes a particular currency to rise or fall sharply, it moves further than careful analysis might indicate as many investors simultaneously act in the same way. Once the markets realise that the currency has overshot, it will partially retrace its movements and settle at an intermediate level.

Indications of overshooting

There are three indications that a currency may be seriously misvalued. First, its exchange rates with other currencies may not be moving towards covered interest parity, suggesting that the markets expect a sharp rise or fall in the immediate future. Second, a country may run a large and persistent balance-of-payments deficit or surplus. Although it is not uncommon for a country to have a balance-of-payments deficit or surplus for many years, a large deficit or surplus can indicate that the currency is far too strong or weak relative to the currencies of major trading partners.

The third indication of misvaluation is when the before-tax prices of traded goods in one country are very different from the prices in another. This approach draws on the theory of purchasing power parity, which holds that a given amount of money should be able to purchase similar amounts of traded goods in different countries. One simple guide to purchasing power parity is The Economist's Big Mac Index, which uses the cost of a hamburger in different countries, expressed in dollars, to estimate whether currencies are overvalued or undervalued relative to the dollar. More exhaustive analyses, which study the prices of various products in different countries, are published by the World Bank and private firms.

Managing floating rates

When they decide that exchange rates have veered far from levels they deem appropriate, governments and their central banks may endeavour to move the market. This is not difficult. If a government or a central bank manages to reduce investors' expectations of inflation, its currency will strengthen. If the central bank is able to reduce short-term interest rates while keeping inflation in check, the country's currency will weaken relative to the currencies of countries whose real interest rates have not decreased.

In many cases, however, a government or central bank wishes to alter exchange rates without making fundamental changes in economic policy. It might deem its interest-rate policy appropriate for reducing unemployment, for example, even as it makes known its dissatisfaction with exchange rates. Trying to move exchange rates under such circumstances is more a psychological exercise than an economic one. The effort is bound to fail, because an economic policy can be used to achieve only one target at a time. If monetary policy is being used to achieve the goal of lowering unemployment, it cannot simultaneously be used to achieve a desired exchange rate.

In these circumstances, authorities often resort to intervention to support a currency that has been falling or drive down a currency that has been rising. Intervention, which is always done in secret, usually involves the use of a country's foreign-currency reserves to buy domestic currency in the markets, thereby strengthening the domestic currency's price. In some cases, central banks have intervened by purchasing their currency in the forward markets rather than in the spot market. Either method can inflict heavy losses on investors and traders who have bet aggressively that the currency will fall. Knowing of this danger, the foreign-exchange markets are highly sensitive to the slightest hints from government officials that they would like to see exchange rates change.

The amount of money central banks can spend on intervention, however, is small relative to the amount of currency traded each day. It is also finite, limited by the amount of the country's reserves. As a result, neither intervention nor official comments that hint at intervention will affect exchange rates for long unless the country's economic policies are changed as well. Otherwise, traders will quickly sense that the central bank is losing its desire to intervene or is running short of reserves, and exchange rates will resume their previous course.

Obtaining price information

Except when a government supports a fixed exchange rate, there is no single posted price at which currencies are traded. Banks, electronic information systems such as Reuters and electronic currency-trading systems display price quotations on customers' screens. Normally, a dealer provides both a buy price, giving the amount of one currency it will pay for each unit of another, and a higher sell price at which customers may obtain currency. The spread between the buy and sell prices provides the dealer's profit and covers the cost of running the trading operation. The prices any dealer offers on screen, however, are strictly indicative; recent trades may or may not have occurred at these prices, and a customer may not be able to obtain a quoted price. Most dealers offer much more favourable rates on large trades than on small ones.

Many daily newspapers and websites offer currency-price tables. These contain exchange rates drawn from those offered by dealers on the previous trading day, so they do not necessarily represent rates that will be available on the day of publication. These are normally rates offered on large commercial transactions, and are much more favourable than those available to the tourists who read them closely. Table 2.5 offers an extract from a typical currency-price table.

This table was published in the United States, and therefore states all prices in terms of US dollars; in other countries, the table would normally quote prices in the local currency. The countries listed are those whose currencies trade most actively against the dollar. Prices are reported in two different ways: columns two and three give the number of dollars required to buy one unit of the relevant currency on the last two trading days, and columns four and five give the number of units of the other currency that could be purchased for $1.

Forward rates

As well as spot rates, Table 2.5 gives forward rates for the most heavily traded currencies, the pound sterling and the Canadian dollar. These represent the prices an investor would pay for currency to be delivered in one, three or six months. For the Canadian dollar, the forward rates are above the spot rates, indicating that investors expect Canada's real interest rates to rise compared with US interest rates over the coming months, causing exchange rates to strengthen as well. The pound sterling is expected to weaken slightly against the US dollar over the next six months.

TABLE 2.5 **Typical newspaper currency prices**

Country	Exchange rate ($ equivalent)		Currency per $	
	Tuesday	Monday	Tuesday	Monday
Argentina	0.2590	0.2590	3.8601	3.8601
Australia	0.8119	0.7996	1.2316	1.2506
Bahrain (dinar)	2.6525	2.6532	0.3770	0.3769
Brazil	0.5227	0.5227	1.9077	1.9077
Canada	0.8955	0.8950	1.1167	1.1173
1-month forward	0.8960	0.8955	1.1161	1.1167
3-months forward	0.8969	0.8960	1.1149	1.1161
6-months forward	0.8985	0.8975	1.1130	1.1142
Chile	0.001876	0.001879	533.09	532.32
UK	1.6281	1.6288	0.6142	0.6139
1-month forward	1.6281	1.6287	0.6142	0.6140
3-months forward	1.6279	1.6280	0.6143	0.6143
6-months forward	1.6276	1.6279	0.6144	0.6143

Cross-rates

A different kind of table is required to report currency cross-rates. Table
2.6 lists the identical currencies across the top and down the left-hand
side. The individual cells in the table offer each country's exchange
rate with respect to the other country, without requiring that either
currency be converted into a third currency, such as dollars. Hence, 10
Danish kroner would purchase 2.148 Swiss francs on this date, while
one Swiss franc would buy 4.655 krone. In practice, however, cross
trading is limited to the most heavily traded currencies. A Japanese
firm would have no difficulty exchanging yen directly for euros. But
a Malaysian firm wishing to purchase Polish zlotys would first have
to exchange ringgit for a major currency, such as euros or dollars, and
then exchange these for zlotys.

TABLE 2.6 **Currency cross-rates**

	C$	DKr	7	¥	NKr	SKr	SFr	£	US$
Canada (C$)		4.673	0.628	74.5	5.185	5.514	1.004	0.414	0.669
Denmark (Dkr)	2.140		1.345	159.4	11.100	11.800	2.148	0.885	1.432
Euro (6)	1.592	7.438		118.6	8.252	8.777	1.598	0.659	1.065
Japan (¥)	1.342	6.272	0.843		6.959	7.401	1.347	0.555	0.898
Norway (NKr)	1.929	9.013	1.212	143.7		10.640	1.936	0.798	1.290
Sweden (SKr)	1.814	8.474	1.139	135.1	9.402		1.820	0.750	1.213
Switzerland (SFr)	0.996	4.655	0.626	74.2	5.165	5.494		0.412	0.666
UK (£)	2.417	11.300	1.519	180.1	12.530	13.330	2.426		1.617
US ($)	1.495	6.985	0.939	111.4	7.750	8.243	1.501	0.618	

Note: Danish kroner, Norwegian kroner and Swedish kronor per 10; yen per 100.

Currency indexes

Evaluating changes in the exchange rate between two currencies is simple enough. Evaluating how a particular currency has performed over time, however, is much trickier, as the performance of that currency against many other currencies must be considered.

Trade-weighted exchange rate

The most widely used method for doing this is constructing a trade-weighted exchange rate, which is an index incorporating a currency's performance against a basket containing the currencies of all its trading partners. The weighting is done based on the share of the country's trade that can be attributed to each trading partner. For example, Mexico's trade-weighted exchange rate depends heavily on the exchange rate between the peso and the dollar, as the United States accounts for about two-thirds of Mexico's foreign trade; and about half of the Czech Republic's trade-weighted exchange rate is determined by the exchange rate between the koruna and the euro. The index is arbitrarily set equal to 100 in some base year, and then measures how the currency has subsequently fared.

FIG 2.2 **Trade-weighted exchange rates**
2010=100

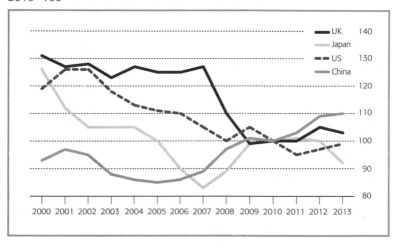

Source: Bank for International Settlements

Figure 2.2 shows the weighted exchange rates for four currencies prepared by the Bank for International Settlements on the basis of their trade with other economies. Other methods of calculating trade weights would produce different changes in the currencies' measured performance.

These indexes suffer from problems common to all indexes, such as failing to accommodate changes in trade patterns since the start date. Nonetheless, they make clear two basic facts of life in the currency markets. First, no currency is strong forever, so buy and hold is not a profitable strategy in foreign-exchange markets. Second, currencies can fluctuate greatly over comparatively brief periods of time, offering potentially huge gains to investors who are astute enough to guess which way the markets will go.

3 Money markets

THE TERM "MONEY MARKET" refers to the network of corporations, financial institutions, investors and governments which deal with the flow of short-term capital. When a business needs cash for a couple of months until a big payment arrives, or when a bank wants to invest money that depositors may withdraw at any moment, or when a government tries to meet its payroll in the face of big seasonal fluctuations in tax receipts, the short-term liquidity transactions occur in the money market.

The money markets have expanded significantly in recent years as a result of the general outflow of money from the banking industry, a process referred to as disintermediation. Until the start of the 1980s, financial markets in almost all countries were centred on commercial banks. Savers and investors kept most of their assets on deposit with banks, either as short-term demand deposits, such as cheque-writing accounts, paying little or no interest, or in the form of certificates of deposit that tied up the money for years. Drawing on this reliable supply of low-cost money, banks were the main source of credit for both businesses and consumers.

Financial deregulation and the ease of moving money electronically caused banks to lose market share in both deposit gathering and lending. This trend has been encouraged by legislation, such as the Monetary Control Act of 1980 in the United States, which allowed market forces rather than regulators to determine interest rates. Investors can place their money on deposit with investment companies that offer competitive interest rates without requiring a long-term commitment. Many borrowers can sell short-term debt to the same sorts of entities, also at competitive rates, rather than negotiating loans from bankers. The money markets are the mechanism that brings these borrowers and investors together without the comparatively costly intermediation of banks. They make it possible for borrowers to meet short-run liquidity needs and deal with irregular cash flows without resorting to more costly means of raising money.

There is an identifiable money market for each currency, because interest rates vary from one currency to another. These markets are not independent, and both investors and borrowers will shift from one currency to another depending upon relative interest rates. However, regulations limit the ability of some money-market investors to hold foreign-currency instruments, and most money-market investors are concerned to minimise any risk of loss as a result of exchange-rate fluctuations. For these reasons, most money-market transactions occur in the investor's home currency.

The money markets do not exist in a particular place or operate according to a single set of rules. Nor do they offer a single set of posted prices, with one current interest rate for money. Rather, they are webs of borrowers and lenders, all linked by telephones and computers. At the centre of each web is the central bank whose policies determine the short-term interest rates for that currency. Arrayed around the central bankers are the treasurers of tens of thousands of businesses and government agencies, whose job is to invest any unneeded cash as safely and profitably as possible and, when necessary, to borrow at the lowest possible cost. The connections among them are established by banks and investment companies that trade securities as their main business. The constant soundings among these diverse players for the best available rate at a particular moment are the force that keeps the market competitive.

The worldwide financial crisis that started in 2007 was felt strongly in the money markets. Money-market investors tend to be highly risk averse; that is, they value the absolute safety of their funds more than the higher return they would receive for taking risks. As many banks and industrial companies showed signs of financial distress, investors became concerned about the accuracy of their accounts and were reluctant to extend credit even on an extremely short-term basis. The "freezing" of the money markets blocked normal lending activity in the United States and much of Europe for an extended period, helping drive those economies into recession.

Data from the Bank for International Settlements, which compiles statistics gathered by national central banks, indicate that around $13 trillion of money-market instruments were in circulation worldwide in 2012. This represented a significant drop from the $14 trillion outstanding in December 2008, but was still far above the $6 trillion figure at the end of 2001.

What money markets do

There is no precise definition of the money markets, but the phrase is usually applied to the buying and selling of debt instruments maturing in one year or less. The money markets are thus related to the bond markets, in which corporations and governments borrow and lend based on longer-term contracts. Similar to bond investors, money-market investors are extending credit, without taking any ownership in the borrowing entity or any control over management.

Yet the money markets and the bond markets (which are discussed in Chapter 4) serve different purposes. Bond issuers typically raise money to finance investments that will generate profits – or, in the case of government issuers, public benefits – for many years into the future. Issuers of money-market instruments are usually more concerned with cash management or with financing their portfolios of financial assets.

A well-functioning money market facilitates the development of a market for longer-term securities. Money markets attach a price to liquidity, the availability of money for immediate investment. The interest rates for extremely short-term use of money serve as benchmarks for longer-term financial instruments. If the money markets are active, or "liquid", borrowers and investors always have the option of engaging in a series of short-term transactions rather than in longer-term transactions, and this usually holds down longer-term rates. In the absence of active money markets to set short-term rates, issuers and investors may have less confidence that longer-term rates are reasonable and greater concern about being able to sell their securities should they so choose. For this reason, countries with less active money markets, on balance, also tend to have less active bond markets.

Investing in money markets

Short-term instruments are often unattractive to small investors, because the high cost of learning about the financial status of a borrower can outweigh the benefits of acquiring a security with a life span of three months. For this reason, investors typically purchase money-market instruments through funds, rather than buying individual securities directly.

Money-market funds

The expansion of the money markets has been fuelled by a special type of entity, the money-market fund, which pools money-market securities, allowing investors to diversify risk among the various company and government securities held by the fund. Retail money-market funds cater for individuals, and institutional money-market funds serve corporations, foundations, government agencies and other large investors. The funds are normally required by law or regulation to invest only in cash equivalents, securities whose safety and liquidity make them almost as good as cash.

Money-market funds are a comparatively recent innovation. They reduce investors' search costs and risks. They are also able to perform the role of intermediation at much lower cost than banks, because money-market funds do not need to maintain branch offices, accept accounts with small balances and otherwise deal with the diverse demands of bank customers. Also, unlike banks, money-market funds typically are not required to set aside a portion of investors' funds to cover possible losses on investments, enabling them to pay higher interest rates to investors than banks can. The spread between the rate money-market funds pay investors and the rate at which they lend out these investors' money is normally a few tenths of a percentage point, rather than the spread of several percentage points between what banks pay depositors and charge borrowers.

The shift of short-term capital into investment funds rather than banks is most advanced in the United States, which began

FIG 3.1 **Money-market fund assets and demand deposits in the United States**
Year end, $bn

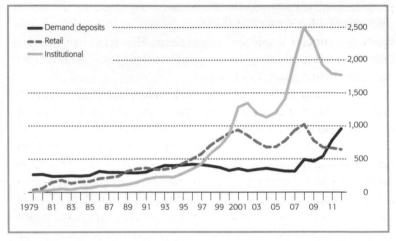

Source: Federal Reserve Board

deregulating its financial sector earlier than most other countries. The flow of assets into money-market funds is related to the gap between short-term and long-term interest rates; assets in US money-market funds fell between 2001 and 2005, as extremely low short-term interest rates encouraged investors to put their money elsewhere. The same phenomenon led investors in many countries to reduce their holdings of money-market assets after 2008, as interest rates fell to the extent that many money-market funds were paying annual interest rates well below 1%. Figure 3.1 illustrates the shift.

According to the Investment Company Institute, assets of money-market funds worldwide were $4.8 trillion at the end of 2012, representing a 17% decrease since 2008. Investors in US money-market funds owned 56% of these assets. Money-market funds are relatively undeveloped in a number of countries with vibrant stock and bond markets, including Germany, Japan and the UK.

Stable value

In many cases, money-market funds have attracted investors by promoting the idea that while interest rates may fluctuate, the fund's shares have a fixed value. In the United States, money-market funds typically maintain a value of $1 per share. This fixed value makes money-market funds attractive relative to bank deposits, whose value does not fluctuate from day to day.

The difficulty with promoting stable value is that the values of money-market securities owned by a fund may fluctuate. In particular, short-term securities issued by a company may lose much or all of their value if the issuer encounters financial distress or declares bankruptcy. In such cases, the money-market fund may be able to maintain its stable value only if the investment company that operates it puts in sufficient money to make up for the diminished value of the securities the fund owns; otherwise, the per-share value of the fund will need to fall, causing losses for investors. A management company is not legally required to support its money-market funds, but it may choose to do so to protect the reputations of other funds it operates.

The vulnerability of money-market funds proved to be a problem in 2009, when the failures of certain banks destroyed the value of their securities held by some money-market funds. In some of these cases, funds recognised the losses by reducing their per-share value below the normal level – an event known in the United States as "breaking the buck". Central banks feared that panicked investors would flee the funds, causing even greater losses to investors as funds dumped securities and endangering businesses that routinely sold money-market securities to meet their cash needs. The US Federal Reserve and some other central banks stepped in to guarantee the value of money-market funds for limited periods, effectively giving money-market investors the same protection generally accorded to bank depositors.

Following that crisis, regulators in several countries sought to require money-market funds to have fluctuating per-share values, with each day's value depending upon the value of the securities owned by the fund. The managers of money-market funds have strongly resisted this change, because they believe announcing that investors could lose some of their principal would make such funds less attractive.

Individual sweep accounts

The investment companies that operate equity funds and bond funds usually provide money-market funds to house the cash that investors wish to keep available for immediate investment. People with large amounts of assets often invest in money-market instruments through sweep accounts. These are multipurpose accounts at banks or stockbrokerage firms, with the assets used for paying current bills, investing in shares and buying mutual funds. Any uncommitted cash is automatically "swept" into money-market funds or overnight investments at the end of each day, in order to earn the highest possible return.

Institutional investors

Money-market funds are by no means the only investors in money-market instruments. All sizeable banks maintain trading departments that actively speculate in short-term securities. Investment trusts (mutual funds) that mainly hold bonds or equities normally keep a small proportion of their assets in money-market instruments to provide flexibility, in part to meet investors' requests to redeem shares in the trust without having to dispose of long-term holdings. Pension funds and insurers, which typically invest with long time horizons, also invest a proportion of their assets in money-market instruments in order to have access to cash at any time without liquidating long-term positions. Businesses in the United States owned $575 billion of money-market instruments, including commercial paper and shares in money-market funds, at June 2013. Certain types of money-market instruments, particularly bank certificates of deposit, are often owned directly by individual investors.

Interest rates and prices

Borrowers in the money markets pay interest for the use of the money they have borrowed. Most money-market securities pay interest at a

TABLE 3.1 **Domestic money-market instruments worldwide**
Year end, $bn

	1994	2000	2006	2008	2011
Commercial paper	858	2,089	2,793	2,424	2,149
Treasury bills	1,993	1,888	3,621	4,958	5,640
Other short-term paper	1,386	1,931	4,531	5,375	3,705
Total	4,237	5,909	10,946	12,757	11,493

Source: Bank for International Settlements

fixed rate, which is determined by market conditions at the time they are issued. Some issuers prefer to offer adjustable-rate instruments, on which the rate will change from time to time according to procedures laid down at the time the instruments are sold. Because of their short maturities, most money-market instruments do not pay periodic interest during their lifetimes but rather are sold to investors at a discount to their face value. The investor can redeem them at face value when they mature, with the profit on the redemption serving in place of interest payments.

The value of money-market securities changes inversely to changes in short-term interest rates. Because money-market instruments by nature are short term, their prices are much less volatile than the prices of longer-term instruments, and any loss or gain from holding the security in the short time until maturity rather than investing at current yields is small.

Types of instruments

There are numerous types of money-market instruments. The best known are commercial paper, bankers' acceptances, treasury bills, government agency notes, local government notes, interbank loans, time deposits and paper issued by international organisations. The amount issued during the course of a year is much greater than the amount outstanding at any one time, as many money-market securities are outstanding for only short periods of time.

Commercial paper

Commercial paper is a short-term debt obligation of a private-sector firm or a government-sponsored corporation. In most cases, the paper has a lifetime, or maturity, greater than 90 days but less than nine months. This maturity is dictated by regulations. In the United States, most new securities must be registered with the regulator, the Securities and Exchange Commission, prior to issuance, but securities with a maturity of 270 days or less are exempt from this requirement. Commercial paper is usually unsecured, although a particular commercial paper issue may be secured by a specific asset of the issuer or may be guaranteed by a bank.

The market for commercial paper first developed in the United States in the late 19th century. Its main advantage was that it allowed financially sound companies to meet their short-term financing needs at lower rates than could be obtained by borrowing directly from banks. At a time when US bank deposits were not insured, short-term corporate debt was not necessarily a riskier investment choice for savers than a bank deposit. In the wake of the Great Depression, during which the government created a deposit-insurance scheme, the popularity of commercial paper fell. By the early 1980s, annual issuance of commercial paper in the United States was only about one-fifth the annual volume of bank lending.

Commercial paper became hugely more popular in the 1980s. At a time of high inflation and soaring short-term interest rates, regulations limited the interest that banks could pay depositors. Money-market funds enabled investors to earn higher rates than banks could offer, and strong non-banking firms discovered that they could raise money more cheaply by selling commercial paper to money-market funds than by borrowing from banks. These events caused the commercial paper market to thrive. It has continued to grow rapidly, with occasional interruptions due to conditions in the financial markets. Issuance fell sharply amid financial crisis in 2007–08.

Because financial deregulation came earlier in the United States than elsewhere, the US commercial paper market was the first to develop. However, commercial paper markets have developed rapidly in other countries, and the US share of worldwide issuance has fallen.

In the years prior to the financial crisis, commercial paper issuance by financial firms expanded enormously, as shown in Table 3.2. This category includes, for example, firms that finance industrial equipment, aircraft leasing companies and the financing subsidiaries of automobile manufacturers. These firms, which compete with banks, often find it profitable to use commercial paper to fund loans to individual borrowers without the expense and regulatory complications of becoming a bank and gathering deposits. However, as many banks and non-bank financial firms encountered difficulties from 2008, investors were reluctant to purchase their commercial paper. Consequently, some of these firms failed because they were unable to raise funds to pay off maturing commercial paper.

TABLE 3.2 **Corporate commercial paper outstanding in the United States**
Seasonally adjusted, year end, $bn

	1992	1996	2000	2004	2008	2012
Financial	407	601	1,206	1,268	731	508
Non-financial	146	187	398	120	202	208
Total	553	788	1,606	1,388	922	716

Source: Federal Reserve Board

Commercial paper was slow to develop in most other countries, as they lacked a legal framework for it. The exception is Canada, where outstandings reached C$164 billion in 2006, before the financial crisis led to a sharp contraction in the market and government intervention to assure payment. The market stabilised at around C$54 billion in 2010–13, less than one-third of its maximum size

In addition to domestic issues, $506 billion of commercial paper was outstanding on international markets at June 2013. This amount refers to paper that was sold outside the issuer's country and was not denominated in the currency of the country where it was issued. Approximately 40% of international commercial paper was denominated in dollars, 30% in euros and most of the remainder in sterling. The share of international commercial paper denominated in euros increased until 2011, as it could be traded throughout the euro zone with no currency risk, but euro-denominated issuance diminished amid renewed financial crisis. The largest single source of international commercial paper issuance is Germany, reflecting the importance of German banks and the difficulty of issuing such securities on the German domestic markets, followed by the United States, the UK, the Netherlands and Spain.

Many large companies have continual commercial paper programmes, bringing new short-term debt on to the market every few weeks or months. It is common for issuers to roll over their paper, using the proceeds of a new issue to repay the principal of a previous issue. In effect, this allows issuers to borrow money for long periods of time at short-term interest rates, which may be significantly lower than long-term rates. The short-term nature of the obligation lowers the risk perceived by investors. Thus, although gross issuance of international commercial paper in sterling in the first quarter of 2013 came to $86 billion, net issuance, after repayment of previously outstanding paper, was only $10 billion, reflecting the fact that $76 billion of sterling-denominated commercial paper matured during the quarter.

These continual borrowing programmes are not riskless. If market conditions or a change in the firm's financial circumstances preclude a new commercial paper issue, the borrower faces default if it lacks the cash to redeem the paper that is maturing. This occurred to several major US and European companies in 2001 and 2002 and to banks in several countries between 2008 and 2012: the credit-rating agencies lowered their ratings, making it impossible for them to sell new commercial paper and thus confronting them with dire shortages of cash. Some of the companies were able to avert bankruptcy thanks to last-minute loans from banks, but others were forced to declare themselves bankrupt. Companies that wish to issue commercial paper typically obtain "back-up" credit lines from banks, which they can draw on to repay outstanding commercial paper in the event they are unable to roll it over. Banks' reluctance or inability to extend such credit lines was one reason commercial paper issuance has declined since 2008. The use of commercial paper also creates a risk that if interest rates should rise, the total cost of successive short-term borrowings may be greater than had the firm undertaken longer-term borrowing when rates were low.

Bankers' acceptances

Before the 1980s, bankers' acceptances were the main way for firms to raise short-term funds in the money markets. An acceptance is a promissory note issued by a non-financial firm to a bank in return for a loan. The bank resells the note in the money market at a discount and guarantees payment. Acceptances usually have a maturity of less than six months.

Bankers' acceptances differ from commercial paper in significant ways. They are usually tied to the sale or storage of specific goods, such as an export order for which the proceeds will be received in two or three months. They are not issued at all by financial-industry firms. They do not bear interest; instead, an investor purchases the acceptance at a discount from face value and then redeems it for face value at maturity. Investors rely on the strength of the guarantor bank, rather than of the issuing company, for their security.

In an era when banks were able to borrow at lower cost than other types of firms, bankers' acceptances allowed manufacturers to take advantage of banks' superior credit standing. This advantage has largely disappeared, as many other big corporate borrowers are considered at least as creditworthy as banks. Although bankers' acceptances are still a significant source of financing for some companies, their importance has diminished considerably as a result of the greater flexibility and lower cost of commercial paper. The amount outstanding in the United States peaked at $74 billion in 1974, and fell steadily to near zero by 2000. They are more extensively issued in some other countries, notably Canada, where C$64 billion was outstanding in 2013.

Treasury bills

Treasury bills, often referred to as t-bills, are securities with a maturity of one year or less, issued by national governments. Treasury bills issued by a government in its own currency are generally considered the safest of all possible investments in that currency. Such securities account for a larger share of money-market trading than any other type of instrument.

The mix of money-market and longer-term debt issuance varies considerably from government to government and time to time. Like other borrowers, governments will want to undertake long-term borrowings when the gap between short-term and long-term interest rates is low, but will prefer shorter-term borrowings when the cost of long-term debt is relatively high. The US government, for example, sought to reduce the average length of its borrowing, starting in 1996, to reduce interest costs, but then announced in 2005 that it would resume issuance of 30-year bonds to finance an increased national debt. By 2013, approximately $1.6 trillion in US Treasury bills with a maturity of one year or less was outstanding, amounting to less than one-eighth of the public debt of nearly $12 trillion. Similarly, the Canadian government increased short-term borrowing from about one-fifth of total borrowings in 2000 to more than one-quarter in 2013. The government of Japan had exhibited a strong preference for long-term bonds, but sharply increased its issuance of short-term securities after 2001. The German government makes relatively little use of money-market instruments, relying more heavily on longer-term borrowings. France emphasised short-term government debt in 2004, but then replaced much of it with longer-term debt in 2005. The UK has traditionally avoided issuing short-term treasury securities, but it expanded the stock of short-term treasury debt from £2 billion in 2001 to more than £70 billion at various times in the 2012/13 fiscal year.

In cases where a government is unable to convince investors to buy its longer-term obligations, treasury bills may be its principal source of financing. This is the main reason for the steep growth in treasury-bill issuance by the governments of emerging-market countries during the 1980s. Many of these countries have histories of inflation or political instability that have made investors wary of long-term bonds, forcing governments as well as non-government borrowers to use short-term instruments. As countries develop reputations for better economic and fiscal management, they are often able to borrow for longer terms rather than relying exclusively

TABLE 3.3 **Domestic treasury bills outstanding**

	$bn, year end
1996	2,002
1998	1,826
2000	1,833
2002	2,317
2004	3,413
2006	3,621
2008	4,958
2011	5,640

Source: Bank for International Settlements

on short-term instruments. At the end of 1999, for example, 53% of the Brazilian government's debt was due within one year, but short-term borrowing diminished as the government was able to obtain longer-term financing at more favourable rates.

Some emerging-market countries have issued treasury bills denominated in foreign currencies, mainly dollars, in order to borrow at lower rates than prevail in their home currency. This strategy requires frequent refinancing of short-term foreign-currency debt. When a sudden fall in the value of the currency raises the domestic-currency cost of refinancing that debt, the government may not be able to meet its obligations unless foreign investors are willing to purchase new treasury-bill issues to repay maturing issues. This caused debt crises in Mexico in 1995, Russia in 1998 and Brazil in 1999.

The overall size of the treasury-bill market changes considerably from year to year, depending upon the status of governments' fiscal policies. The market shrank in the late 1990s as a result of the shift from budget deficits to budget surpluses, which reduced government debt outstanding in the United States, Canada, most EU countries and some emerging markets, but then expanded after 2000 as many governments increased their budget deficits to combat recession. The market grew rapidly from 2008 as the United States and many European countries experienced large government deficits (see Table 3.3).

Government agency notes

National government agencies and government-sponsored corporations are heavy borrowers in the money markets in many countries. These include entities such as development banks, housing finance corporations, education lending agencies and agricultural finance agencies.

Agencies of the US government became some of the most important money-market borrowers, dramatically increasing their issuance of short-term debt during the 1990s and early 2000s. This includes the paper of such agencies as the Tennessee Valley Authority, an electricity utility, and the Federal Home Loan Bank System, the central authority for savings institutions.

Local government notes

Local government notes are issued by state, provincial or local governments, and by agencies of these governments such as schools authorities and transport commissions. The ability of governments at this level to issue money-market securities varies greatly from country to country. In some cases, the approval of national authorities is required; in others, local agencies are allowed to borrow only from banks and cannot enter the money markets.

One common use for short-term local government securities is to deal with highly seasonal tax receipts. Such securities, called tax anticipation notes, are issued to finance general government operations during a period when tax receipts are expected to be low, and are redeemed after a tax payment deadline. Local governments and their agencies may also issue short-term instruments in anticipation of transfers from a higher level of government. This allows them to proceed with spending plans even though the transfer from higher authorities has not yet been received.

Interbank loans

Loans extended from one bank to another with which it has no affiliation are called interbank loans. Many of these loans are across international boundaries and are used by the borrowing institution to re-lend to its own customers. As of December 2012, banks had

$19 trillion outstanding to banks in other countries, with almost all of it maturing within one year. These flows of interbank lending are an important mechanism whereby the easing or tightening of credit conditions in one country is felt in other countries.

Banks lend far greater sums to other institutions in their own country. Overnight loans are short-term unsecured loans from one bank to another. They may be used to help the borrowing bank finance loans to customers, but often the borrowing bank adds the money to its reserves in order to meet regulatory requirements and to balance assets and liabilities.

The interest rates at which banks extend short-term loans to one another have assumed international importance. Many financial instruments have interest rates tied to the London inter-bank offered rate (Libor), which is supposedly the average of rates charged by important banks in the UK for overnight loans to one another. In 2012, authorities in the UK accused numerous banks of "rigging" Libor by submitting false information about rates being charged on loans to other banks. This resulted in Libor being set artificially high, requiring borrowers to pay excessively high interest rates on floating-rate loans tied to Libor.

A newer interest rate, Euribor, the rate at which European banks lend to each other, fulfils the same function for financial instruments denominated in euros. In the United States the Fed funds rate, the rate at which banks with excess reserves lend to those that are temporarily short of reserves, is the primary policy lever of the Federal Reserve Board, and hence a closely watched economic indicator. Each of these rates is applied only to loans to healthy, creditworthy institutions. A bank that believes another bank to be in danger of failing will charge sharply higher interest rates or may refuse to lend at all, even overnight, lest the unsecured loan be lost if the borrower fails.

Time deposits

Time deposits, another name for certificates of deposit or CDs, are interest-bearing bank deposits that cannot be withdrawn without penalty before a specified date. Although time deposits may last for as long as five years, those with terms of less than one year compete with other money-market instruments. Time deposits with terms as brief as 30 days are common. Large time deposits are often used by corporations, governments and money-market funds to invest cash for brief periods. Banks in the United States held $1.5 trillion in large time deposits in mid-2013. Nearly half that amount was held in the US offices of banks based in other countries.

International agency paper

International agency paper is issued by the World Bank, the Inter-American Development Bank and other organisations owned by member governments. These organisations often borrow in many different currencies, depending upon interest and exchange rates.

Repos

Repurchase agreements, known as repos, play a critical role in the money markets. They serve to keep the markets highly liquid, which in turn ensures that there will be a constant supply of buyers for new money-market instruments.

A repo is a combination of two transactions. In the first, a securities dealer, such as a bank, sells securities it owns to an investor, agreeing to repurchase the securities at a specified higher price at a future date. In the second transaction, days or months later, the repo is unwound as the dealer buys back the securities from the investor. The amount the investor lends is less than the market value of the securities, a difference called the haircut, to ensure that it still has sufficient collateral if the value of the securities should fall before the dealer repurchases them.

For the investor, the repo offers a profitable short-term use for unneeded cash. A large investor whose investment is greater than the amount covered by bank insurance may deem repos safer than bank deposits, as there is no risk of loss if the bank fails. The investor profits in two ways. First, it receives more for reselling the securities than it paid to purchase them. In effect, it is collecting interest on the money it advances to the dealer at a rate known as the repo rate. Second, if it believes the price of the securities will fall, the investor can sell them and later purchase equivalent securities to return to the dealer just before the repo must be unwound. The dealer, meanwhile, has obtained a loan in the cheapest possible way, and can use the proceeds to purchase yet more securities.

In a reverse repo the roles are switched, with an investor selling securities to a dealer and subsequently repurchasing them. The benefit to the investor is the use of cash at an interest rate below that of other instruments.

Repos and reverse repos allow dealers, such as banks and investment banks, to maintain large inventories of money-market securities while preserving their liquidity by lending out the securities in their portfolios. They have therefore become an important source of financing for dealers in money-market instruments. Many dealers and investors also take positions in the repo market to profit from anticipated interest-rate changes, through matched book trading. This might entail arranging a repo in one security and a reverse repo in another, both to expire on the same day, in the expectation that the difference in the prices of the two securities will change.

Investors like repos partly because of their flexibility. The average maturity of a repo is only a few days, but it is possible to arrange one for any desired term. An investor can arrange an overnight repo, which carries the lowest interest rate but must be repaid the following day; a term repo, which is settled on a specific date usually 3–6 months hence and carries a slightly higher rate; or an open repo, which continues until one or the other party demands its termination at a rate close to the overnight repo rate. Historically, most repos have involved national government notes or, in the United States, the notes of federally sponsored agencies, although other types of securities have come to be used more frequently. But in the 2007–08 crisis investors became reluctant to accept non-government securities as collateral for repos because of uncertainty about those securities' true value. The decrease in US repo activity reduced banks' ability to lend, helping turn the financial crisis into an economic downturn.

The repo market was originally a result of government regulations limiting the interest banks could pay on short-term deposits. It grew rapidly in the United States, the largest single market. Even after a decline in the wake of the financial crisis, an average of $279 billion of repo loans was outstanding on an average day in 2013. The

European repo market was slower to develop and until recently was small. However, a survey found an average €5.6 trillion of repos on banks' books in December 2012, triple the amount in 2001. Roughly 60% of the European repo market is denominated in euros, with the remainder mainly in sterling and dollars.

In Japan, *gensaki*, repos with Japanese government bonds, have been traded since 1976. The *gensaki* market declined during the 1980s as a result of the increased use of commercial paper and a tax on transactions. By 1998 the average amount of *gensaki* outstanding was only about $90 billion. As part of its 1998 financial-market reform programme the Bank of Japan, the central bank, announced its intention to revive the Japanese repo market, but as of 2013 it remained modest in size.

Futures and the money markets

Investors in the money markets use futures contracts on money-market rates for a variety of purposes, including hedging and cash management. By buying or selling a futures contract on a short-term interest rate or a short-term debt security, an investor can profit if the relevant rate is above or below the chosen level on the contract's expiration date. Interest-rate futures can also be used to cover, or hedge, the risk that money-market instruments will decrease in value because of interest-rate changes. Futures markets in many countries trade contracts based on three-month government securities, and there are also contracts based on overnight bank lending rates. Institutional investors use futures contracts, along with short-term notes and commercial paper, as an integral part of their money-market strategies. (Futures markets are discussed in Chapter 8.)

How trading occurs

Trading in money-market instruments occurs almost entirely over telephone links and computer systems. The banks and non-bank dealers in money-market instruments sign contracts, either with one another or with a central clearing house, committing themselves to completing transactions on the terms agreed.

Some clearing houses are government entities, such as the Central

Moneymarkets Office of the Bank of England, whereas others, such as the Depository Trust Company in New York and Euroclear in Brussels, are co-operative institutions owned by the banks and dealers active in the market. When a trade occurs, one or both parties is responsible for reporting the event electronically to the clearing house, which settles the trade by debiting the bank account of the dealer responsible for the purchase and crediting the account of the selling dealer. Most money-market instruments exist only in electronic book-entry form and are held by the clearing house at all times; after a trade, the clearing house simply holds the instrument on behalf of the new owner instead of the previous one. The clearing house thus reduces counterparty risk – the risk that the parties to a transaction might not live up to their obligations. It generally does not serve as an investigative or enforcement agency, so if there is a dispute between the putative buyer and seller as to the terms of a trade it must be resolved by the parties themselves or in the legal system.

Because of the large amounts of money involved, the collapse of an important bank or securities dealer with many unsettled trades could pose a threat to other banks and dealers as well. For this reason, clearing houses have been striving to achieve real-time settlement, in which funds and securities are transferred as quickly as possible after the transaction has been reported.

Credit ratings and the money market

Ratings agencies are private firms that offer opinions about the creditworthiness of borrowers in the financial markets. The issuers of treasury bills, agency notes, local government notes and international agency paper usually obtain ratings before bringing their issues to market. Some commercial paper issues are rated, although in many cases the ratings agency expresses its view of an issuer's multi-year commercial paper programme rather than judging each issue separately. Participants in interbank lending and buyers of bankers' acceptances look for a rating not of the particular deal, but of the financial institutions involved.

Three firms, Moody's Investor Services, Standard & Poor's (S&P) and Fitch, rate money-market issuers around the world. Their ratings scales for short-term corporate debt appear in Table 3.4. Some of these agencies maintain separate scales for rating short-term government debt, commercial paper and banks' strength. Many other ratings agencies specialise in individual industries or countries.

TABLE 3.4 **Short-term credit ratings**[a]

	Moody's	S&P	Fitch Ratings
Very strong capacity to pay	Prime-1	SP-1+	F1, F1+
Strong capacity to pay	Prime-2	SP-1	F2
Adequate ability to pay	Prime-3	SP-2	F3
Speculative ability to pay	Not prime	SP-3	B, C
In default			D

a Exact definitions used by agencies may differ.
Source: Ratings agencies

Tier importance

These ratings have a great impact on the market. In the United States, money-market funds invest overwhelmingly in Tier 1 commercial paper, defined as paper having the highest short-term ratings from at least two ratings agencies. Funds are prohibited from investing more than 5% of their assets in Tier 2 paper, defined as paper that does not qualify for Tier 1. As a result, comparatively little commercial paper is issued by firms that cannot qualify for Tier 1, and there is almost no below-investment-grade paper available in the market. Similarly, banks that do not have high financial strength ratings will have difficulty attracting certificates of deposit, and the lowering of a bank's rating by any of the ratings agencies will cause depositors to demand higher interest rates or to flee altogether.

Money markets and monetary policy

The money markets play a central role in the execution of central banks' monetary policy in many countries. Until recently, the job of national central banks, which indirectly seek to regulate the amount of credit in the economy in order to manage economic growth and inflation, involved mainly purchasing and selling government debt to government-securities dealers in open-market operations. These operations involve adding money to or draining money out of the banking system, which encourages or constrains banks' lending and thereby affects spending and demand in the economy.

These days, however, central banks in countries with well-developed financial systems often manage monetary policy through the repo market rather than with direct purchases and sales of securities. Under this system, the central bank enters into a repurchase agreement with a dealer. The money it pays the dealer passes to the dealer's bank, adding reserves to the banking system. When the repo matures the dealer returns the money to the central bank, draining the banking system of reserves unless the central bank enters into new repo transactions to keep the reserves level unchanged.

If the central bank wishes to drain reserves from the system, it engages in a matched sale–purchase transaction, selling securities from its portfolio to dealers with agreements to repurchase them at future dates.

Central bank interest rates

In many countries, central banks can also lend directly to the money markets by providing credit to financial institutions at posted rates. Such loans are mainly for the purpose of helping institutions that have experienced sudden withdrawals of funds or otherwise face a lack of liquidity. Central bank loan rates are often less attractive than those available in the private sector, so as to encourage financial institutions to borrow in the money markets before turning to the central bank. Central bank rates change much less frequently than rates in the money markets. The main central bank loan rate in the United States and Japan is called the discount rate. The corresponding rate in the UK is the base rate and in Canada the Bank of Canada rate. The rate at which the European Central Bank (ECB) lends to banks in the euro zone is its marginal lending rate.

Open-market operations have a direct impact on interest rates in the money markets. A central bank's use of money-market rates to accelerate or retard economic growth affects investors' expectations of inflation, which in turn influence longer-term rates. Open-market operations thus permit central banks to exercise at least limited influence over medium-term and long-term interest rates.

Watching short-term interest rates

Central banks, governments and investors pay close attention to short-term interest rates.

Spreads

In particular, spreads, the differences in interest rates on different instruments, are highly sensitive indicators of market participants' expectations.

One important set of spreads is that between uncollateralised loans and repos. As repos are fully collateralised, there is almost no risk that repayment will be disrupted. Uncollateralised loans among banks, however, are at risk if a bank should fail. The spread between these two types of lending thus reflects perceived creditworthiness. Comparing spreads in various countries is instructive. During winter 1998, for example, the average spread between uncollateralised three-month loans and three-month repos was 21 basis points (hundredths of a percentage point) in the UK, 5.6 basis points in the United States, 8 basis points in France and 58 basis points in Japan, the much wider spread reflecting the general view that many Japanese banks were extremely weak.

The spreads between different categories of commercial paper are closely watched by the Federal Reserve in the United States and by the Bank of Canada. The spread between paper rated AA and that with a weaker A2-P2 rating is usually 15–20 basis points. A widening may indicate that investors are worried about a deteriorating economy, which would be more likely to cause financial distress for issuers of A2-P2 paper than for issuers of stronger AA-rated paper. A spread between top-rated commercial paper issued by financial companies and that issued by non-financial companies also indicates anxiety in the markets, as in good times paper from financial and non-financial issuers bears similar interest rates. The ECB's reliance on repos to implement monetary policy means that the two-week euro repo rate has become an important indicator. The spread between two-week repos on German government securities and short-term notes also receives considerable attention in the markets.

Overnight rates

Rates paid on overnight bank deposits also receive close attention. In some countries this is known as the call rate; in the euro-zone countries it is called Eonia (euro overnight index average). Differences in rates for money-market instruments of different maturities are among the most sensitive economic indicators. An example is Japan, where in 2005, after several years of poor economic growth and deepening problems in the banking sector, the economy began to show signs of recovery. Interest rates were extremely low throughout the year. In late August 2005, the closely watched call rate on overnight bank deposits earned interest at an average annual rate close to zero, and money placed on deposit for three months earned an average of 0.02%. One month later, as shown in Figure 3.2, the overnight rate was still negligible, but the rate on three-month deposits had begun to move up as borrowers increased their demand for funds.

FIG 3.2 **Money-market rates in Japan**
Annualised weekly average

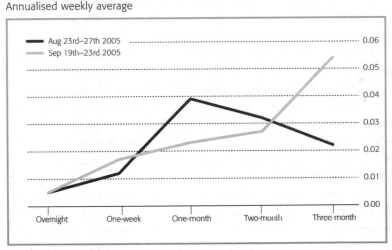

Source: Bank of Japan

In more technical language, the yield curve, which traces the interest-rate yields of securities of different maturities from the same issuer, steepened during the month, at least at the long end. Why? An investor with a three-month time horizon can choose to make 91 consecutive overnight investments rather than a single investment for three months. The three-month rate can therefore be thought of as a forecast of overnight rates for the coming three months. It is usually higher than the overnight rate to compensate for inflation, which could erode the value of the investor's principal over time. The drop in the three-month rate during December indicates that at the end of the month investors no longer expected overnight rates to rise as much as they had thought likely at the start of December. As overnight rates are strongly influenced by the policies of the central bank, this suggests that investors thought it less likely that the Bank of Japan would push up interest rates soon, presumably because economic conditions had not improved as much as had been expected. (The yield curve is discussed in more detail in Chapter 4.)

The prime rate

The prime rate was established decades ago as the interest rate charged by banks in the United States to their best corporate borrowers, and it once received a great deal of attention in the news media. Although big corporate borrowers are no longer affected by the prime rate, it is the basis for some variable-rate consumer credit, including credit-card loans and home-equity loans. Thus a rise in the prime rate often curtails consumer spending. The rate, however, changes only infrequently and by increments of 0.25%, rather than daily in response to immediate money-market conditions. Another US money-market rate, that for US Treasury securities adjusted to an average maturity of one year, is used as the basis for many adjustable-rate mortgage loans. Its economic impact has increased as more Americans have taken out adjustable-rate mortgages, although in the United States, unlike some other countries, interest rates on individual mortgages of this type change only once a year.

UK mortgage rates

In contrast, changes in the variable mortgage rates in the UK are passed on to homeowners within a matter of weeks and therefore have an almost immediate impact on the economy. These rates usually change in increments of 0.25%, and lenders are free to alter them, along with the mortgage payments they govern, as often as desired. This has made mortgage rates one of the UK's most sensitive economic indicators.

4   Bond markets

THE WORD "BOND" means contract, agreement, or guarantee. All these terms are applicable to the securities known as bonds. An investor who purchases a bond is lending money to the issuer, and the bond represents the issuer's contractual promise to pay interest and repay principal according to specified terms. A short-term bond is often called a note.

Bonds were a natural outgrowth of the loans that early bankers provided to finance wars starting in the Middle Ages. As governments' financial appetites grew, bankers found it increasingly difficult to come up with as much money as their clients wanted to borrow. Bonds offered a way for governments to borrow from many individuals rather than just a handful of bankers, and they made it easier for lenders to reduce their risks by selling the bonds to others if they thought the borrower might not repay. The earliest known bond was issued by the Bank of Venice in 1157, to fund a war with Constantinople.

Today, bonds are the most widely used of all financial instruments. The size of the global bond market in early 2013 exceeded $90 trillion, of which roughly $70 trillion traded on domestic markets, and another $21 trillion traded outside the issuer's country of residence.

In the United States, the largest single market, over $850 billion worth of bonds change hands on an average day, and the value of outstanding bonds at March 2013 exceeded $39 trillion. Table 4.1 shows the countries with the largest domestic debt markets.

Bond issuance grew rapidly in many countries from 2009 to 2013, for a variety of reasons. Poor economic conditions encouraged many governments to run large budget deficits, funded by the sale of

TABLE 4.1 **Outstanding amounts of domestic debt securities**[a]
$trn

	December 2004	December 2008	December 2012[b]
US	24.7	24.6	33.0
Japan	15.7	11.1	14.4
China	0.8	2.2	3.8
France	3.3	2.9	3.6
Italy	3.9	3.3	3.0
Germany	3.4	2.6	2.6
Brazil	0.7	0.9	2.1
Canada	1.3	1.0	1.7
Spain	1.3	1.7	1.6
UK	1.7	1.2	1.6
South Korea	0.8	0.9	1.3

a Excludes asset-backed and money-market instruments.   b Figures for some countries are for March.
Source: Bank for International Settlements

government bonds, in order to stimulate their economies. Extremely low long-term interest rates made it attractive for many companies to issue bonds even if they had no immediate need for the money. The improved economic health of some major countries, notably China, Brazil and Mexico, enabled companies in those countries to borrow far more cheaply than in the past in both domestic and foreign currency, contributing to an emerging-market bond boom that ended in 2013.

Bonds are generally classified as fixed-income securities. They are often thought of as dull, low-risk instruments for conservative investors, and as defensive vehicles for preserving capital in unsettled markets. Before the 1970s these stereotypes were true, but bond markets have changed dramatically since then. Some bonds do not guarantee a fixed income. Many bear a high degree of risk. All that bonds have in common is that they are debt securities which entitle the owner to receive interest payments during the life of the bond and repayment of principal, without having ownership or managerial control of the issuer.

Why issue bonds?

Bonds are never an issuer's only source of credit. All the businesses and government entities that choose to sell bonds have already borrowed from banks, and many have received financing from customers, suppliers or specialised finance companies. The principal reason for issuing bonds is to diversify sources of funding. The amount any bank will lend to a single borrower is limited. By tapping the vastly larger base of bond-market investors, the issuer can raise far more money without exhausting its traditional credit lines with direct lenders.

Bonds also help issuers carry out specific financial-management strategies. These include the following:

- **Minimising financing costs.** Leverage, the use of borrowed money, enables profit-making businesses to expand and earn more profit than they could by using only the funds invested by their shareholders. Firms generally prefer bonds to other forms of leverage, such as bank loans, because the cost is lower and the funds can be repaid over a longer period. A bond issue may or may not increase the issuer's leverage, depending upon whether the bonds increase the total amount of borrowing or merely replace other forms of borrowing.

- **Matching revenue and expenses.** Many capital investments, such as a toll bridge or a copper smelter, take years to complete but are then expected to produce revenue over a lengthy period. Bonds offer a way of linking the repayment of borrowings for such projects to anticipated revenue.

- **Promoting intergenerational equity.** Governments often undertake projects, such as building roads or buying park land, which create long-lasting benefits. Bonds offer a means of requiring future taxpayers to pay for the benefits they enjoy, rather than putting the burden on current taxpayers.

- **Controlling risk.** The obligation to repay a bond can be tied to a specific project or a particular government agency. This can insulate the parent corporation or government from responsibility if the bond payments are not made as required.

- **Avoiding short-term financial constraints.** Governments and firms may turn to the bond markets to avoid painful steps, such as tax increases, redundancies or wage reductions, which might otherwise be necessary owing to a lack of cash.

The issuers

Four basic types of entities issue bonds.

National governments

Bonds backed by the full faith and credit of national governments are called sovereigns. These are generally considered the most secure type of bond. A national government has strong incentives to pay on time in order to retain access to credit markets, and it has extraordinary powers, often including the ability to print money and to take control of foreign-currency reserves, which can be used to make payments.

The best-known sovereigns are those issued by the governments of large, wealthy countries. US Treasury bonds, known as Treasuries, are the most widely held securities in the world, with $11.9 trillion in private ownership in mid-2013. Other popular sovereigns include Japanese government bonds, called JGBs; the German government's Bundesanleihen, or Bunds; the gilt-edged shares issued by the British government, known as gilts; and OATs, the French government's *Obligations assimilables du trésor*. Governments of so-called emerging economies, such as Brazil, Argentina and Russia, also issue large amounts of bonds.

Another category of sovereigns includes bonds issued by entities, such as a province or an enterprise, for which a national government has agreed to take responsibility. Investors' enthusiasm for such bonds will depend, among other things, on whether the government has made a legally binding commitment to repay or has only an unenforceable moral obligation. In many countries the amount of debt for which the national government is potentially responsible is high. In the United States, for example, federally sponsored agencies had $2.1 trillion in bonds outstanding as of 2013, down from a peak of $3.2 trillion in 2008. Although much of this does not represent legal obligations of the US government, it would come under heavy pressure to pay if one of the issuing agencies were to default – and in 2008, the government rescued two federally sponsored housing lenders, Fannie Mae and Freddie Mac, to avert such defaults.

Lower levels of government

Bonds issued by a government at the sub-national level, such as a city, a province or a state, are called semi-sovereigns. Semi-sovereigns are generally riskier than sovereigns because a city has no power to print money or to take control of foreign exchange.

The best-known semi-sovereigns are the municipal bonds issued by state and local governments in the United States, which are favoured by some investors because the interest is exempt from US federal income taxes and income taxes in the issuer's state. About $3.7 trillion worth were outstanding in 2013. Canadian provincial bonds, Italian local government bonds and the bonds of Japanese regions and municipalities are also widely traded. Many countries, however, deliberately seek to keep sub-sovereign entities away from the bond markets. This serves to limit their indebtedness, but also assures a steady flow of loan business to banks. The Spanish government's inability to limit borrowing by regional governments forced it to bail out four heavily indebted regions in 2012 in order to protect bondholders. Brazil ended a 15-year ban on bond issuance by state governments in 2013. In the United States, Detroit, Michigan, formerly one of the country's largest cities, was forced to restructure its debts through a bankruptcy proceeding in mid-2013, causing owners of its bonds to lose a large part of their investment.

There are many categories of semi-sovereigns, depending on the way in which repayment is assured. A general-obligation bond gives the bondholder a priority claim on the issuer's tax revenue in the event of default. A revenue bond finances a particular project and gives bondholders a claim only on the revenue the project generates; in the case of a revenue bond issued to build a municipal car park, for example, bondholders cannot rely on the city government to make payments if the car park fails to generate sufficient revenue. Special-purpose bonds provide for repayment from a particular revenue source, such as a tax on hotel stays dedicated to service the bonds for a convention centre, but usually are not backed by the issuer's general fund.

Public-sector debt, including sovereign and semi-sovereign issues, accounts for about 50% of all domestic debt worldwide. The total amount of public-sector debt outstanding in early 2013 was almost $45 trillion, of which $43 trillion was issued by governments within their domestic bond markets and $1.6 trillion was issued internationally.

Corporations

Corporate bonds are issued by business enterprises, whether owned by private investors or by a government. Large firms may have many debt issues outstanding at a given time. In issuing a secured obligation, the firm must pledge specific assets to bondholders. In the case of an electricity utility that sells secured bonds to finance a generating plant, for example, the bondholders might be entitled to take possession of and sell the plant if the company defaults on its bonds, but they would have no claim on other generating plants or the revenue they earn. The holders of senior debt have first claim on the company's revenue and assets if the firm defaults, save those pledged to secured bondholders. The holders of subordinated debt have no claim on assets or income until all other bondholders have been paid. A big firm may have several classes of subordinated debt. Mezzanine debt is a bond issue that has less security than the issuer's other bonds, but more than its shares.

Securitisation vehicles

An asset-backed security is a type of bond on which the required payments will be made out of the income generated by specific assets, such as mortgage loans or future sales. Some asset-backed securities are initiated by government agencies, others by private-sector entities. These sorts of securities are assembled by an investment bank, and often do not represent the obligations of a particular issuer. (Asset backed securities are discussed in Chapter 5.)

The distinctions between the various categories of bonds are often blurred. Government agencies, for example, frequently issue bonds to assist private companies, although investors may have no legal claim against the government if the issuer fails to pay. National governments may lend their moral support, but not necessarily their full faith and credit, to bond issues by state-owned enterprises or even by private enterprises. Corporations in one country may arrange for bonds to be issued by subsidiaries in other countries, eliminating the parent's liability in the event of default but making payment dependent upon the policies of the foreign government.

Bond futures

Futures contracts on interest rates are traded on exchanges in many countries. These contracts allow investors to receive payment if an interest rate is above or below a specified level on the contract's expiration date. Large investors use such contracts as an integral part of their bond-investment strategies. (Futures and interest-rate options contracts are discussed in Chapter 8. Forward contracts, which can also be used to manage the risk that interest rates will change, are discussed in Chapter 9.)

The biggest national markets

Corporate bonds and some asset-backed securities are the main components of the private-sector debt market. This market has been growing rapidly overall, although some countries have seen decreases in the size of their private-sector bond markets from time to time (see Table 4.2).

As Table 4.2 illustrates, a disproportionate share of the world's private-sector debt securities is issued in the United States. This is largely the result of deliberate efforts to retard the development of bond markets in many other countries. In Japan, the Bond Issue Arrangement Committee, a bankers' group encouraged by the government, controlled costs and the timing of issuance until 1987, and a bankers' cartel kept fees high. In Germany, regulations up to 1984 prohibited companies from selling bonds with terms of less than five years and required approval from the finance ministry for each issue. France barred corporate issues with terms of less than seven years before 1992, required Treasury approval of the details of each issue, and required a committee of bankers and public officials to

TABLE 4.2 **Outstanding private-sector domestic debt securities**
$bn

	1998	2004	2008	2012
US	5,984	13,661	16,773	20,872
Japan	1,453	2,030	1,964	4,036
UK	388	367	397	3,454
France	477	959	1,484	2,483
China	134	190	793	2,210
Germany	1,140	1,033	1,229	2,177
Netherlands	246	399	566	1,900
Italy	364	877	1,482	1,711
Spain	142	423	1,205	1,453
Total	11,302	22,346	29,879	n/a

Source: Bank for International Settlements

approve the timing so that private-sector issues would not interfere with the government's borrowing plans. Such restrictions encouraged the use of bank financing rather than bonds. The European corporate-bond market has grown rapidly since the introduction of a single currency in 1999 created a large pool of investors who could purchase a bond denominated in euros without exposing themselves to the risk of exchange-rate changes.

In the Asia-Pacific region, bond issuance increased fivefold between 2007 and 2013, as many countries that previously had small domestic bond markets, notably China and South Korea, experienced significant market growth. This was partly the result of low interest rates around the world, but also reflected the rapid growth of the corporate sector and regulatory changes, which gave investors increased confidence in owning long-term obligations.

Issuing bonds

National regulations detail the steps required to issue bonds. Each issue is preceded by a lengthy legal document, variously called the offer document, prospectus or official statement, which lays out in detail the financial condition of the issuer; the purposes for which the debt is being sold; the schedule for the interest and principal payments required to service the debt; and the security offered to bondholders in the event the debt is not serviced as required. Investors scrutinise such documents carefully, because details specific to the issue have a great impact on the probability of timely payment. In some cases, regulators must review the offer document to determine whether the disclosures are sufficient, and may block the bond issue until additional information is provided. Issuers in the United States may file a shelf registration to obtain advance approval for a large volume of bonds, which can be sold in pieces, or tranches, whenever market conditions appear favourable. Most other countries have not adopted this innovation.

Underwriters and dealers

Issuers sell their bonds to the public with the help of underwriters and dealers. An issue may be underwritten by a single investment banking firm or by a group of them, referred to as a syndicate. Many syndicates include investment banks from different countries, the better to sell the bonds internationally. The issuer normally chooses one or two firms to be the lead underwriters. They are responsible for arranging the syndicate and for allocating a proportion of the bonds to each of the member firms. Formerly, dozens of firms competed in the underwriting business. However, mergers and acquisitions among banks have led to the creation of a handful of huge investment banks, which dominate bond underwriting throughout the world.

The underwriters may receive a fee from the issuer in return for arranging the issue and marketing it to potential investors. Alternatively, they may purchase the bonds from the issuer at a discount and resell them to the public at a higher price, profiting from the mark-up. If the investment bankers underwrite the issue on a firm commitment basis, they guarantee the price the issuer will receive and take the risk of loss if purchasers do not come forward at that price. They may instead underwrite the bonds with only their best efforts, in which case the issuer receives whatever price investors will pay and the underwriter takes no risk if the bonds fail to sell at a particular price. The underwriters may sell bonds at a discount to dealers, who take no underwriting risk but handle sales to smaller investors.

National governments often distribute their bonds through primary dealers without the assistance of underwriters. Primary dealers have the obligation, and often the exclusive right, to participate in the government's bond sales, and then resell the bonds to investors.

Swaps

The fact that an issuer has sold a particular bond issue need not mean that the issuer is paying the expected amount of interest on that issue. Increasingly, issuers make use of interest-rate swaps to obtain the financing schedule they desire. For example, an issuer might issue $100m of five-year notes at a fixed interest rate, and then immediately enter into a swap transaction whereby an investment bank meets those fixed payments and the issuer makes floating-rate payments to the bank. Whether such a transaction saves costs or reduces risk for the issuer depends upon the swap spread – the difference between a fixed rate and the current floating rate for a swap of a given maturity.

Setting the interest rate

The interest rate on a bond issue can be determined by a variety of methods. The most common is for the underwriter to set the rate based on market rates on the day of issuance. This, however, involves a certain amount of guesswork, and can lead either to excessive costs for the issuer if the interest rate is set too high, or to the underwriter being stuck with unsold bonds if the rate is set too low. Most syndicates prohibit their members from selling the bonds at less than the agreed price for a certain period of time, to keep the syndicate members from competing against one another.

An alternative method of determining interest rates involves auctions. There are several auction techniques used in the bond markets. Competitive-bid auctions allow investors or dealers to offer a price for bonds being issued at a particular interest rate (or, alternatively, to offer an acceptable interest rate for bonds being sold at par value). The offered price may go higher (or the offered rate lower) in successive rounds of bidding. The bonds may all be sold at the single highest price at which there are sufficient offers to sell the entire issue, or, in a multiple-price auction, each bidder that wins a share of the bonds will pay the last price it bid. In a sealed-bid auction bids are submitted in writing. One popular type of sealed-bid auction is a Dutch auction, in which the issuer sets an interest rate and bidders then submit schedules stating how many bonds they would buy at various prices; the bonds are sold at the highest price at which the entire issue is taken up.

Selling direct

New technology has made it practical for some issuers to sell their bonds directly to investors over the internet, without the intermediation of underwriters or dealers. This is likely to lead to lower costs for some issuers, and to reduce the profits of investment banks and brokers that underwrite and sell bonds.

The first online issue was an offering of $55m by the city of Pittsburgh, Pennsylvania, in November 1999. Since then, volume has grown rapidly. Originally online offers were limited to institutional investors, but as the market has developed sales direct to individual investors have become more common. Depending on the arrangements, investors may be able to learn about the issues, read financial materials and submit "indications of interest" – tentative offers – over the internet, and in some cases may actually place bids online during a specified auction period. Although investment banks often are involved in online bond issues, they commonly receive smaller fees for distributing new issues online than for traditional underwritings, as less work is required to identify potential purchasers and determine market receptivity to the offering.

Many national governments issue at least some of their bonds through a system that allows investors to bid in electronic auctions. This method saves money for investors by allowing them to circumvent the dealers that used to control government bond issuance. In one such auction, in December 2012, two-thirds of the ten-year bonds being sold by the US Treasury were purchased directly by investors rather than by bond dealers.

No more coupons

In the past, bond purchasers were given certificates as proof of their ownership. The certificates would often come with coupons attached, one for each interest payment due on the bonds. The investor would detach the appropriate coupon and take it to the bank or securities broker in order to receive the payment.

Paper bonds are now uncommon. They are still used for some registered bonds, which are issued in the name of the holder, and for bearer bonds, which are not registered in a particular name and may be sold by whoever has physical possession. Most debt securities, however, are issued as book-entry bonds, existing only as electronic entries in the computer of the trustee, the bank that is responsible for making interest payments on behalf of the issuer and, eventually, for redeeming the bonds. Tax authorities increasingly insist that bonds be issued in the name of a specific bondholder, as interest payments on bearer bonds are difficult to tax.

The changing nature of the market

Until the 1970s the bond market was principally a primary market. This meant that investors would purchase bonds at the time of issuance and hold the bonds until the principal was repaid. Their highly predictable cash flow made bonds attractive assets to investors such as life insurance companies and pension funds, the obligations of which could be predicted far in advance. The basic investment strategy was to match assets and liabilities. An investor would estimate its financial requirements in a certain future year, often 10 or 20 years hence, and would then search for bonds of acceptable quality that would be repaid at that time. Successful bond investors were those who managed to buy bonds offering slightly higher yields than other bonds of similar quality.

Since the late 1970s, the reasons for investing in bonds have changed. Many investors now actively trade bonds to take advantage of price differences, rather than holding them over the long term. Two developments have brought about this change. First, computers have made it possible for traders to spot price differences quickly. Second, whereas investors previously valued all their bonds at the original purchase price until they were sold, accounting rules now require that under certain conditions bonds be valued at their current market value, or "marked to market". As this requires the owner to record any loss or gain during each reporting period regardless of whether a bond is sold, there may be no advantage in holding rather than selling it.

Secondary dealing

Some corporate bonds trade on stock exchanges, where they are exchanged between one investor and another. The vast majority of bond trading, though, occurs in the over-the-counter market, between an investor and a bond dealer. Investors may place trade orders over the telephone or an internet link to a particular dealer, although large institutional investors, such as pension funds and mutual funds, are likely to use more sophisticated electronic systems providing access to multiple dealers.

Whatever the system, an institutional investor wishing to purchase or sell a bond makes its desire known, usually by contacting several dealers. Dealers which hold or are willing to hold inventories of that bond respond with a bid price if they are offering to buy, or an asking price if they are offering to sell. Government bonds are traded by many dealers, and the spread between bid and ask prices is often razor-thin. Popular corporate issues will be actively traded by a dozen or more dealers, but usually have wider bid-ask spreads than government bonds. Smaller issues by corporations or sub-sovereigns can be difficult to trade, as there may be only one or two dealers interested in buying or selling the bonds. In some cases, it may not be possible to acquire a particular bond as none of the investors owning that bond is offering it for sale.

Electronic trading

Much effort and money has gone into building electronic trading systems. By 2002, 81 screen-based bond-trading systems were in operation, some belonging to a single dealer and others bringing many dealers together. The market was unable to support so many competitors and many of these nascent electronic bond exchanges failed. Other electronic systems have sought to enable investors to trade directly with one another, without paying fees to dealers. Electronic trading has been hugely successful in the government bond market, where the number of different securities is small and liquidity – the amount available for investment – is high. Electronic systems are estimated to account for about three-quarters of trading in European government bonds. Most electronic systems also offer online trading of commercial paper, emerging-market bonds and other fixed-income products.

Trading of corporate and municipal bonds has proven surprisingly difficult to automate because of three characteristics of these markets. First, institutional investors often pursue strategies that require near-simultaneous transactions. For example, an investor may wish to sell the DuPont bonds in its portfolio and purchase Dow Chemical bonds, which are currently cheaper. But this transaction is interesting only if the investor can complete both legs – it does not wish to sell DuPont and then find that it cannot obtain the Dow bonds. Such transactions may be difficult to consummate without discussion with dealers, whose inventories of bonds allow them to assure clients that the entire transaction can be completed.

Second, obtaining full price information is a persistent problem in bond trading. As comparatively little bond trading occurs on exchanges, there is no way to ensure that all trades are publicly reported. In the United States rules now require that dealers report certain transactions to a central clearing house, but in some countries only the dealer and its customer know the price at which a particular bond has traded. The prices posted by dealers and released to financial information providers may or may not reflect the prices at which trades have actually occurred.

Third, the number of bonds issued by companies, and by local governments and their agencies, is vast – an estimated 150,000 different debt securities trade in the EU. A large corporation may have dozens of different bonds outstanding, each with different characteristics. Most of these bonds are traded rarely, if ever, after initial issuance. An investor posting an electronic offer to buy or sell such a security is unlikely to find a taker – in market parlance, trading in such issues is illiquid. The investor may be better served by talking to a dealer, who may be willing to trade the bonds or may know of another investor prepared to buy or sell that specific issue.

Electronic trading is likely to lead to increased price transparency, at least for some types of securities, and this will help reduce investors' costs. As the technology has matured, electronic trading systems have taken on an important role in the dealing of large, heavily traded issues. However, they remain less effective mechanisms for buying and selling the millions of smaller bond issues outstanding. The existence of this enormous variety of bonds will continue to assure a role, albeit a lesser one, for bond dealers.

Settlement

Central banks have made considerable efforts to shorten the time between execution of a trade and the exchange of money and payment. The shorter the settlement time, in general, the lower is the risk that a bank or securities firm will be harmed by the collapse of another firm with which it has traded. The collapse of Lehman Brothers, a US investment bank, in September 2008 resulted in an inability to settle a large number of bond transactions, and led to renewed interest in reducing settlement times. Central banks in wealthier countries now require traders in government securities to settle no later than the next business day, and in some countries, such as Japan and the United States, parties that fail to promptly deliver the securities they have agreed to sell are subject to fines. Even so, failure to deliver or accept securities after agreeing to a trade remains a stubborn problem in the bond market.

Types of bonds

Increasing varieties of bonds are available in the marketplace. In some cases, an issuer agrees to design a bond with the specific characteristics required by a particular institutional investor. Such a bond is then privately placed and is not traded in the bond markets. Bonds that are issued in the public markets generally fit into one or more of the following categories.

Straight bonds

Also known as debentures, straight bonds are the basic fixed-income investment. The owner receives interest payments of a predetermined amount on specified dates, usually every six months or every year following the date of issue. The issuer must redeem the bond from the owner at its face value, known as the par value, on a specific date.

Callable bonds

The issuer may reserve the right to call the bonds at particular dates. A call obliges the owner to sell the bonds to the issuer for a price, specified when the bond was issued, that usually exceeds the current market price. The difference between the call price and the current market price is the call premium. A bond that is callable is worth less than an identical bond that is non-callable, to compensate the investor for the risk that it will not receive all of the anticipated interest payments.

Non-refundable bonds

These may be called only if the issuer is able to generate the funds internally, from sales or taxes. This prohibits an issuer from selling new bonds at a lower interest rate and using the proceeds to call bonds that bear a higher interest rate.

Putable bonds

These give the investor the right to sell the bonds back to the issuer at par value on designated dates. This benefits the investor if interest rates rise, so a putable bond is worth more than an identical bond that is not putable.

Perpetual debentures

Also known as irredeemable debentures, perpetual debentures are bonds that will last forever unless the holder agrees to sell them back to the issuer.

Zero-coupon bonds

These do not pay periodic interest. Instead, they are issued at less than par value and are redeemed at par value, with the difference serving as an interest payment. Zeros are designed to eliminate reinvestment risk, the loss an investor suffers if future income or principal payments from a bond must be invested at lower rates than those available today. The owner of a zero-coupon bond has no payments to reinvest until the bond matures, and therefore has greater certainty about the return on the investment.

STRIPS

An acronym for separately registered interest and principal of securities, STRIPS are an innovation related to zero-coupon bonds. They turn the payments associated with a bond into separate securities, one for each payment involved. Thus a ten-year bond with semi-annual interest payments could be restructured as up to 21 different securities, with 20 representing the right to each of the interest payments to be made over the bond's term and one the right to receive the principal when it is repaid. Each of these securities is effectively a zero-coupon bond, which is sold for less than the related payment and is redeemed at face value. Many national debt-management offices and central banks will strip government bonds at the request of securities dealers. Investment banks may construct similar securities from any bond to meet the needs of particular investors.

Convertible bonds

Under specified conditions and strictly at the bondholder's option, convertible bonds may be exchanged for another security, usually the issuer's common shares. The prospectus for a convertible issue specifies the conversion ratio – the number of shares for which each bond may be exchanged. A convertible bond has a conversion value, which is simply the price of the common shares for which it may be traded. The buyer must usually pay a premium over conversion value, to reflect the fact that the bond pays interest until and unless it is converted. Convertibles often come with hard call protection, which prohibits the issuer from calling the bonds before the conversion date.

Adjustable bonds

There are many varieties of adjustable bonds. The interest rate on a floating-rate bond can change frequently, usually depending on short-term interest rates. The rate on a variable-rate bond may be changed only once a year, and is usually related to long-term interest rates. A step-up note will have an increase in the interest rate no more than once a year, according to a formula specified in the prospectus. Inflation-indexed bonds seek to protect against the main risk of bond investing: the likelihood that inflation will erode the value of both interest payments and principal. Capital-indexed bonds apply an inflation adjustment to interest payments as well as to principal. Interest-indexed bonds adjust interest payments for inflation, but the value of the principal itself is not adjusted for inflation. Indexed zero-coupon bonds pay an inflation-adjusted principal upon redemption.

Structured securities

Bonds that have options attached to them are called structured securities. Callable, putable and convertible bonds are simple examples of structured securities. Another traditional example is a warrant bond, a bond which comes with a warrant entitling the holder to buy a different bond under certain conditions at some future date. Many structured securities are far more complex, featuring interest rates that can vary only within given limits, can change at an exponential rate or can even cease to be payable altogether in certain circumstances. The prices of such instruments can be difficult to calculate and depend heavily on the value attached to the option features. (Options are discussed in more detail in Chapter 8.)

Properties of bonds

Every bond, irrespective of issuer or type, has a set of basic properties.

Maturity

This is the date on which the bond issuer will have repaid all the principal and will redeem the bond. The number of years to maturity is the term. In practice, term and maturity are often used interchangeably. Bonds with maturities of 1–5 years are usually categorised as short-term, those with maturities of 5–12 years as medium-term and those with maturities exceeding 12 years as long-term. Few bonds are issued with maturities beyond 30 years, and in many countries the longest maturity is only 10 or 20 years.

Coupon

This is the stated annual interest rate as a percentage of the price at issuance. Once a bond has been issued, its coupon never changes. Thus a bond that was issued for $1,000 and pays $60 of interest each year would be said to have a 6% coupon. Bonds are often identified by their maturity and coupon, for example, "the 6.25s of '24".

Current yield

Current yield is the effective interest rate for a bond at its current market price. This is calculated by a simple formula:

$$\frac{\text{Annual dollar coupon interest}}{\text{Current price}}$$

If the price has fallen since the bond was issued, the current yield will be greater than the coupon; if the price has risen, the yield will be less than the coupon. Suppose a bond was issued with a par value of €100 and a 6% coupon. Interest rates have fallen, and the bond now trades at €105. The current yield is:

$$\frac{€6}{€105} = 5.71\%$$

Yield to maturity

This is the annual rate the bondholder will receive if the bond is held to maturity. Unlike current yield, yield to maturity includes the value of any capital gain or loss the bondholder will enjoy when the bond is redeemed. This is the most widely used figure for comparing returns on different bonds.

Duration

Duration is a number expressing how quickly the investor will receive half of the total payment due over the bond's remaining life, with an adjustment for the fact that payments in the distant future are worth less than payments due soon. This complicated concept can be grasped by looking at two extremes. A zero-coupon bond offers payments only at maturity, so its duration is precisely equal to its term. A hypothetical ten-year bond yielding 100% annually lets the owner collect a great deal of money in the early years of ownership, so its duration is much shorter than its term. Most bonds fall in between. If two bonds have identical terms, the one with the higher yield will have the shorter duration, because the holder is receiving more money sooner.

The duration of any bond changes from one day to the next. The actual calculation can be complicated and can be done in several ways. Different investors may have different views of a bond's duration: one of the critical numbers in the calculation, the discount rate that should be used to attach a current value to future payments, is strictly a matter of opinion; and another, the amounts that will be paid at specific dates, is not always certain.

Traders and investors pay close attention to duration, as it is the most basic measure of a bond's riskiness. The longer the duration, the more the price of the bond is likely to fluctuate before maturity. Divergent estimates of duration are an important reason that investors differ about bond prices: if there is a ten-year bond with a 6% coupon and semi-annual interest payments, an investor who estimates the duration to be 7.6 years would be willing to pay a higher price than one who estimates it to be 7.7 years.

Ratings of risk

Before issuing bonds in the public markets, an issuer will often seek a rating from one or more private ratings agencies. The selected agencies investigate the issuer's ability to service the bonds, including such matters as financial strength, the intended use of the funds, the political and regulatory environment, and potential economic changes. After completing its investigation, an agency will issue a

TABLE 4.3 **What bond ratings mean**[a]

	Moody's	Standard & Poor's	Fitch Ratings
Highest credit quality; issuer has strong ability to meet obligations	Aaa	AAA	AAA
Very high credit quality; low risk of default	Aa1 Aa2 Aa3	AA+ AA AA–	AA
High credit quality, but more vulnerable to changes in economy or business	A1 A2 A3	A+ A A–	A
Adequate credit quality for now, but more likely to be impaired if conditions worsen	Baa1 Baa2 Baa3	BBB+ BBB BBB–	BBB
Below investment grade, but good chance that issuer can meet commitments	Ba1 Ba2 Ba3	BB+ BB BB–	BB
Significant credit risk, but issuer is presently able to meet obligations	B1 B2 B3	B+ B B–	B
High default risk	Caa1 Caa2 Caa3	CCC+ CCC CCC–	CCC CC C
Issuer failed to meet scheduled interest or principal payments	C	D	D

a Firms' precise definitions of ratings vary.

rating that represents its estimate of the default risk, the likelihood that the issuer will fail to service the bonds as required. This rating is normally paid for by the issuer, although in some cases an agency will issue a rating on its own initiative.

Three well-known companies, Moody's Investors Service and Standard & Poor's, both based in New York, and Fitch, based in New York and London, dominate the ratings industry. The firms' ratings of a particular issue are not always in agreement, as each uses a different methodology. Table 4.3 interprets the default ratings of the three international firms. There are also many ratings agencies that operate in a single country, and several that specialise in a particular industry, such as banking or insurance.

All the ratings agencies emphasise that they rate only the probability of default, not the probability that the issuer will experience financial distress or that the price of its bonds will fall. Nonetheless, ratings are important in setting bond prices. Bonds with lower ratings almost always have a greater yield than bonds with higher ratings. If an agency lowers its rating on a bond that has already been issued, the bond's price will fall. Government regulations or internal procedures restrict the amount many pension funds and insurance companies can invest in bonds that have a high probability of default, those rated as "below investment grade".

Ratings have increased in importance because of the growing number of bonds with "step-up" and acceleration provisions. Under a typical step-up, a bond might be issued with a 7% coupon, but if the issuer's credit rating is lowered, the coupon immediately increases to 7.25%. If the issue has an acceleration provision, the bonds could become repayable immediately upon a downgrade. In either case, the lowering of an issuer's credit rating can have serious adverse consequences, both for the issuer and for the investors who hold its securities.

Bond defaults during the financial crisis that began in 2008 called attention to the fact that issuers typically pay ratings agencies for rating a bond, potentially creating a conflict of interest in so far as an agency might be concerned about losing business if it issues a low rating. This has resulted in calls for changes in the ratings system. Such changes have proven difficult to mandate, however, as a system based on payments by investors may not be financially viable.

Interpreting the price of a bond

The price of a bond is normally quoted as a percentage of the price at which the bond was issued, which is usually reported as 100. In most countries, prices are quoted to the second decimal place. Thus a bond trading at 94.75% of its issue price will be quoted at 94.75 in most countries, indicating that a bond purchased for $10,000 when issued is currently worth $9,475. A price exceeding 100 means that the bond is worth more now than at the time it was issued.

The prices of non-government bonds are often reported in terms of the spread between a particular bond and a benchmark. In the United States, confusingly, high-grade corporate bonds are usually quoted in terms of a spread over US Treasury yields at similar maturity; if the current yield on ten-year Treasuries is 5.20%, a bond quoted at +220 would yield 7.40% at its current price. High-yield bonds, however, are quoted as a percentage of the face value. For floating-rate instruments, the spread is often expressed in terms of the London inter-bank offered rate (Libor), a key rate in the London market. In some cases, both the bid and ask prices are quoted.

The interest rates on government bonds may be affected by the expectation that a particular bond issue will be repurchased rather than by economic fundamentals alone. This has made government bonds an increasingly unstable benchmark in some countries, and investors have been looking for other measures by which to judge the pricing of non-government bonds.

Interest rates and bond prices

Interest-rate changes within the economy are the single most important factor affecting bond prices. This is because investors can profit from interest-rate arbitrage, selling certain bonds and buying others to take advantage of small price differences. Arbitrage will quickly drive the prices of similar bonds to the same level.

Bond prices move inversely to interest rates. The precise impact of an interest-rate change depends upon the duration of the bond, using the basic formula:

$$\text{Price change} = \text{duration} \times \text{value} \times \text{change in yield}$$

Assume that an investor has just paid C$1,000 for a bond priced at 100, denominated in Canadian dollars with a 6% coupon and a term of ten years to maturity. This bond might initially have a duration of 7.66 years. If Canadian interest rates for ten-year borrowings suddenly fall, investors will flock to the bond with a 6% coupon and bid up the price. Suppose that the market rate for ten-year borrowings in Canada drops to 5.9% immediately after the bond is issued. The price change can then be calculated as:

$$7.66 \times C\$1,000 \times (0.060 - 0.059) = C\$7.66$$

So this bond would now have a market value of C\$1,007.66 and a price of 100.77. Conversely, if Canadian interest rates for ten-year borrowings rise, the value of the bond will decrease until the current yield is in line with the market.

As this example illustrates, the prices of long-term bonds can be much more volatile than the prices of short-term bonds because of their longer duration. In the face of the same interest-rate change, the price of a bond with a duration of 12.5 years would have risen by 1.25%, and the price of a bond with a duration of 2.3 years would have risen by 0.23%. This relationship can be visualised using price/yield curves, drawn on a graph with the vertical axis denoting bond prices and the horizontal axis representing interest rates. As Figure 4.1 shows, a given increase in yield will cause the price of a bond with long duration to fall much more than the price of a bond with shorter duration, and a given decrease in yield will cause its price to rise more. This graphical relationship is known to bond investors as convexity.

FIG 4.1 **The price/yield curve**

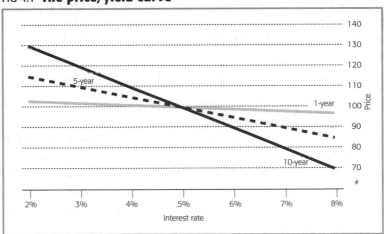

Inflation and returns on bonds

Interest rates can be thought of as having two separate components. The first is recompense for inflation, the change in prices that is expected to occur during the term of a borrowing. The second is the payment the bond investor exacts for the use of its money after taking inflation into account. The sum of these components is the nominal interest rate. Bond coupons and bond yields are both nominal interest rates.

The payment to the investor beyond expected inflation is the real interest rate. The real interest rate cannot be known precisely, but there are ways to estimate it. For example, the current yield on a bond that is indexed for inflation could be compared with the yield on a bond with the same maturity date not indexed for inflation. The difference between these two rates can be understood as the inflation premium investors demand for buying bonds that are not indexed. If the expected inflation rate increases, the yield on such bonds will have to increase for the investor to receive the same real return, which means that the price of the bond must fall. Thus the bond markets are closely attuned to economic data concerning employment, wage increases, industrial capacity utilisation and commodity prices, all of which may be indicators of future inflation.

Exchange rates and bond prices and returns

Many bond buyers invest internationally. To purchase bonds denominated in foreign currencies, they must convert their home currency into the relevant foreign currency. After eventually selling the bonds, they must convert the foreign-currency proceeds back into their home currency. Their return is thus highly sensitive to exchange-rate movements.

For example, consider a Japanese investor that spent $10,000 to purchase a US bond at a time when ¥1 was worth 0.0083 cents (an exchange rate of ¥120 to $1). The bond would therefore have cost ¥120,000. Assume that by the time the investor wishes to sell the bond, the yen has depreciated against the dollar by 10%, so that ¥1 is now worth 0.0075 cents (an exchange rate of ¥133.33 to $1). Even if the price of the bond is unchanged, the value of the investment would be ¥133,330, a gain of 11.11%.

The effects of currency movements can overwhelm the returns on the bonds themselves. Table 4.4 compares average bond-market returns in local currency and in dollars for 2012, a year in which persistently low interest rates limited the returns on bonds in many countries. Among these six countries, France provided the best return for foreigners investing in dollars, as the prices of French bonds rose strongly while the value of the euro changed little against the dollar.

TABLE 4.4 **Returns on government bonds, 2012**
%

	Canada	France	Japan	UK	Australia	US
Return in local currency	2.24	10.15	1.77	2.83	5.61	2.03
Return in US dollars	2.23	10.25	1.57	2.72	5.62	2.03

Sources: Bloomberg; Federal Reserve Board

Thus the strengthening of a country's currency can increase the demand for its bonds and raise prices, other things remaining the same. However, other things rarely remain the same. As explained in Chapter 2, the main reason for a change in the exchange rate between two countries is a change in their relative interest rates. Why this occurs will determine the effect on bond prices. In the example above, if the yen is weaker against the dollar because Japanese interest rates have fallen, bond prices in the United States might strengthen. If, however, the yen is weaker against the dollar because US interest rates have risen, bond prices in the United States might fall. In summary, the relationship between exchange-rate changes and bond prices is not always predictable.

The yield curve

The interest rate that lenders require of any borrower will depend on the term of the borrowing. The yield curve depicts the various rates at which the same borrower is able to borrow for different periods of time. The most closely watched yield curve in any country is that of the national government, which is the closest approximation to a risk-free yield. Other yield curves, such as the one for corporate borrowers, are best understood in comparison with the risk-free yield.

The yield curve is drawn against two axes, the vertical showing yield (expressed in percentage points) and the horizontal giving the term in years. Most of the time the yield curve is positively sloped, going from the lower left corner of the chart to the upper right. In this case, very short-term borrowings would have the lowest yield, with the yield increasing as the term lengthens. The reasons for this shape are readily understandable, as lenders and investors wish to be compensated for the greater risk that inflation will erode the value of their asset over a longer period.

The precise shape of the yield curve varies slightly from day to day and can change significantly from one month to the next. If long-term interest rates rise relative to short-term interest rates, the curve is said to steepen; if short-term rates rise relative to long-term rates, the curve flattens. One way to think about this is to regard the yield curve as a forecast of future short-term interest rates. Bond issuers and investors, of course, always have the option of repeatedly purchasing money-market instruments rather than making long-term commitments, so a steeper yield curve implies that they expect money-market yields to be higher in future than they are now. The yield curve is said to be inverted if short-term interest rates are higher than long-term rates. An inverted yield curve is usually a sign that the central bank is constricting the flow of credit to slow the economy, a step often associated with a lessening of inflation expectations. This can make investors in longer-term instruments willing to accept lower nominal interest rates than are available on shorter-term instruments, giving the curve an inverted shape.

The steepness of the yield curve is not related to the absolute level of interest rates. It is possible for the curve to flatten amid a general rise in interest rates, if short-term rates rise faster than long-term rates. Figure 4.2 gives examples of yield-curve changes for government bonds in the United States, the UK, Germany and Japan on two days in 2013.

In the time between these two days, interest rates in the United States, the UK and Germany rose sharply at the "long" end of the yield curve, but increased much less for maturities of less than 12 months.

FIG 4.2 **Yield curves for government securities on two days in 2013**
Annualised % yield

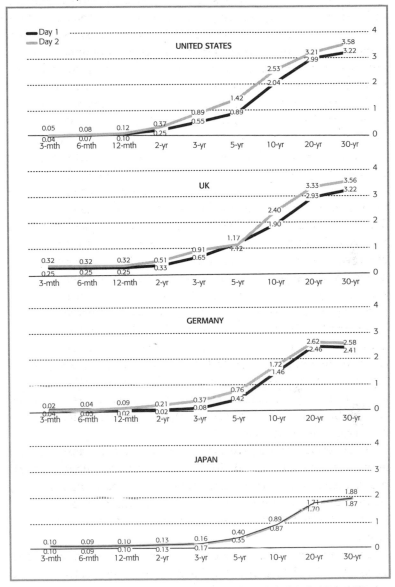

Sources: US Treasury; Deutsche Bundesbank; Bank of England; Bloomberg

This is referred to as a "steepening" of the yield curve, meaning that the cost of long-term borrowing rose relative to the cost of short-term borrowing. In this situation, investors in these countries probably saw decreases in the value of their holdings of long-term bonds, but may have shifted their funds from short-term to long-term securities as long-term rates became more attractive. In Japan, however, yields on government bonds of all maturities changed little between these two days.

Many investors and traders actively sell bonds of one maturity and buy bonds of another as changes in the yield curve alter relative prices. For example, in early 2013 the interest rate on ten-year US Treasuries was 1.5 percentage points above that on two-year Treasuries. By mid-year ten-year bonds were yielding 1.8 percentage points above two-year bonds. An investor who had sold two-year Treasuries and used the proceeds to purchase ten-year Treasuries early in the year would have made a poor decision, as the ten-year bonds performed more poorly in relative terms over that period.

Spreads

In general, investors who buy bonds first make a decision about asset allocation. That is, they determine what proportion of a portfolio they wish to hold in bonds as opposed to cash, equities and other types of assets. Next, they are likely to allocate the bond portfolio broadly among domestic government bonds, domestic corporate bonds, foreign bonds and other categories. Once the asset allocation has been determined, the decision about which particular bonds to purchase within each category is based largely on spreads.

A spread is the difference between the current yields of two bonds. It is usually expressed in basis points, with each basis point equal to one-hundredth of a percentage point. To simplify matters, traders in most countries have adopted a benchmark, usually a particular government bond, against which all other bonds are measured. If two bonds have identical ratings but different spreads to the benchmark, investors may conclude that the bond with the wider spread offers better relative value, because its price will rise relative to the other bond if the spread narrows.

Changes in spreads indicate which risks are currently most worrying to investors. Consider the European government bond market, where the benchmark has been the ten-year Bund issued by the German government. Until the late 1990s there was a substantial spread between Bunds and the bonds issued by governments in Italy, Spain and several other European countries. However, as 12 EU countries moved towards the establishment of a single currency, the euro, on January 1st 1999, the spreads within the euro zone narrowed. Investors who had purchased bonds with wide spreads against the Bund profited as spreads narrowed. Conversely, spreads of Greek government bonds "blew out" against Bunds in 2012, as investors came to see Greece as a far riskier borrower than Germany. Even at a time of rising interest rates, when bond prices generally fall, traders astute enough to foresee changes in spreads can do well.

Corporate bond spreads can also widen or narrow if investors sense a change in the issuer's creditworthiness. If a firm's sales have been weak, investors may think there is a greater likelihood that the firm will be unable to service its debt, and will therefore demand a wider spread before purchasing the bond. Conversely, investors frequently purchase bonds when they expect that the issuer's rating will be upgraded by one of the major credit agencies, as the upgrade will cause the bond's price to rise as its yield moves closer to the benchmark interest rate.

Enhancing security

An issuer frequently takes steps to reduce the risk bondholders must bear in order to sell its bonds at lower interest rate. There are three common ways of doing this:

- **Covenants** are legally binding promises made at the time a bond is issued. A simple covenant might limit the amount of additional debt that the issuer may sell in future, or might require it to keep a certain level of cash at all times. Covenants are meant to protect bondholders not only against default, but also against the possibility that management's future actions will lead ratings agencies to downgrade the bonds, which would reduce the price in the secondary market.

- **Bond insurance** is frequently sought by issuers with unimpressive credit ratings. A bond insurer is a private firm that has obtained a top rating from the main ratings agencies. An issuer pays it a premium to guarantee bondholders that specific bonds will be serviced on time. With such a guarantee, the issuer is able to sell its bonds at a lower interest rate. Bond insurance is a particularly popular enhancement for municipal bonds in the United States, and its popularity has also increased in Europe. However, several bond insurance companies experienced credit-rating declines following issuer defaults on insured securities in 2007–08, and some were unable to meet their obligations. This led some municipal issuers to issue uninsured bonds instead of insured securities.

- **Sinking funds** ensure that the issuer arranges to retire some of its debt, on a prearranged schedule, prior to maturity. The issuer can do this either by purchasing the required amount of its bonds in the market at specified times, or by setting aside money in a fund overseen by a trustee, to ensure that there is adequate cash on hand to redeem the bonds at maturity.

Repurchase agreements

The role of repurchase agreements, or repos, is essential to the smooth functioning of the market.

Repos were discussed in Chapter 3, but to summarise: a repo is a contract in which a seller, usually a securities dealer such as an investment bank, agrees to sell bonds in return for a cash loan, but promises to repurchase the bonds at a specific date and price. For the seller, a repo offers a low-cost way of borrowing money to finance the purchase of more bonds. For the buyer, a repo is a low-risk alternative to keeping cash in the bank, as the securities serve as collateral. A reverse repo is the same operation with the parties switching sides, so that the securities dealer trades money for securities belonging to an investor.

The largest part of the repo market is the overnight market. However, big investors often enter into term repos for longer periods. In such cases, repos can offer an inexpensive way to take a large position ahead of expected changes in bond prices. Suppose, for example, that an investor expects long-term interest rates to fall. It might arrange a reverse repo, selling long-term bonds to a dealer, taking the dealer's loan and buying yet more long-term bonds. If long-term interest rates fall before the repo matures, the investor sells both sets of bonds at a profit, earning far more than if it had simply bought and held bonds. Conversely, however, the investor's loss from this leveraged transaction would be magnified if interest rates move in the opposite way.

High-yield debt – or junk

One of the most important bond-market developments in recent years is the issuance of debt by entities with weak credit ratings. Such bonds are called high-yield debt or below-investment-grade debt. They are better known to the public as junk bonds.

Until the 1980s firms and government agencies rated "below investment grade" were largely shut out of the debt markets. Starting in about 1983, institutional investors in the United States began to allocate a small proportion of their assets to bonds that did not meet normal investment criteria. Early high-yield bonds were frequently used to finance leveraged buy-outs, with the issuers using the borrowed money to buy up all the shares in a firm and operate it as a privately held business. Today they may be used for many different purposes. About 38% of the corporate bonds traded in the United States in 2012 were high-yield bonds.

High-yield markets were slower to develop in Europe and Asia. High-yield bond issuance in the UK and Japan is small, but many firms and governments in emerging economics issue securities that are not rated investment grade and are traded as high-yield bonds. Figure 4.3 traces the growth of the high-yield market in the United States and Europe. The high-yield market was hit badly by the financial crisis in 2007–08. By definition, high-yield issuers face higher default risk, and usually have high debt burdens relative to income. The risk of default in a weakening economy caused investors to turn away from high-yield bonds in 2008, when US issuance fell 67% and issuance in Europe ceased altogether, but the market recovered strongly in 2009 and set new records in 2012.

FIG 4.3 **High-yield bond issuance**
$bn

Sources: Securities and Financial Markets Association; Association for Financial Markets in Europe

Some high-yield corporate bonds are issued under provisions allowing payment-in-kind (PIK) if the issuer is unable to make a scheduled interest payment. This means that under specified conditions, the issuer can give its creditors additional bonds in lieu of cash payment. PIK provisions are proposed most frequently when there is a high probability that the issuer will be unable to make interest and principal payments as scheduled. Certain PIK bonds have a "toggle" feature that allows the issuer to decide whether to pay interest in cash or kind each time a payment is due. Investors, however, understandably prefer payment in cash, and they may extract onerous terms, such as extremely high interest rates, in return for their willingness to accept PIK or toggle provisions in a bond issue.

Some bonds that carried investment-grade ratings when they were issued now trade as high-yield bonds because the issuer's financial condition has deteriorated. These are known as fallen angels. When the condition of the issuer of a below-investment-grade bond improves significantly, the bond may gain an investment-grade rating. In this case, traders refer to it as a rising star. In 2008, according to

Standard & Poor's, 152 European high-yield issuers were downgraded. By 2013, as corporate profits improved, the number of rising stars around the world increased more rapidly than the number of fallen angels, according to S&P.

Below-investment-grade bonds usually trade at a substantial spread to Treasuries and high-grade corporate bonds. On average, rates on high-yield bonds in the US market are about 400 basis points higher than the rates on Treasuries of similar maturity. The bonds with the lowest ratings almost always have the widest spreads. But spreads among high-yield bonds, and between high-yield bonds and Treasuries, can vary considerably depending on the economy. In December 2000, as the US economy was weakening, the average yield reached 941 basis points above Treasuries. In return for offering higher interest, high-yield bonds carry a much larger risk of default, especially at times of economic stress. In 2008, 126 high-yield issuers defaulted in Europe, on 2.5% of outstanding bonds, and 4% of US high-yield bonds defaulted. By the spring of 2013, the average yield on high-yield bonds briefly fell to about 400 basis points above Treasuries, as investors thought strong profits were increasing the likelihood that high-yield issuers would be able to service their debts.

International markets

The bond markets have long since ceased to be domestic markets. As restrictions on the cross-border flow of capital have been reduced or eliminated, investors have increasingly been able to buy bonds regardless of the national origin of the issuer and the currency of issue. About $2.5 trillion of corporate bonds trade outside the issuer's home country, along with about $1.6 trillion of government debt and $16 trillion issued by banks and other financial institutions. More than half of the world's most heavily traded securities, US Treasury bonds, are now owned by investors outside the United States, as shown in Figure 4.4.

The issuance of bonds outside the issuer's home country can occur in two ways:

■ **Foreign bonds** are issued outside the issuer's home country and are denominated in the currency of the country where

FIG 4.4 **Foreign ownership of US Treasury bonds**
Year end, %

Source: Federal Reserve Board

they are issued. Special names are used to refer to many such issues. Yankee bonds are dollar-denominated securities issued in the United States by non-US issuers. Bonds issued in sterling by issuers from outside the UK are known as bulldog bonds, and the term samurai bonds refers to yen bonds placed by foreign issuers in the Japanese market. Since 2007, non-Chinese investors have been able to buy dim sum bonds, issued in Hong Kong, London or Singapore but denominated in Chinese yuan.

■ **Eurobonds** are denominated in neither the currency of the issuer's home country nor that of the country of issue, and are generally subject to less regulation. Thus a sterling-denominated bond offered in London by a Japanese firm would be considered a foreign bond, and the same security offered in London but denominated in dollars or Swiss francs would be called a Eurobond. (The market for Eurobonds is discussed in Chapter 6.)

Why would an issuer choose an international issue rather than a domestic one? First, it may wish to match its borrowing to the income that is intended to pay for that borrowing. A French firm intending to build an electrical generation plant in Turkey, for example, might borrow in Turkish liras rather than in euros because the electricity will be priced and sold in liras. Second, the greater liquidity of the main bond markets, particularly New York and London, means that borrowers from other countries can often obtain lower interest rates than at home, even after taking currency risk into account. This is especially true for issuers from countries where financial markets are underdeveloped and investors' willingness to purchase local-currency bonds is limited. Third, an international issue is often undertaken to establish the issuer's reputation among international investors, to ease the way for future borrowings or share offerings.

As illustrated in Tables 4.1 and 4.2, the United States has by far the world's largest domestic bond market, accounting for almost half of all bonds in circulation. International bonds of US issuers equal only one-sixth of the amount outstanding domestically. The picture is very different for many other countries. Germany and the UK have disproportionately large shares of the international bond market, with German issuers having sold more bonds internationally than domestically. China, which until recently had underdeveloped financial markets, now trails only the United States in terms of the size of its domestic corporate-bond market, and Chinese companies have issued large quantities of bonds in other currencies to finance their expansion abroad.

Emerging-market bonds

Until the 1990s, only the most creditworthy of issuers could issue bonds in the international markets. Governments unable to obtain investment-grade ratings on their sovereign debt were restricted to borrowing from banks or from domestic credit markets. Companies in these countries were excluded from the international debt markets as well because, with few exceptions, the ratings agencies impose a sovereign ceiling, meaning that no borrower in a country can be rated as high as its national government. If the sovereign debt of the national government was deemed to be a poor credit risk, the country's corporate debt was automatically treated the same way.

Over the past two decades, however, investors have come to accept

FIG 4.5 **Emerging-market bonds outstanding**
$bn

Source: Bank for International Settlements

the debt of these so-called emerging-market countries as a separate category of investment. The main characteristic of emerging-market debt, apart from a below-investment-grade credit rating, is high price volatility. On average, weekly changes in the price of emerging-market bonds are about four times as great as changes in the price of government and corporate bonds issued in the more developed markets.

Firms and governments in dozens of emerging economies have issued bonds internationally. Total issuance grew nearly tenfold between 1991 and 1997. It then slowed in the wake of the financial crises in Asia in 1998, as shown in Figure 4.5, before resuming rapid growth early in 2000. Issuance fell to near zero in late 2001 and early 2002, as financial crises in Turkey and Argentina, combined with the global economic slowdown, curbed investor interest. Net issuance fell to nearly zero in 2008 as investors shied away from risk, but then grew strongly in 2011 and 2012. Brazil, Russia and China are the emerging economies with the largest quantities of bonds outstanding. The euro has displaced the dollar as the main currency of issuance.

The main cause of the emerging-market bond boom from 1994

to 1997, apart from the general fall in interest rates throughout the world, was exchange-rate policy. The governments of many emerging-market countries either fixed their exchange rates against certain foreign currencies or pegged them, allowing them to change in a pre-announced way. As interest rates in the more advanced economies were much lower than those in emerging markets, businesses took advantage of the opportunity to sell international bonds in the expectation that their domestic currency income could easily be exchanged for enough foreign currency to service the bonds. However, when market forces made it impossible for governments in Thailand, South Korea, Indonesia and several other countries to maintain their currency pegs in 1997, the currencies fell sharply. Similar events occurred in Russia in 1998. Many issuers, unable to afford the foreign exchange required to service their bonds, defaulted.

When the markets became more welcoming to emerging-market issues in 1999, corporate bonds were more prominent than they had been previously. Corporate bonds accounted for about 30% of emerging-markets issuance in the first quarter of 2000. However, as the world economy slowed in 2000 and many countries entered recession in 2001, investors shunned both government and corporate bonds from most emerging economies. Net issuance of bonds by companies based in developing countries was nil in 2000 and 2001. When the Argentine government imposed foreign-exchange controls and then defaulted on its debt in 2001 and 2002, Argentine companies were unable to service their own debts and were forced into default as well, reminding investors that changes in government policy are always a risk to holders of corporate bonds.

Issuance of international bonds by companies in emerging-market economies was muted in the immediate aftermath of the financial crisis that began in 2007, as many of these companies made greater use of their domestic bond markets to borrow without exposing themselves to risks from currency shifts. Emerging-market companies returned to the international bond markets in 2011 and 2012, often using foreign-currency bond issues to finance acquisitions of companies in other countries.

Bond indexes

The return on bonds depends greatly upon external forces, particularly interest rates. This makes it difficult to measure investment managers' success on an absolute scale, as even the best managers will earn negative returns (lose money) when interest rates rise. Leading investment banks have therefore constructed bond indexes against which to judge the overall performance of a particular bond portfolio.

Indexes serve to answer several different questions. First, how does the total return on a particular bond, including interest payments as well as changes in market value, compare with the total return on bonds from similar issuers? A large number of indexes track the return on narrow categories of bonds to offer a measuring stick. Second, how well has a particular manager done? A large institutional investor might divide its bond portfolio among many managers, asking them to follow diverse strategies. Comparing them with one another would not reveal how well each has pursued the desired strategy. Comparison with appropriate indexes, however, would show whether it was worthwhile for the investor to pay the manager, or whether a better return could have been obtained simply by tracking the index by purchasing precisely those bonds. Third, do particular bond-investment strategies persistently underperform other strategies? If one index lags another year after year, an investor has reason to wonder whether the mix of bonds tracked by the lagging index is a sensible investment.

Bond indexes come in two basic types:

■ **Benchmark.** The simplest, the benchmark index, tracks the performance of a bond issue that is deemed an appropriate benchmark for an entire category of bonds. This type of index is particularly useful for sovereign bonds, as there is only a single sovereign issuer in each country that issues bonds of varying terms. In countries whose governments issue long-term bonds, the benchmark bond is normally an issue with ten years to maturity.

■ **Weighted.** The other common type of index measures the total return of an identifiable group of bonds. The index number is set equal to 100 at an arbitrary start date. Such indexes are usually weighted, which means that the importance of any bond in the index is based on the size of the issue compared with the total size of all issues included in the index. The performance of an index depends heavily on which bonds are included, because the spreads of the individual bonds will change in various ways. There are hundreds of weighted indexes. For example, three major Japanese investment banks publish weighted indexes of the Japanese bond market. The Nomura Bond Performance Index includes issues with an investment-grade rating and at least ¥1 billion of bonds outstanding. The Nikko Bond Performance Index has similar selection criteria, but with a starting date of December 1979. The Daiwa Bond Index, in contrast to the other two, includes only issues with at least ¥5 billion outstanding. None of these three indexes can be said to be superior to the others; they simply take slightly different snapshots of the market.

Index shortcomings

Despite their widespread use, weighted bond indexes are problematic for several reasons:

- **Inconsistency.** No index can track precisely the same bonds over time, because most bonds eventually mature or are called, and many cease to be actively traded.

- **Uncertain pricing.** Calculating changes in a bond index requires a determination of the price change on each bond in the index. Many bonds, however, trade infrequently, so there may be no recent transactions to provide current price information. Even if transactions have occurred, the compiler of the index may not be able to learn the price. The compiler must therefore seek to estimate the price of the bond, rather than relying on actual transactions. As a result, a bond index is inherently far less precise than an index of shares that are traded on a daily basis.

- **Disqualification.** A bond may be dropped from an index if it ceases to meet the criteria for inclusion, particularly if it is upgraded or downgraded by ratings agencies. Such an event will force portfolio managers who are tracking the index to sell the bond at the same time as many other money managers are selling the same bond for the same reason, exacerbating its price decline. This occurred, for example, when South Korea lost its AA credit rating in 1997 and managers who were tracking AA-bond indexes were forced to dump South Korean bonds at a loss. In December 2001, Argentina's weighting in the JP Morgan Emerging Market Bond Index Plus (EMBI +) was reduced by half after the government implemented an exchange of bonds which had been included in the index, but which it was no longer able to service.

■ **Poor diversification.** Some indexes include few issuers, forcing fund managers who are tracking the index to have undiversified portfolios. This was a problem for managers of emerging-market portfolios in 1998: Russia had a heavy weighting in the EMBI + because it had issued large amounts of bonds. The more bonds the Russian government issued, the more bonds portfolio managers needed to buy to track the index, leaving them with large losses when the government suspended payments on many bonds.

5 Securitisation

TRADITIONALLY, INVESTORS HAVE FAVOURED BONDS for their safety and predictability. A fixed-rate bond promises guaranteed cash flows: the amount and date of each interest payment are specified when the bond is issued, as are the dates on which the bond may be redeemed. The investor therefore knows precisely how much money it will receive 5, 10 or 20 years in the future, and the conditions, if any, under which the bond may be called prior to maturity.

An asset-backed security is a type of bond offering no such certainty. The security, in most cases, is not backed by the full faith and credit of a government or a private company. Rather, a creditor, most often a lender, issues securities supported by a stream of income the issuer expects to receive in the future from specific assets. There is no assurance that the income will be received as anticipated. Some of it might not arrive at all. Sometimes the assets will be liquidated earlier than expected, resulting in less interest income than the bondholders assumed they would receive. As a result, future cash flows can only be guessed at rather than known with a high degree of confidence.

In return for accepting this uncertainty, investors in asset-backed securities are able to achieve higher returns than on regular government or corporate bonds. At the same time, the securities are far more readily bought and sold (they have greater liquidity, in market parlance) than the individual assets underlying them, making it easier for investors to get into or out of a particular type of investment. These advantages made asset-backed securities hugely popular in the years prior to 2007. However, some types of asset-backed securities experienced large losses in 2007–08, and issuance fell sharply as it became apparent that the prices of some securities did not adequately reflect the risk. By 2013, issuance of asset-backed securities in Europe and the United States had fallen roughly 80% from its peak.

Asset-backed securities are sold either with fixed rates of interest or with floating rates. They can be broadly divided into two categories:

- **Mortgage-backed securities.** These are supported by first mortgages on residential property.
- **Non-mortgage securities.** These can be backed by assets of any other sort, including housing-related loans other than first mortgages.

Mortgage-backed securities accounted for approximately 80% of the asset-backed securities outstanding throughout the world at the end of 2008. Securitisation of other sorts of assets grew rapidly in many countries in the first years of the 21st century. The value of non-mortgage asset-backed securities outstanding was more than $2 trillion at December 2004. Worldwide issuance peaked in 2006 at around $1.1 trillion, excluding mortgage-backed securities. Issuance plummeted after 2008, and in 2012 was in the range of $283 billion worldwide. Table 5.1 shows the amount of asset-backed securities issued in various countries in 2012.

TABLE 5.1 **Issuance of non-mortgage asset-backed securities** 2012

	$bn
US	184
France	20
UK	16
Germany	14
South Korea	10
Spain	6
Australia	5
Japan	5
Italy	4
Other countries	19
Total	283

Source: Dealogic

The securitisation process

Securitisation is the process by which individual assets, which on their own may be difficult to sell or even to attach a value to, are aggregated into securities that can be sold in the financial markets. The earliest known securitisations occurred in Denmark, where mortgage bonds have served to finance house purchases for many years. Mortgage securities became widely used in the United States in the 1970s. Since then, innovation has led to the securitisation of other sorts of assets, and asset-backed securities have taken root in several countries in Europe and Asia.

The securitisation process begins with the creation of the assets that will later be securitised. This usually occurs in the normal course of business: a mortgage bank extends a mortgage to a homebuyer; a bank gives a customer a credit card; a studio releases a feature film. Under normal circumstances, such an asset is carried on the firm's books, with the money earned by that asset, such as loan payments, to be reported as income in whatever future year it is received.

Securitisation involves transforming, or packaging, such assets into securities that can be sold to third parties. Securitisation is accomplished with the help of an investment bank, which sets up a trust whose sole purpose is to own the assets being securitised. Usually, each trust is created to own a pool composed of a single type of asset, such as $100m of automotive loans. The trust will purchase the assets in the pool from the firm that created them, using money raised by the sale of asset-backed securities to investors. The owners of the securities are entitled to receive whatever income the assets generate, and in most cases to a pro-rata share of the assets themselves. When individual assets owned by the trust are retired – for example, when an individual loan is paid off – the size of the trust diminishes. Eventually, all the assets will be retired, at which point the trust will terminate.

In general, the diversity of the assets underlying an asset-backed security provides safety to investors. However, some lenders may attempt to securitise a large proportion of the loans they originate and hold onto few of them, giving them little incentive to make sure that the individual loans are sound. The securitisation of unsound loans was a major contributor to the financial crisis that began in 2007, and caused large losses to both investors and the banks that originated the securities. As a result of these problems, financial regulators in many countries have required banks to maintain ownership of a significant portion of the loans that they bundle into securities and to hold capital – shareholders' funds – to protect against a decline in value of the portion they own. These new regulations have made securitisation more costly and therefore less attractive.

Recourse to guarantees

In many cases, investors in an asset-backed trust benefit from certain guarantees. Governments frequently guarantee part or all of the payment on residential mortgages to encourage housing construction. The original lender may also guarantee loan payments to induce investors to buy its assets. In this situation, the lender sells the assets to the trust with recourse, meaning that the trust will seek reimbursement from the lender if an individual borrower should fail to pay interest or principal as scheduled.

Why securitise?

The impetus for securitisation lies in the benefits it brings to firms that choose to securitise their assets. Securitisation may prove attractive for several reasons:

- It enables a firm to specialise in particular aspects of a complex business in which it might have a special advantage, rather than participating in all areas of the business. Many large financial companies have become successful by taking unorthodox approaches to one specialised task, such as lending to owners of mobile homes or identifying the characteristics of potentially profitable credit-card customers. A firm might have no unusual expertise in other parts of the business, such as managing the assets once they have been created. Selling off the assets through securitisation allows the firm to focus on what it does best, where it can add the greatest value.

- Selling assets allows issuers to change their risk profile. Among the risks facing recording artists, for example, is the possibility that changing tastes will result in fewer sales of their albums. By securitising certain recordings, artists can receive a specified amount of revenue immediately. They might lose the opportunity to reap huge profits from a release that turns out to be a hit, but also shed the risk that they will fall from popular favour and experience declining sales. If an artist so desires, it may even be possible to structure the transaction so that, if more than a specified quantity of songs is sold, the artist receives a portion of the windfall profit.

- Issuers may wish to reduce their need for capital. Take the case of a bank that is required by regulators to maintain capital according to the size and type of its assets. When the bank extends a loan, the loan's market value appears as an asset on its balance sheet, and the bank must then set aside the appropriate amount of capital to cover potential declines in the value of that asset. The institution may find that having much of its capital tied up in this way limits opportunities to use that capital for purposes that may generate better returns for shareholders, such as financing new investment or acquiring other firms. Securitising the assets allows the bank to remove them wholly or partially from its balance sheet, thereby freeing up capital for other uses. The bank will no longer receive the interest payments on the loans, but it has shed the risk that the loans will not be serviced in a timely manner. It can either return the unneeded capital to shareholders or use it to build up parts of the business, such as the origination of loans that are to be securitised, which may enable it to earn better returns for shareholders.

- The sale of securitised assets creates publicly available prices. Some types of assets, such as property or equipment leases, are complicated to trade and, because they are unique, can be difficult to value. Asset-backed securities are usually much easier to trade than the underlying assets themselves. If securities backed by office-building mortgages are selling for half the price they were two years ago, investors, regulators and managers will have a reasonable idea of what a lender's portfolio of commercial mortgages might be worth even when those specific assets have not been securitised.

Market development

Until the start of the 21st century, securitisation was a huge business in the United States and almost non-existent elsewhere. Several factors encouraged its development. First, the regulatory climate was generally favourable to innovation and even encouraged it by making it less costly for banks to securitise loans than to make loans and hold them on their own balance sheets. Second, the US legal system did not stand in the way. In countries such as Japan and Italy, by contrast, laws intended to protect the rights of borrowers delayed the development of the securitisation of assets, as it was uncertain whether a trust would have clear title to any assets it might purchase from an issuer. A third influence has been the willingness of investors to perform the complicated mathematical analysis required to determine the value of asset-backed securities. In some countries, investors who were accustomed mainly to buying and holding bonds and equities were not used to such sophisticated analysis, and were slow to accept asset-backed products.

The securitisation market changed dramatically after 2000. First, securitisation became popular in Europe and in parts of Asia (see Figure 5.1). Japan began to permit securitisation in 1993 as a means of allowing troubled banks to dispose of assets, such as property held as collateral for debtors who have defaulted. Taiwan passed a law to encourage securitisation in June 2003. Asset-backed securities were issued for the first time in India in 2002, and the first security from China came to market in 2006.

This rapid growth was supported by the growth of a special type of security, the collateralised debt obligation (CDO). CDOs were developed in the early 1990s, but only after 2000 did they begin to include large quantities of asset-backed securities. The sponsor of a CDO might raise money from investors, borrow additional amounts, and use the money to purchase asset-backed securities or other

FIG 5.1 **Issuance of asset-backed securities, excluding mortgages**
$bn

Sources: Securities Industry and Financial Markets Association; European Securitisation Forum; Dealogic

assets. The issuance of CDOs holding asset-backed securities almost quadrupled from 2004 to 2006 (Table 5.2).

TABLE 5.2 **Global issuance of structured-finance CDOs**

	$bn
2000	68
2004	158
2008	62
2010	9
2012	58

Source: Securities Industry and Financial Markets Association

The stage of rapid growth in asset-backed securities issuance was followed by a sharp worldwide decline starting in the second half of 2007. As economic troubles mounted around the world, an increasing number of borrowers defaulted on automotive loans, home-equity loans and other loans that had been securitised. This meant that investors in the asset-backed securities did not receive the interest payments they had anticipated, and the securities themselves lost value. Many asset-backed securities that had received high ratings from the credit-rating agencies went into default, shaking confidence in the market and leading to a drop in securitisation activity.

Mortgage-backed securities

Mortgages are by far the most important source of asset-backed securities. Such securities give investors the right to interest payments from a large number of mortgage loans, which are bundled together into securities. Most mortgage-backed securities are based on residential mortgages, but there is also a significant market in commercial mortgage-backed securities (CMBS). These are usually based on pooled loans of a single type, such as mortgages on hotels or office buildings.

Fannie Mae led the way

Although the Danes are credited with first developing the idea of issuing mortgage bonds, the most important step in the creation of the modern market for asset-backed securities was the establishment of the Federal National Mortgage Association (FNMA) in 1938. This company, known as Fannie Mae and originally a US government agency, was established to create a secondary market in mortgages. The primary mortgage market involved the decision by a private company, known as the originator, to lend to a homebuyer. When it purchased such a loan from the originator in the secondary market, Fannie Mae made it possible for the originator to make yet more loans, providing a substantial impetus to the housing market. With Fannie Mae as a model, private-sector entities began to purchase individual mortgages in secondary-market transactions as early as 1949, and US government regulators formally permitted thrift institutions to buy and sell mortgages in 1957.

From its earliest days, Fannie Mae took steps that were essential to the growth of the secondary market. It established standard procedures to be used in originating the mortgages it would buy, including methods of valuing property, rules for assessing individual borrowers' creditworthiness, and rules relating mortgage eligibility to income. It also set rules to govern servicing, the collection of interest and principal payments from borrowers, which most often was handled by the originator. Such standards eventually smoothed the development of mortgage-backed securities: although each mortgage backing a particular security would be different in detail, investors could be assured that every individual mortgage complied with the same general standards.

Pass-through certificates

Initially, Fannie Mae used government money to purchase mortgages from the lenders that had originated them, with the interest payments on the mortgages serving to repay the government. Then, in the 1960s, investment bankers hit upon an idea for tapping private investment by turning mortgages into securities, rather than buying and selling individual mortgages. These new securities were called pass-through certificates, so named because the principal and interest due monthly from the mortgagors of the loans backing the security would be passed directly to the investors. Pass-throughs, first issued in 1970, were the first modern asset-backed securities.

CMBS

Many different types of mortgages are securitised. As well as a lively market for single-family mortgage securities, there is substantial issuance of commercial mortgage-backed securities, known as CMBS. These may be based on mortgages for apartment buildings, housing for the elderly, retail developments, warehouses, hotels, office buildings and other sorts of structures. CMBS were first issued by Resolution Trust Corporation, a US government agency established to dispose of the assets of failed thrift institutions in the early 1990s. Discovering that it could dispose of these loans far more quickly by securitising them than by selling them off one by one, Resolution Trust Corporation issued nearly $18 billion of securities before ceasing operations in 1998.

Following in its footsteps, investment banks began to routinely securitise commercial mortgages, primarily for sale to life insurance companies. Total CMBS issuance in the United States and Europe reached $300 billion in 2007. However, a weakening world economy led to higher vacancy rates in commercial properties and falling rents, hurting CMBs investors. New securitisations of commercial mortgages were negligible in 2008–09. Since then, the market has recovered in the United States but remained sluggish in Europe.

REMICs

Another important step in the development of securitisation came in 1986, when the US Congress amended the tax laws to provide for real estate mortgage investment conduits, known as REMICs. These are a legal device to ensure that the income produced by a mortgage-backed security is taxable to the investors who have purchased the securities, but not to the trust that nominally owns the underlying mortgages and collects the payments from individual mortgagors. Many mortgage-backed securities in the United States are now issued through REMICs.

US agency securities

Several entities sponsored by the US government promote secondary markets for mortgage-backed securities. Collectively, the securities

TABLE 5.3 **US agency mortgage-backed securities**
$bn

	Amount issued	Amount outstanding at year end
1998	955	2,018
2000	583	2,492
2002	2,044	3,158
2004	1,393	2,274
2006	1,239	3,846
2008	1,366	4,956
2010	1,920	5,517
2012	1,575	5,656

Source: Securities Industry and Financial Markets Association they issue are known as agency securities. The agency securities market has burgeoned into one of the biggest financial markets of any kind (see Table 5.3). The total amount outstanding in mid-2013 was $5.7 trillion. Average daily trading volume in 2013 exceeded $250 billion, a drop from the peak of nearly $350 billion in 2008. Between 2008 and 2013, many newly issued agency securities were purchased by the Federal Reserve Board in an effort to hold down interest rates and stimulate the economy. In general, agency securities are called after the agency that issued them, and each agency's securities have slightly different characteristics.

Fannie Maes

Fannie Maes are issued by the former Federal National Mortgage Association, which began its existence as a US government enterprise. After becoming a shareholder-owned company using Fannie Mae as its name, the corporation failed in 2008. It was placed under the conservatorship of the government, which injected funding to keep it afloat. It has continued to issue securities backed by loans made in different parts of the country, enabling investors to reduce the risk that economic woes in a particular region will cause a disproportionate number of the securities in a particular pool to go into default. The interest rates on the individual loans in a fixed-rate mortgage pool may vary within a range of 2.5 percentage points. Based on these individual interest rates, Fannie Mae issues each security bearing a specific rate of interest, and guarantees that investors will receive timely payment of principal and interest each month, even if individual borrowers fail to pay. The company makes its money from the difference between the rates individuals pay to borrow and the lower interest rates paid to investors in pass-throughs, plus various fees. The amount of outstanding Fannie Maes exceeds $2.7 trillion. The company's failure did not directly affect its outstanding mortgage-backed securities and it continues to issue mortgage securities.

Ginnie Maes

Ginnie Maes are securities issued by private lenders under the auspices of the Government National Mortgage Association, a

US government corporation. The GNMA (hence the name Ginnie Mae) was split off from Fannie Mae in 1968, and is intended to promote home ownership among families of modest means. Each individual mortgage in a Ginnie Mae pool is guaranteed by some government agency, such as the Veterans Administration, which guarantees mortgages for former members of the US armed forces. The lender groups the mortgages to form a pool of loans having similar payment characteristics and maturities, and then receives Ginnie Mae permission to issue securities based on these mortgages. The lender is responsible for collecting interest and principal from individual borrowers and sending monthly payments to the holders of the securities it has issued, but the full faith and credit of the government guarantees that investors will receive all principal and interest payments due. The face value of outstanding Ginnie Maes exceeded $1.4 trillion in 2013.

Freddie Macs

Freddie Macs are issued by the Federal Home Loan Mortgage Corporation (FHLMC), a private-sector corporation established under a US government charter. Like Fannie Mae and Ginnie Mae, Freddie Mac operates only in the secondary market and does not lend money directly to individual borrowers. The corporation is obliged by government regulation to devote a share of its mortgage financing to low-income and moderate-income families. Its securities are similar to those issued by Fannie Mae, with which it competes, and do not constitute obligations of the government. Also like Fannie Mae, losses as a result of increased defaults by mortgage borrowers led to the company being placed under government conservatorship in 2008, but Freddie Mac continues to purchase loans and issue mortgage-backed securities. In mid-2013 it had $1.6 trillion in mortgage-backed securities outstanding.

Farmer Macs

Farmer Macs are pass-throughs of mortgages on farms and rural homes. The Federal Agricultural Mortgage Credit Corporation (FAMCC), a shareholder-owned company established by the US government, securitises both agricultural mortgages and loans guaranteed by the US Department of Agriculture, some of which are not mortgages. The company guarantees interest and principal payments to the purchasers of its securities, and its guarantee is backed by a $1.5 billion line of credit from the US Treasury. The volume of Farmer Mac securities is much smaller than that of the other government-sponsored participants in the US secondary mortgage market.

Mortgage securities outside the United States

More than $200 billion worth of residential mortgage securities was issued outside the United States in 2013, principally in western Europe. Securitisation helped inflate housing bubbles in a number of European countries, notably Ireland and Spain (see Table 5.4), where subsequent residential property collapses contributed to severe economic distress. Here are examples of how markets for mortgage-backed securities have developed in a number of countries outside the United States.

TABLE 5.4 **Residential mortgage securities outstanding in Europe**
€bn

	2000	2004	2008	2010	2012
Belgium	1	4	49	62	71
Germany	5	7	28	22	17
Ireland	3	4	58	69	51
Italy	5	35	126	144	98
Netherlands	11	63	255	290	269
Spain	12	50	190	191	127

Canada

NHA MBS are mortgage-backed securities issued under the National Housing Act by Canada Mortgage and Housing Corporation, an agency of the Canadian government. The corporation purchases and securitises mortgages issued by authorised private-sector lenders in Canada. Its pass-through securities are backed by single-family mortgages, mortgages on multi-family buildings, mortgages on social housing, or a combination of the three. Interest and principal payments are guaranteed by the corporation, and thus by the Canadian government. The corporation had C$382 billion (US$382 billion) of mortgage-backed securities outstanding at December 2012.

Denmark

Denmark has over $360 billion of mortgage-backed securities outstanding, a huge amount for a small country. This is because almost all home mortgages in Denmark are securitised. Danish mortgage securities are backed by fixed-rate residential mortgages with terms of 10–30 years, although, as in the United States, individual borrowers are free to pay off a mortgage before its maturity date without penalty. Unlike US mortgage-backed securities, those in Denmark combine commercial and residential properties, and investors typically receive interest payments quarterly rather than monthly. The underlying mortgages remain on the balance sheet of the mortgage bank that originated them, and are not sold to a trust.

Germany

Pfandbriefe are securities issued by certain mortgage banks or state banks in Europe. *Pfandbriefe* were a German creation, but Spanish and French financial institutions also are major issuers. There are two basic varieties: *Hypothekenpfandbriefe*, which account for about 40% of outstanding *Pfandbriefe* and are backed by residential mortgages meeting standards established by the German government; and *Oeffentliche Pfandbriefe*, which are backed by public-sector debt from Germany or other European countries.

Pfandbriefe differ from other asset-backed securities in that they are issued directly by banks, rather than through special-purpose vehicles, and the assets remain on the banks' balance sheets. Also *Pfandbriefe*, unlike other asset-backed securities, are not backed by a fixed pool of assets. The issuing bank can add to the asset pool from time to time and is legally responsible if the assets fail to generate enough income to pay the bondholders. For these reasons, investors in *Pfandbriefe*, unlike investors in most other types of asset-backed securities, must pay close attention to the financial strength of the bank issuing the securities, as it is the ultimate guarantor of payment. Most German mortgages are not securitised through *Pfandbriefe*, as only mortgages not exceeding 60% of the value of the property are eligible. *Pfandbriefe* issuance has fallen from approximately €1 trillion per year in 2003–05 to around €600 billion in 2010–12, with mortgages accounting for nearly half of total issuance.

The UK

The first mortgage-backed security in the UK was a £50m issue for National Home Loans in 1987. A total of £1 billion of mortgage-backed securities was issued that year in the UK, and the market has grown steadily since. Expansion has been retarded by the unique characteristics of the British residential mortgage market. A high proportion of mortgages have floating rates that adjust frequently; long-term fixed-rate mortgages are uncommon; and borrowers are able to increase the amount of an outstanding mortgage or to change lenders at little cost. These characteristics make many British mortgages unsuitable for packaging into long-term securities. Nonetheless, British issuance of mortgage-backed securities grew quickly even after the collapse of the housing market in 2008. The face value of British mortgage-backed securities outstanding was £355 billion at the end of 2012.

Other parts of Europe

Elsewhere in Europe, issuance of mortgage-backed securities was insignificant before the creation of the euro. Issuance in the euro zone began to grow rapidly in 2004, but fell just as rapidly after peaking in 2008. Strictly private-sector transactions underlie almost all mortgage-backed securities in other European countries, as there is no European equivalent of Fannie Mae or Ginnie Mae.

Japan

In Japan, development of mortgage-backed securities was hindered by laws allowing mortgagors to object to the resale of their mortgages.

The first attempt to issue a mortgage-backed security failed in 1998. However, several issues were completed successfully in 2000. The Japan Housing Finance Agency, created in 2007, has programmes modelled on Fannie Mae and Ginnie Mae, and has become a substantial issuer of mortgage-backed securities.

China

The People's Bank of China, the central bank, authorised the issuance of mortgage-backed securities in April 2000. However, there was no issuance until 2005 and the market remains small.

Australia

The mortgage securitisation market used to be important in Australia, peaking at $74 billion of issuance in 2006, when many mortgage-backed securities were targeted at foreign investors. However, it has declined sharply since 2007, with securitisation largely replaced by banks' bond issuance as a method of mortgage funding. Approximately A$100 billion (US$103 billion) worth of mortgage-backed securities remains outstanding, but new issuance has been scant.

Non-mortgage securities

As investors became accustomed to purchasing mortgage-backed securities, financial-market participants naturally began considering the possibilities of other types of asset-backed securities. The most avid participants in this process are banks, which use securitisation to play a role as intermediaries between borrowers and investors rather than as the ultimate providers of the borrowed funds. Many non-bank lenders have also turned to securitisation to fund their activities, particularly as securitisation allows them to grow far more rapidly than they could if they had to raise capital to support a large portfolio of loans. Table 5.5 shows the change in the amount of securities based on assets other than mortgages in the United States. Table 5.6 contains similar information for Europe.

TABLE 5.5 **Asset-backed securities outstanding in the United States, excluding mortgages**
$bn

	1996	2000	2004	2008	2012
Automotive loans	71	133	232	138	142
Credit-card loans	181	306	391	314	128
Home-equity loans	52	152	454	396	468
Manufactured-housing loans	15	37	42	20	13
Student loans	10	41	115	240	235
Other	76	403	594	1,565	714
Total	405	1,072	1,828	2,673	1,700

Source: Securities Industry and Financial Markets Association

TABLE 5.6 **Asset-backed securities outstanding in Europe, excluding mortgages**
€bn

	2000	2004	2008	2010	2012
Automotive loans	5	21	51	51	64
Consumer loans	7	18	63	69	67
Credit-card loans	9	27	40	28	28
Leases	4	23	40	36	30
Other	21	57	104	94	87
Total	46	146	298	278	276

Source: Securities Industry and Financial Markets Association

Credit-card securities

These were at one time the largest single category of non-mortgage asset-backed securities in both the United States and Europe. Many large banks have securitised part or all of their credit-card portfolios in order to put their capital to more profitable uses. However, securitisation has fallen sharply from its peaks before the financial crisis. Some $123 billion of credit-card securities, typically offering floating interest rates, were outstanding in the United States in 2013, barely one-third of the peak level of 2008. In Europe, $29 billion of credit-card asset-backed securities were outstanding in 2013, mainly in the UK. One reason for the reduced volume of issuance is that many banks have curtailed credit-card lending and consumers have been more reluctant to take on credit-card debt.

Home-equity loans

Securities backed by home-equity loans, often guaranteed by second liens (which offer security only after the borrower's debt to holders of the first mortgage has been satisfied), flourished in the United States before 2008. They became popular after tax-law changes removed preferences for other types of consumer borrowing. Many mortgage loans to risky borrowers, known as subprime loans, traded as home-equity securities in the asset-backed securities market, and thousands of these securities failed to perform as anticipated as the borrowers on the underlying mortgages defaulted. The amount of outstanding home-equity asset-backed securities has fallen in every calendar quarter since spring 2007, as existing home-equity loans are repaid or written off and few new loans are made. Only $4 billion of home-equity asset-backed securities were issued in 2012, down from a peak of $483 billion in 2006.

Automotive loans

Often securitised by the finance arms of automobile manufacturers, automotive loans are well-established in the asset-backed market. Some $149 billion of auto-loan securities were outstanding in the United States in mid-2013, as well as $64 billion in Europe and smaller amounts in Australia, Canada and the United Arab Emirates. Issuance depends on both the volume of automotive sales and the willingness of banks or automobile companies to finance those sales from their own resources; 2012, which saw a recovery in US auto sales, also saw a large increase in auto-loan securitisations. Unlike most credit-card and home-equity securities, asset-backed securities based on auto loans typically have fixed interest rates. There are also substantial amounts of securities backed by loans on aircraft ($17 billion worldwide at the end of 2012), shipping containers ($5 billion), rail cars, and agricultural and construction equipment.

Manufactured-housing securities

Introduced in the early 1990s, manufactured-housing securities had been considered high-risk loans unsuited for securitisation, as borrowers often had modest incomes, lending procedures were not uniform, and the homes themselves were not considered likely to appreciate in value from year to year. However, once non-bank lenders began to offer and securitise manufactured-housing loans, high interest rates made them attractive to investors. Some $15 billion of securities backed by manufactured housing were sold in the United States in 1999. Many of the loans went into default as economic growth slowed and unemployment rose in 2000 and 2001. Few new securities of this type have been issued since 2002, and amounts outstanding have fallen as borrowers have repaid their loans. By 2013, $12 billion of manufactured-housing securities were outstanding, down from a peak of $52 billion in 2000.

Student loans

Student loans have been securitised only since June 1993. Most student-loan securitisation is conducted by the Student Loan Marketing Association (SLMA), a shareholder-owned company established by the US government. The company, known as Sallie Mae, purchases student loans in the secondary market and packages them for sale as securities. Figure 5.2 shows the amount outstanding, which accounted for 14% of all US asset-backed securities by 2013.

Assorted others

Novel types of asset-backed securities are frequently offered for sale. Small-business loans have successfully been securitised by several banks, even though they constitute a fairly heterogeneous asset. Life insurance policies have been securitised, as have property insurance policies protecting against natural disasters. Film distribution companies, such as The Walt Disney Co, have successfully securitised the anticipated revenue from groups of films, and in 1998 a singer,

FIG 5.2 **Student loan securities outstanding**
$bn

Source: Securities and Financial Markets Association

David Bowie, securitised future revenue from recordings that had already been issued. Securities backed by anticipated ticket revenue have been used to build sports stadiums in several US cities. Unlike loan securitisations, however, sports and entertainment securitisations are usually one-of-a-kind deals and do not account for a large proportion of the market. They pose some significant risks not present in other types of securitisation, as the value of the securities depends heavily on the ability and willingness of particular entertainers or athletes to promote their product in future.

Asset-backed commercial paper

The assets that support medium-term and long-term securities can also be used to back commercial paper, a security with a maturity of less than 270 days. Fully supported paper has repayment guaranteed by a source other than the underlying assets, such as a surety bond or a letter of credit, and repayment of partially supported asset-backed paper depends primarily on the cash flow from the pool of assets. The paper is issued by a trust or other special-purpose vehicle, which uses the proceeds to purchase assets such as receivables. The trust may purchase these assets from a single firm or from several different firms.

Asset-backed commercial paper was created to meet investor demand for high-quality commercial paper in the face of limited corporate issuance. In effect, by repackaging long-term obligations, investment banks are able to market securities with the desired term. In 2007, however, what was designed as a very low-risk product for investors suffered serious disruptions as investors backed away, fearful of deterioration in the quality of the underlying assets. In the United States, the value of asset-backed commercial paper outstanding fell from $1.2 trillion in July 2007 to $839 billion five months later, as issuers were unable to roll over their paper. The Federal Reserve Board was concerned that money-market mutual funds would be unable to sell their asset-backed commercial paper holdings to meet investors' redemption requests, and it offered the funds emergency financing for a limited period. A similar problem arose in the Canadian market for asset-backed commercial paper, leading to a mandatory restructuring programme supported by the federal government and three provinces.

In mid-2013, approximately $280 billion of asset-backed commercial paper was outstanding in the United States, one-quarter of the 2006 level. The amount outstanding in Europe was €14 billion, down from a peak of €58 billion in early 2007.

Structured finance

The basics of asset-backed securities are reasonably simple: the issuer pools the assets that are to underlie the securities, and then issues securities giving the owners the right to income from those assets. But matters can get far more complicated. A significant portion of the asset-backed market consists of structured securities: securities designed to allow the investor to accept a greater or smaller amount of risk in return for a greater or smaller expected return. The best-known structured securities are collateralised mortgage obligations, or CMOs, but there are many non-mortgage variants as well. CMOs are popular with institutional investors, with $831 billion of the securities outstanding at March 2013.

To create structured securities, the issuer divides the securities backed by a pool into sections, called tranches or classes, with different characteristics. One CMO created from a mortgage-backed security, for example, might consist of all principal and interest payments received during the first three years. A second tranche might consist of payments received in years 4–7, and so on. Non-mortgage securities can be structured in a similar way. Usually, 3–5 separate securities are created from each pool of assets. The highest-risk tranches often are marketed to individual investors, who may be enticed by the high yields without fully understanding the risks involved.

In many cases, issuers and their investment bankers design asset-backed securities to meet the needs of particular investors with regard to the timing of income, regulatory restrictions on investments, or tax considerations. One widely used technique is to create STRIPS – securities that treat the interest-bearing component of the security separately from the repayment of principal. These components behave very differently from one another. Interest-only STRIPS, for example, will lose value when interest rates fall, as more borrowers will pay their loans early and thus pay less interest than anticipated, even as the corresponding principal-only STRIPS gain in value as their owners receive principal payments sooner than expected. Of equal concern to investors, however, may be that the interest received by the owners of interest-only STRIPS may, in some countries, be taxed at a higher rate than the capital gains earned by the owners of the principal-only STRIPS.

The optionality factor

This structuring creates a way to attach an explicit price to the optionality that is inherent in most asset-backed securities. The optionality stems from the fact that in most cases the borrower of a loan that has been securitised has the right to repay early, and in some cases may have the right to extend the loan rather than repaying as scheduled. The shortest-term tranche, usually called the A tranche, is least likely to be affected by repayments and is therefore the most stable among the structured securities. The next segment, the B tranche, could be expected to be more volatile, and investors will require a higher interest rate to purchase it. The most volatile tranche of a structured security is the support tranche, which is entitled to principal and interest payments in the most distant time period and therefore, by design, is the tranche that absorbs most of the prepayment and extension risk. For CMOs, the support tranche is referred to as the planned amortisation class, or the Z tranche. This tranche offers high returns when interest rates are stable. When rates rise or fall significantly, however, individuals may be more inclined to repay their loans or to extend payment, and the value of the Z tranche can fluctuate widely. For this reason, it is sometimes referred to in the market as "toxic waste".

Pricing

The price of a fixed-rate asset-backed security is usually expressed as an interest-rate yield compared with the yield of an appropriate benchmark, most often government bonds of similar maturity. Floating-rate asset-backed securities are usually priced from a widely used floating interest rate, such as the London inter-bank offered rate (Libor). The difference between the yield of an asset-backed security and that of its benchmark varies greatly and depends upon many factors:

■ **Credit risk.** When an economy is strong, borrowers are expected to have little difficulty meeting their obligations and the premium required by investors in asset-backed securities will be small. If the economy is seen to be slowing or in recession, however, investors in asset-backed securities will demand wider spreads to compensate for the risk that individual borrowers will encounter financial distress and default on their loans. This spread widening was clearly in evidence in 2007–09 amid increasing borrower defaults and deteriorating economic performance. For example, the spread of BBB-rated asset-backed securities in Europe widened from around one percentage point in September 2007 to 15 percentage points at the end of 2008, as investors anticipated defaults on credit-card and automobile loans. The extent of spread widening, however, depended very much on the characteristics of the securities: spreads on mortgage-backed securities from Spain widened much more than those on securities from France, as investors expected much more deterioration in the Spanish housing market.

■ **Rating.** Credit-rating agencies evaluate asset-backed securities with methods similar to those used for corporate securities. In particular, they closely scrutinise the financial strength of any firm or government agency that purports to guarantee payment of interest and/or principal if the securities fail to perform as expected. Higher-rated asset-backed securities can be expected to trade much closer to their benchmarks than lower-rated securities.

■ **Asset characteristics.** Two pools of credit-card loans or fixed-rate mortgages may appear similar yet have very different characteristics. Investors quantify and study the characteristics of the assets, such as the weighted average maturity, the weighted average age of the underlying loans and the delinquency rate, in order to compare the expected cash flows of different pools.

■ **Prepayment risk.** One of the greatest risks faced by investors in asset-backed securities is that individual borrowers may pay part or all of the principal of their loans ahead of schedule. This occurs most often at a time of falling interest rates, and can force the owners of securities to reinvest the prepaid funds at a lower rate of interest than they had expected to receive. Also, some tranches of structured securities may lose a large part of their value if prepayments are greater than expected. Large investors in asset-backed securities have developed elaborate mathematical models to estimate prepayment rates, but these models are often subject to significant error.

■ **Extension risk.** This is the reverse of prepayment risk. If market interest rates rise, the average term of the loans in a pool may be higher than expected as borrowers avoid prepayment, causing investors in the securities to be stuck with a comparatively low-yielding asset for longer than they anticipated. Extension risk, like prepayment risk, is difficult to model accurately.

■ **Underwriting risk.** Some of the banks that originate asset-backed securities are known to be scrupulous in making the underlying loans. These securities will generally have lower yields than similar securities issued by banks that are thought to be less careful about underwriting loans.

■ **Servicing risk.** Servicing is the collection of principal and interest payments from individual borrowers. The servicer receives a fee for collecting each payment and passes the remainder of the payment to the trustee to be paid out to the investors. Some servicers are far more successful than others at collecting timely payments and dealing with borrowers who are in default. The quality of the servicer will be reflected in the price of each security.

Buying asset-backed securities

Their comparatively high yield makes asset-backed securities attractive investments. Most types of asset-backed securities, including mortgage-backed securities, are sold in small denominations and can be purchased from brokerage firms. Some securities, notably *Pfandbriefe*, are traded on stock exchanges. However, because the value of an individual asset-backed security may be dramatically altered by prepayments or other factors that are difficult to project, owning a single security can be risky for an unsophisticated investor. For this reason, individuals may be better off investing in a fund that owns many asset-backed securities than purchasing the securities directly.

Measuring performance

On average, mortgage-backed and asset-backed securities produce substantially higher returns than government or corporate bonds of similar maturity and asset quality. However, the returns on asset-backed securities are often far more volatile than those of other types of fixed-income securities, and some types of asset-backed securities may be far more volatile than others. Investing in individual asset-backed securities requires considerable quantitative skill. Investors can obtain highly detailed information about the individual loans in each security, as well as the characteristics of the borrowers and the rate at which the loans are being repaid. The extent to which repayment rates, late payments and defaults differ from expectations can greatly affect the value of the securities.

Several investment banks publish indexes of the performance of asset-backed securities. The performance of these indexes can readily be compared with the performance of corporate-bond indexes. Many US agency mortgage securities are owned by mutual funds that hold only this type of security, and the annual rates of return of these funds are widely published in newspapers and online.

Tracking the performance of more esoteric varieties of asset-backed securities can be difficult. Because of their unique characteristics, these securities often trade in comparatively illiquid markets, and this makes it difficult to attach a meaningful value to them.

6 International fixed-income markets

MOST FINANCIAL-MARKET ACTIVITY takes place wholly within the boundaries of a single country and is denominated in that country's currency. A large and growing share, however, now crosses national boundaries, as individuals move capital into currencies that seem to offer greater returns, and as borrowers search the globe for money at the lowest price.

This international market for money can be divided into two segments. In some cases, investors and borrowers will arrange transactions in a country other than their own, using that country's currency. In other cases, a transaction will be arranged in a currency other than that of the country where it occurs. At one time, the former were known simply as foreign transactions, and the latter were referred to as Euromarket transactions. The distinction between the two has blurred, however, as this chapter will explain.

A brief history of the Euromarkets

The idea of using the money of one country to transact business in another is not new. Such offshore dealings have gone on for centuries, often with the aim of avoiding taxes, regulation or confiscation. The name Euromarket was first applied to the acceptance of offshore deposits in 1957, at the height of the cold war, when Moscow Narodny Bank decided to transfer its dollar deposits out of the United States to foreclose the possibility that the US government would confiscate Soviet assets. The Russians had their dollars transferred from New York to a French bank that had the cable address EUROBANK, and soon all dollars deposited in European banks took the name Eurodollars.

Market surge

These dollars helped create a new financial market as a result of the Bretton Woods system of fixed exchange rates, around which the economy of the non-communist world was organised after the second world war. This system still had aspects of a gold standard: if a country had a balance-of-payments deficit, it would settle the imbalance by paying gold to its creditor countries. In theory, the loss of that gold would lead the country's central bank to contract the money supply, which would slow the economy, which would in turn reduce demand for imports and thus bring the balance of payments back into balance.

By the late 1950s, however, the United States seemed to be running a persistent balance-of-payments deficit, and government officials grew concerned that the country's gold stocks were running low. One cause of the problem was thought to be that foreigners were issuing too many securities in the United States and then exchanging the proceeds for foreign currency to use in their home countries. This worsened the US payments imbalance, putting yet more pressure on gold reserves. The US government responded with a set of policies, of which the centrepiece was the interest equalisation tax, recommended by President John Kennedy in July 1963 and enacted in August 1964. By claiming 15% of the interest received by Americans on stocks and bonds issued by Europeans (securities from Canada, Japan and less-developed countries were exempt), the tax was intended to reduce capital outflows and thus staunch the loss of gold.

Back in business

The tax accomplished its immediate objective as the so-called Yankee bond market, in which foreigners sold dollar-denominated bonds in the United States, quickly dried up. The financing needs that had given rise to Yankee bonds remained, however, and European financial markets were still in sufficient disarray from the war that they could not raise large amounts of capital. Investment bankers quickly hit upon the idea of selling dollar-denominated bonds in London, where, as long as they were not sold to US residents, the securities would be unaffected by the US tax.

The first Eurobond, a $15m offering by Autostrade, an Italian motorway company, was issued in 1963. In 1964, 76 separate Eurobond issues raised almost $1.2 billion, and the Eurobond market was firmly established. When the interest equalisation tax was extended to bank loans in 1965, banks moved much of their dollar-based international lending to London as well. As British banking regulations did not apply to foreign banks lending in foreign currencies, banks from around the world flocked to London to set up offices. By the time the interest equalisation tax was removed in 1974, the Euromarket was a prominent part of the international financial scene.

The international bond market today

The international market is neither an exchange nor a particular group of products. Rather, the term refers to a decentralised system in which currencies held outside their home countries are reloaned without being converted to another currency. Most dealings in the international market take the form of bank loans to customers and short-term loans from one bank to another. The securities markets, however, account for a large and rapidly growing share of international activity. The size

FIG 6.1 **Outstanding international debt securities**
$bn

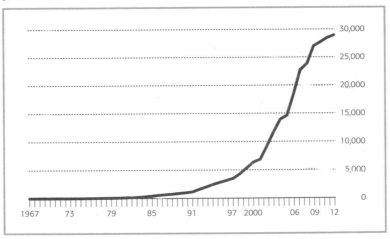

Source: Bank for International Settlements

FIG 6.2 **Domestic and international bond markets**
Amounts outstanding, $bn

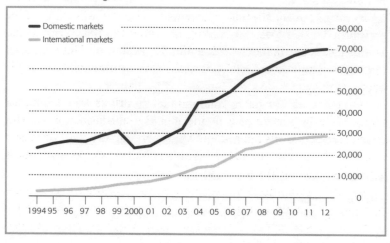

Source: Bank for International Settlements

FIG 6.3 **International bond new issue volume**
$bn

Source: Bank for International Settlements

of the market, expressed in terms of securities outstanding, is shown in Figure 6.1.

By comparison, there are approximately $70 trillion of debt securities of all types outstanding in domestic financial markets. The international markets, with about $22 trillion of debt securities outstanding, thus constitute 24% of the total worldwide market for debt securities.

As Figure 6.2 illustrates, international securities are playing an increasingly important role in the global securities markets. The international markets are also growing more rapidly than domestic markets. The precise number of securities traded is unknown, but it is thought to be well over 100,000.

As with domestic debt instruments, international instruments come in three main varieties: bonds, medium-term notes and short-term commercial paper. The issuance of new bonds and notes has been increasing rapidly, as shown in Figure 6.3.

Although these instruments are sometimes referred to as Eurodollar paper, the term is a misnomer. The US dollar is only one of the currencies used in the international market. It is equally possible to issue securities denominated in yen (Euroyen), Swiss francs, New Zealand dollars (Eurokiwis) and any other freely convertible currency. Historically, the US dollar and the yen have been the main currencies of issuance, with the D-mark a distant third. When the single European currency, the euro, was created at the start of 1999, it quickly became the most important vehicle for issuance of international securities. However, as shown in Table 6.1, euro-denominated issuance faded in 2011 and 2012 as the financial crisis prompted many European banks to retrench and, in the process, to reduce their outstanding debt. (It should be noted that the Euromarket and the market for euro-denominated securities are by no means the same thing; euro-denominated securities issued in a country that has adopted the euro as its currency are domestic instruments, not international ones.) Use of the yen for international bond issuance also declined, leaving the dollar once again as the main currency of issuance.

A borrower's decision to issue bonds in a particular currency does not mean that the borrower requires that currency to finance investments. The larger and more sophisticated borrowers tapping the

TABLE 6.1 **Net international bond and note issues, by currency**
$bn

	2000	2004	2008	2012
Euro	425	924	954	76
US dollar	554	380	690	567
Pound sterling	92	134	564	15
Swiss franc	0	13	31	−11
Yen	11	27	21	−23
Canadian dollar	−3	26	31	−32
Australian dollar	−1	30	12	11
Hong Kong dollar	5	7	−7	−3

Source: Bank for International Settlements

international market for financing will borrow in whichever currency offers the most attractive interest rates at a given time and then, through the foreign-exchange markets, obtain the desired currency. The large share of issuance occurring in US dollars in most years therefore reflects favourable dollar interest rates and the large pool of investors preferring to purchase dollar-denominated securities, rather than the issuers' need for dollars.

Money-market instruments

As well as bonds, which have maturities of up to 30 years, and medium-term notes, with maturities of 1–5 years, short-term instruments are also traded in the international markets. Commercial paper, sometimes referred to as euro-commercial paper, is debt with a maturity of less than 270 days, issued by corporate borrowers. There is also a lively international market in other short-term paper, sometimes called short-term euronotes. These are mainly tradable bank deposits, similar to certificates of deposit, and government securities maturing within one year. Demand for international money-market instruments, modest until then, shot up in 1999 with the adoption of the single European currency, then fell as low long-term rates made issuance of long-dated bonds more attractive. The issuance of international money-market instruments fell sharply in the wake of the financial crisis in 2008, as investors lost confidence in the strength of many borrowers' finances. When the market revived, in 2012, investors shied away from commercial paper, forcing borrowers to raise short-term funds in other ways (see Table 6.2).

TABLE 6.2 **Net issuance of international money-market instruments**
$bn

	2000	2004	2008	2010	2012[a]
Commercial paper	55.2	40.4	70.6	−64	−8.1
Other short-term paper	97.0	20.9	11.1	78.0	124.6

a Data as of June 30th.
Source: Bank for International Settlements

Historically, the majority of international money-market instruments have been traded in US dollars, with yen, Swiss francs, pounds sterling, D-marks and Hong Kong dollars also being used significantly. Since 2002, however, the euro has vied with the dollar as the main currency of issuance. Although euro-denominated issuance slowed, as of 2013 the value of euro-denominated bonds traded in international markets substantially exceeded the value of dollar-denominated bonds.

In comparison with domestic money markets, trading in international money-market instruments remains small. In some periods, the amount of short-term securities outstanding in international markets actually falls. For example, although $527 billion of international money-market instruments were issued in the second quarter of 2013, some $516 billion of such instruments issued previously were repaid during the quarter, resulting in net issuance of $11 billion.

The issuers

As many aspects of the international markets are unregulated, there are no restrictions as to who may issue bonds. However, investors generally require that issuers obtain ratings from credit-rating agencies, just as they do with most domestic issues of bonds and commercial paper. There is a considerable market in bonds that are rated below investment grade. This is a significant attraction for companies in countries where there is no domestic market for below-investment-grade bonds.

Companies and governments in many different countries turn to the international markets for financing. Their decisions on whether they should sell bonds domestically or in international markets depend on relative interest rates, exchange-rate expectations and the uses to which the funds raised will be put. The biggest issuers of international debt securities are financial institutions, but their share of all bonds outstanding in international markets fell from 80% in 2008 to 47% in 2013. Multinational corporations, national governments and international organisations such as the World Bank and the European Investment Bank are also important issuers.

These proportions vary greatly from country to country. Public-sector issuers, for example, account for the majority of the outstanding international debt securities issued by entities in Argentina and Turkey. At the other extreme, private-sector borrowers account for the lion's share of the bonds and short-term paper sold internationally by entities from India, Switzerland and the United States. Table 6.3 lists the countries whose corporations and governments are the largest borrowers in the international markets.

During the 1990s many borrowers in emerging economies entered the international debt markets for the first time. Previously, both firms and governments in less advanced economies had raised capital mainly through bank borrowings, which typically have higher interest rates and shorter terms than bonds. After years of inflation, stabilisation programmes and other economic reforms made countries such as Mexico and Argentina more attractive to foreign investors, and relaxation of financial regulations has permitted firms in these countries to sell bonds abroad more readily. Typically,

TABLE 6.3 **International debt securities outstanding, by nationality of issuer**
$bn

	2000	2004	2008	2012
US	1,762	3,354	6,036	2,904
UK	563	1,403	2,747	2,831
Germany	913	2,332	2,897	2,050
France	314	930	1,613	1,774
Netherlands	293	690	1,118	1,436
Italy	209	683	1,232	1,112

Source: Bank for International Settlements

corporations from emerging-market countries succeed in selling bonds internationally only after the national government has obtained ratings from credit-rating agencies and completed a sovereign bond issue. Both government and corporate issuers in these countries typically break into the market with bonds maturing in as little as two or three years, but they are able to issue securities with longer maturities as they become better known to investors.

The growth of emerging-market issuance has been erratic owing to the financial and exchange-rate crises that have afflicted major borrowers. In 1994, for example, issuers from emerging countries sold $32.5 billion of debt in the international markets, but issuance fell to $22 billion the following year, after Mexico was forced to devalue its peso in December 1994. Some $72 billion was sold during 1997, but in 1998, as exchange-rate problems ravaged Thailand, South Korea, Russia and several other countries and threatened to spill over into Latin America, emerging-market debt issuance fell to $24.3 billion. The prices of these securities are often volatile as well, offering highly attractive returns for investors at some points and declining sharply at other times. In early 2002, after Argentina effectively defaulted on its bonds and devalued its currency, Argentine government bonds were selling for as little as one-quarter of their face value. Emerging-market bond issuance was robust in 2011 and 2012 as extremely low interest rates in Europe, North America and Japan drove investors to purchase riskier securities in search of higher yields, but the emerging-market bond boom ended abruptly in mid-2013 as interest rates in the United States began to rise. Table 6.4 lists the biggest emerging-market borrowers.

TABLE 6.4 **Emerging-market issuers of debt securities, amount outstanding**
$bn

	1996	2000	2004	2008	2012
Brazil	29	56	73	118	270
Russia	1	18	23	141	235
China	14	18	15	44	173
South Korea	44	50	67	107	168
Mexico	43	66	59	88	145
UAE	–	–	3	60	111
Poland	1	5	25	44	82
Turkey	13	23	31	52	74
India	5	5	7	41	61
Venezuela	3	11	16	34	59
South Africa	4	7	18	35	54
Argentina	30	72	93	54	51
Malaysia	10	15	23	33	50
Philippines	7	16	25	32	45
Hungary	14	10	17	37	38

Source: Bank for International Settlements

Types of instruments

The variety of instruments traded in the international markets is similar to that available in the domestic markets of countries with advanced financial systems:

■ **Fixed-rate bonds.** These are the most widely traded instrument, accounting for approximately three-quarters of all bonds and notes outstanding in the international market. In recent years there have been some huge fixed-rate issues, with some corporate issuers raising as much as $14 billion in a single international bond offering.

■ **Floating-rate bonds.** Almost all issued by financial institutions, these accounted for 28% of the total amount of bonds outstanding in international markets in 2013. They were more important in earlier years, but extremely low long-term interest rates in 2012 and 2013 encouraged many borrowers to issue fixed-rate bonds instead.

■ **Equity-linked bonds.** These constitute less than 2% of the paper traded in the international market. Almost all of them are convertible, meaning they can be exchanged for the issuer's shares at a predetermined time and price. Equity-linked bonds are issued almost exclusively by non-financial corporations.

The swaps market

Neither the type nor the currency of an international bond issue provides a clear indication of the obligations the borrower has taken on. This is because the international bond markets are tightly linked to the swaps market. Swaps are derivative instruments that permit the user to exchange one set of payment obligations for another. Often, an issuer will sell bonds of whatever type and currency offers the most attractive interest rate at the time of issue and simultaneously enter a swap so that it can make payments in the form desired.

Swaps can make financial reports misleading. For example, an industrial firm that entered the international markets to issue £100m of fixed-rate ten-year bonds with a 6% coupon might be assumed to face a £6m annual interest payment, when in reality it swapped the payments for floating-rate US dollar payments, the size of which will depend upon US interest rates. If US interest rates were to rise suddenly, the firm could thus find itself in financial distress even though it has no dollar-denominated borrowings.

The most common transactions are fixed-for-floating swaps in the same currency. In such deals, the issuer exchanges payment obligations with a counterparty, usually a bank. An issuer of fixed-rate bonds would exchange its fixed payment obligation for the obligation to pay a floating interest rate on a similar amount of principal. Conversely, an issuer of floating-rate bonds might trade its payment obligation for a fixed-rate payment. The desirability of such a transaction depends on swap spreads, the premiums banks demand for agreeing to take on fixed-rate payments (which are usually higher but stable) and to cede floating-rate payments (which are usually lower but variable). There is a lively market in swaps, and market participants can easily obtain current swap spreads from financial information providers.

In the case of long-term bonds, swaps lasting until the bonds' maturity may be difficult to obtain in the market. In such a case, an issuer might arrange a fixed-for-floating swap for five or ten years, after which it would reassume the obligation to make fixed payments or, perhaps, arrange another swap transaction. Table 6.5 shows the growth of the market for interest-rate swaps of different maturities. The figures, in trillions of dollars, represent the face value of obligations being swapped, not the much smaller amounts that individual participants have at risk as interest rates change.

TABLE 6.5 **Notional value of interest-rate swaps and forwards**
$trn

Maturity	2000	2004	2008	2010	2012
0–1 year	21.7	52.5	125.4	177.1	177.7
1–5 years	21.2	65.5	120.2	121.9	158.0
Over 5 years	12.3	42.2	121.8	116.9	105.6

Source: Bank for International Settlements

The volume of new interest-rate swaps is obviously much larger than the volume of new international bond issues, as most swaps are related to domestic bond issues or other types of obligations. The swaps market was almost entirely a telephone market up to 2002, but an electronic swaps trading system sponsored by major banks began in 2002 and trading now occurs mainly via computer. Most swaps trading occurs over the counter in private arrangements between dealers and their clients, but regulatory changes in many countries may force a large proportion of trading to move to formal exchanges, potentially lowering costs and providing greater protection against default.

Global bonds

A global bond is an issue that is marketed simultaneously in the international markets and in the domestic market of the currency of issue. The first global bond, a $1.5 billion issue by the World Bank in 1989, was sold simultaneously as a domestic security in the United States and as an international security in what was then known as the Euromarket, with the issuer dedicating separate portions, or tranches, to each market. Until 1999, the number of global issues was small, as a large issue is needed to make the procedure worthwhile. However, a general increase in investor demand for large (and hence more liquid) issues has resulted in several huge global issues. The biggest so far, a $30 billion issue by Roche Holding in February 2009, included bonds denominated in dollars, euros and sterling, with maturities ranging from two to 30 years.

Bond issuance

The method for issuing securities in the international markets is significantly different from that in most domestic markets. The requirement for registration or regulatory approval depends on where the issue will occur and whether the issuer wishes the bonds to trade on an exchange after the issue. In general, disclosures about the issuer's financial condition and other matters may be substantially less than would accompany a domestic issue in many countries of the EU, Canada, or the United States.

Most international bond issues are sold by a syndicate or selling group of investment dealers formed for the purpose. The principal investment bank, the syndicate manager, determines the price at which the issue will be sold and allocates the bonds to the other dealers in the syndicate. Syndicate members handle the bonds on a fixed-price re-offer basis, meaning that they agree to sell the bonds to customers only at the established price as long as the bonds are still in syndicate. Once the issue is sold, the syndicate breaks and the bonds can trade in the secondary market at prices determined by demand and supply.

In certain cases, the issuer and its lead bank will agree on a bought deal. This means that one bank or a syndicate purchases the entire issue and seeks to resell it in the market, taking the risk that it will lose money if it is unable to sell the bonds for more than it has paid the issuer. In other cases, the bonds will be sold on a best-efforts basis, reverting to the issuer in the event that the members of the syndicate are unable to sell them.

Trading

The market for international bonds is largely an over-the-counter market. Although some issuers choose to arrange for their bonds to be traded on bourses, primarily in Luxembourg and London, most dealing occurs over the telephone rather than at exchanges. Several electronic trading systems have been developed, but in the fixed-income realm these are used mainly for trading highly liquid national government securities rather than bonds issues by banks, corporations, or other entities.

The lack of market information has contributed to illiquidity, which is perhaps the most severe problem confronting the international markets. Many international bonds disappear into investors' portfolios and are then held to maturity, which keeps trading volume rather small. For example, the Luxembourg Stock Exchange listed over 27,000 bonds in 2013, but only a handful of the most active bonds traded even once per day, on average.

Trading in international bonds is also restricted by national regulations. Some countries allow dealers to sell bonds only to large, sophisticated investors, known in legal terminology as qualified institutional buyers, called QIBs (pronounced quibs). The US authorities prohibit the sale of international bonds to US residents for 40 days after issue, and require that such bonds be seasoned by being sold first to other investors before Americans may buy them.

Towards international standards

As it is difficult for national regulators to set rules for markets that operate all over the world, the leading dealers created the International Capital Markets Association (ICMA) to establish standard practices. Based in Switzerland, the ICMA is now recognised as a self-regulatory organisation by the British authorities, and all major dealers adhere to its rules. Among other things, the ICMA has established procedures for clearing transactions, including a reporting system so firms can identify and reconcile errors that may have occurred in writing down the name and quantity of a security that has been bought or sold. The ICMA has also agreed on settlement procedures, so that for all international bond trades among its members, money and securities change hands on the third business day after the transaction.

Obtaining price information

There is no central source for price and volume information concerning the international markets. Most issues trade infrequently, if at all. In any case, most transactions are conducted between a customer and a bond dealer, which has no obligation to inform the public about the details of any transaction. Thus the reported price of a bond may be imputed from the prices of other, similar bonds, rather than the price at which a transaction actually occurred.

Nonetheless, financial information services do seek to report the prices of international bonds, and price tables appear in some newspapers and online. Table 6.6, drawn from the *Financial Times*, lists bonds denominated in four different currencies. Following the maturity date, the bond coupon and the rating assigned by Standard & Poor's, the table provides bid prices (prices at which investors or dealers have offered to purchase the bonds) in relation to the initial offering price of 100. The bid yield column calculates the yield the bonds would offer if purchased at the bid price, thus giving an indication of what investors consider to be an appropriate interest rate for bonds of that currency, maturity and credit quality. The next two columns give the change in the yield over the past day and the past month. The last column provides the spread between the yield on the given bond and the yield on a bond of the same maturity issued by the national government whose currency is being used. This number offers the purest measure of credit risk, as it represents the premium investors demand for holding a bond other than a government bond.

TABLE 6.6 **International bond prices**

	Red date	Coupon	S&P rating	Bid price	Bid yield	Day's chge yield	Mth's chge yield	Spread v govt. bonds
US$								
BNP Paribas	6/15	4.80	AA–	78.23	9.64	0.01	0.44	6.32
GE Capital	3/32	6.75	AA+	83.15	8.42	0	0.73	4.15
Euro								
Unicredit	1/20	4.38	A	85.57	6.27	0.03	0.35	3.48
GE Cap Euro Fdg	1/18	5.38	AA+	90.85	6.81	−0.72	−1.17	3.29
Yen								
Deutsche Bahn Fin	12/14	1.65	...	93.43	2.97	−0.04	0.04	2.07
Nomura Sec S3	3/18	2.28	...	91.45	3.56	−0.04	0.12	2.15
Sterling								
Slough Estates	9/15	6.25	...	81.07	10.22	−0.48	−1.39	7.44
ASIF III	12/18	5.00	A+	56.39	12.92	0.19	−0.79	9.13

In Table 6.6 it can be seen that bonds issued by GE Capital in US dollars, maturing in 2032, are yielding 8.42%, but the same company's bonds in euros, maturing in 2018, are yielding only 6.81%. An investor considering a purchase, however, would surely note the fact that the US dollar bonds yield 4.15 percentage points more than US Treasury securities, whereas the euro bonds yield 3.29 percentage points more than European government bonds of similar maturity. The investor would have to decide whether the lower-yielding euro bonds offer better value, relative to other securities available in the market.

Looking ahead

The international bond market developed largely as a response to taxation and regulation in domestic bond markets. It allowed issuers to borrow money in the currency of their choice without being bound by the regulations of the country whose currency they used. Because the bonds were issued in bearer form, without being registered in the buyer's name, they allowed investors to protect their anonymity and, in some cases, avoid taxation.

Over the years, however, many of the distinctive features of the international market have been eroded. As national governments have liberalised their rules for issuing and trading securities and eased restrictions on cross-border capital flows, the advantages of international issues have ceased to loom large. Efforts to impose a withholding tax on bond interest received by individual investors within the EU could eliminate much of the tax advantage of issuing abroad. Global bond issues and the creation of cross-border issues within the EU have blurred the distinction between Eurobonds and other international bond issues. Some securities traditionally considered to be domestic, such as *Pfandbrief* mortgage bonds issued in Germany, are now promoted heavily to foreign investors and are considered international instruments.

These changes have blurred the difference between Eurobonds and foreign bonds. The term international bonds is now applied to both, and the Euromarkets label has fallen out of use. But although the Euromarkets may have faded into history, the international bond markets are flourishing and are likely to grow rapidly.

7 Equity markets

"IT IS USUALLY AGREED that casinos should, in the public interest, be inaccessible and expensive. And perhaps the same is true of Stock Exchanges." So wrote a British economist, John Maynard Keynes, in 1935. Keynes's jibe is not entirely misplaced; more than a few punters approach the stockmarkets in the same spirit as the racetrack or the roulette wheel. Yet for all their shortcomings, as Keynes himself acknowledged, stockmarkets offer one singular advantage: they are the best way to bring people with money to invest together with people who can put that investment to productive use.

The origins of equities

Equity, quite simply, means ownership. Equities, therefore, are shares that represent part ownership of a business enterprise. The idea of share ownership goes back to medieval times. It became widespread during the Renaissance, when groups of merchants joined to finance trading expeditions and early bankers took part ownership of businesses to ensure repayment of loans. These early shareholder-owned enterprises, however, were usually temporary ventures established for a limited purpose, such as financing a single voyage by a ship, and were dissolved once their purpose was accomplished.

The first shareholder-owned business may have been the Dutch East India Company, which was founded by Dutch merchants in 1602 and issued negotiable share certificates that were readily traded in Amsterdam until the company failed almost two centuries later. By the late 17th century, traders in London coffee houses earned their living

TABLE 7.1 **Equity market capitalisation**
May 2013

	Market capitalisation, $bn
US	21,149
Japan	4,222
China	4,038
UK	3,603
Euronext[a]	3,037
India	2,966
Hong Kong	2,873
Canada	2,010
Germany	1,617
Switzerland	1,362
Australia	1,182
Brazil	1,152
Korea	1,146
OMX Nordic Exchange[b]	1,077
Spain	983

a Includes former Amsterdam, Brussels, Lisbon and Paris stock exchanges.
b Includes Copenhagen, Helsinki, Iceland, Stockholm, Tallinn, Riga and Vilnius stock exchanges.
Sources: World Federation of Exchanges; London Stock Exchange Group

dealing in the shares of joint-stock companies. But it was not until the Industrial Revolution made it necessary to raise large amounts of capital to build factories and canals that share trading became widespread. By 2013, the capitalisation of the world's stockmarkets exceeded $58 trillion after the widespread recovery in share prices since 2008. Table 7.1 gives the total stockmarket capitalisation – the value of all shares listed – in several countries; Table 7.2 shows the value of share turnover in various countries.

Raising capital

Raising capital remains the main function of equity markets. But the equity markets are not the only way for firms to raise capital. Before

TABLE 7.2 **The value of share turnover**
$bn

	2000	2004	2008	2012
US	32,994	20,976	70,085	23,227
UK	4,559	5,169	6,272	2,194
Japan	2,640	3.352	5,888	3,605
Germany	2,120	1,541	4,679	1,276
Euronext[a]	4,911	2,472	4,411	1,576
China	–	517	3,849	4,968
Hong Kong	377	439	1,630	1,106
South Korea	381	488	1,432	1,518
Canada	647	651	1,716	1,357
Switzerland	638	791	1,500	585
Australia	226	524	1,213	936

a Comprises Amsterdam, Brussels, Lisbon and Paris stock exchanges.
Source: World Federation of Exchanges

turning to the markets to obtain financing, firms undertake a detailed analysis of alternative methods of meeting their requirements.

Loans

Loans are the main type of financing available to firms that have not issued securities. Lenders such as banks are accustomed to analysing the business plans and financial condition of small firms, and often lend to companies that would have difficulty raising funds in the financial markets. Bank loans, however, are expensive, and banks can lend only a limited amount to a single borrower. Firms which are able to do so often prefer to diversify their borrowing by selling bonds, securities that entitle the holder to payment of interest and repayment of principal at predetermined times. Bonds (discussed in Chapter 4) have the disadvantage of imposing a fixed repayment obligation, which may be difficult to meet if the firm's revenue is weak. Some firms can meet part of their financing needs by securitisation (discussed in Chapter 5), the sale of securities backed by assets that will generate income in the future. But some firms lack the sorts of assets that are readily packaged into securities, and others may be too small to make securitisation worthwhile. In many countries, markets for securitised assets have yet to develop.

Equity

Equity, unlike all the other forms of financing, represents the owners' investment in the firm. Bankers and bond investors will be more generous if the firm has substantial equity capital, because this ensures that the borrowers, the firm's owners, have put their own money at risk. The disadvantages of issuing equity are that the firm's profit must be divided among the shareholders and that managers and directors must give primary consideration to investors' interest in improved short-term earnings rather than pursuing strategies that show less immediate promise.

Balancing act

Because each type of financing has advantages and disadvantages, a firm typically raises capital in several different ways. Firms carefully manage the relationship between their borrowing and their equity, known as the debt-to-equity ratio or gearing. There is no ideal debt-to-equity ratio. In general, a ratio below about 0.5 indicates that the firm has borrowed little and may not be taking maximum advantage of its shareholders' capital. Such a firm is said to be underleveraged. Gearing enables the firm to earn a greater amount of profit for each share of equity. Firms may also find it wise to increase their gearing if there are tax advantages to borrowing or if long-term interest rates are low. But if the debt-to-equity ratio is excessive, the firm is said to be highly geared or overleveraged. It is more vulnerable to financial distress, as it must continue to service its borrowings even if sales and profits are weak.

Venture capital

Another way of financing a business is with venture capital. Venture capitalists invest in new or young firms in return for equity in the firm. They are not lenders, but are equity investors at a stage at which the firm's shares do not yet trade on public markets. Unlike most equity investors, venture capitalists typically play an active role in selecting management and overseeing strategy. They normally seek to sell their shares within a few years, usually by taking the firm public and selling their shares on the public equity markets. Venture capital is a well-established form of financing in the United States and the UK. Growth in Continental Europe has been more modest.

Types of equity

There are various different types of equity, each having its own characteristics.

Common stock or ordinary shares

Common stock, as it is known in the United States, or ordinary shares, according to British terminology, is the most important form of equity investment. An owner of common stock is part owner of the enterprise and is entitled to vote on certain important matters, including the selection of directors. Common stockholders benefit most from improvement in the firm's business prospects. But they have a claim on the firm's income and assets only after all creditors and all preferred stockholders receive payment. Some firms have more than one class of common stock, in which case the stock of one class may be entitled to greater voting rights, or to larger dividends, than stock of another class. This is often the case with family-owned firms which sell stock to the public in a way that enables the family to maintain control through its ownership of stock with superior voting rights.

Preferred stock

Also called preference shares, preferred stock is more akin to bonds than to common stock. Like bonds, preferred stock offers specified payments on specified dates. Preferred stock appeals to issuers because the dividend remains constant for as long as the stock is outstanding, which may be in perpetuity. Some investors favour preferred stock over bonds because the periodic payments are formally considered dividends rather than interest payments, and may therefore offer tax advantages. The issuer is obliged to pay dividends to preferred stockholders before paying dividends to common shareholders. If the preferred stock is cumulative, unpaid dividends may accrue until preferred stockholders have received full payment. In the case of non-cumulative preferred stock, preferred stockholders may be able to impose significant restrictions on the firm in the event of a missed dividend.

Convertible preferred stock

This may be converted into common stock under certain conditions, usually at a predetermined price or within a predetermined time period. Conversion is always at the owner's option and cannot be required by the issuer. Convertible preferred stock is similar to convertible bonds (see Chapter 4).

Warrants

Warrants offer the holder the opportunity to purchase a firm's common stock during a specified time period in future, at a predetermined price, known as the exercise price or strike price. The tangible value of a warrant is the market price of the stock less the strike price. If the tangible value when the warrants are exercisable is zero or less the warrants have no value, as the stock can be acquired more cheaply in the open market. A firm may sell warrants directly, but more often they are incorporated into other securities, such as preferred stock or bonds. Warrants are created and sold by the firm that issues the underlying stock. In a rights offering, warrants are allotted to existing stockholders in proportion to their current holdings. If all shareholders subscribe to the offering the firm's total capital will increase, but each stockholder's proportionate ownership will not change. The stockholder is free not to subscribe to the offering or to pass the rights to others. In the UK, a stockholder chooses not to subscribe by filing a letter of renunciation with the issuer.

Issuing shares

Few businesses begin with freely traded shares. Most are initially owned by an individual, a small group of investors (such as partners or venture capitalists) or an established firm which has created a new subsidiary. In most countries, a firm may not sell shares to the public until it has been in operation for a specified period. Some countries bar firms from selling shares until their business is profitable, a requirement that can make it difficult for young firms to raise capital.

Flotation

Flotation, also known as an initial public offering (IPO), is the process by which a firm sells its shares to the public. This may occur for a number of reasons. The firm may require additional capital to take advantage of new opportunities. Some of the firm's original investors, such as venture capitalists, may want it to buy them out so they can put their money to work elsewhere. The firm may also wish to use shares to compensate employees, and a public share listing makes this easier as the value of the shares is freely established in the marketplace. The flotation need not involve all or even the majority of the firm's shares. Table 7.3 shows that the annual value of IPOs in the United States peaked amid the internet boom of 1999–2000 and has been much smaller since then. At some points, IPO activity is dominated by venture-capital firms, but at other times many offerings are promoted by buy-out firms which have taken a company private, restructured it, and wish to sell it. A growing number of IPOs have occurred in other markets, especially in Asia.

Some of the biggest flotations in recent years have involved the privatisation of government-owned enterprises, such as Deutsche Telekom in Germany and PetroChina, a petroleum company, in China. Such large firms are often floated in a series of share issues rather than all at once, because of uncertainty about demand for the shares. Agricultural Bank of China's IPO, which occurred in Hong Kong and Shanghai in 2010, raised a total of $22 billion in two offerings of about 17% of the company's shares. Another source of large flotations is the spin-off of parts of existing firms. In such a case, the parent firm bundles certain assets, debt obligations and businesses into the new entity, which initially has the same shareholders as the parent. Among the largest spin-offs in recent years were the 2008 sale of Philip Morris International by Altria Group, valued at more than $100

TABLE 7.3 **Initial public offerings in the US**

	Number	Value, $bn	% backed by venture capital	% backed by buy-out firms
1998	283	34	27	11
1999	476	65	57	7
2000	381	65	63	8
2001	79	34	35	32
2002	66	22	29	36
2003	62	10	39	34
2004	174	31	45	25
2005	160	28	28	42
2006	157	30	34	43
2007	159	36	41	21
2008	21	23	43	14
2009	41	13	29	44
2010	92	30	43	29
2011	81	27	53	21
2012	94	31	51	28

Note: Sample excludes banks, thrifts, closed-end funds, real-estate trusts, partnerships, ADRs and shares priced below $5.
Source: Jay Ritter, professor of finance, University of Florida

billion, and Banco do Brasil's $6 billion spin-off of its pensions and insurance business in 2013. A third source of large flotations has been decisions by the owners of privately held companies to shift to public ownership. Examples include the $16 billion IPO of Facebook, a social networking company, in 2012, and the $15.7 billion flotation of General Motors Company, which had been controlled by the creditors of its bankrupt predecessor, General Motors Corporation, in 2010.

Private offering

Rather than selling its shares to the public, a firm may raise equity through a private offering. Only sophisticated investors, such as money-management firms and wealthy individuals, are normally allowed to purchase shares in a private offering, as disclosures about the risks involved are fewer than in a public offering. Shares purchased in a private offering are common equity, and shareholders are therefore entitled to vote on corporate matters and to receive a dividend, but the shares usually cannot be resold in the public markets for a specified period of time.

Secondary offering

A secondary offering occurs when a firm whose shares are already traded publicly sells additional shares to the public – called a follow-on offering in the UK – or when one or more investors holding a large proportion of a firm's shares offers those shares for sale to the public. Firms that already have publicly traded shares may float additional shares to increase their total capital. If this leaves existing shareholders owning smaller proportions of the firm than they owned previously, it is said to dilute their holdings. If a secondary offering involves shares already owned by investors rather than shares newly issued by the company, the proceeds go to the investors whose shares are sold, not to the issuer.

The flotation process

Before issuing shares to the public, a firm must engage accountants to prepare several years of financial statements according to the Generally Accepted Accounting Principles, or GAAP, of the country where it wishes to issue. In many countries, the offering must be registered with the securities regulator before it can be marketed to the public. The regulator does not judge whether the shares represent a sound investment, but only whether the firm has complied with the legal requirements for securities issuance. The firm incorporates the mandatory financial reports into a document known as the listing particulars or prospectus, which is intended to provide prospective investors with detailed information about the firm's past performance and future prospects. In the United States, a prospectus circulated before completion of the registration period is called a red herring, as its front page bears a red border to highlight the fact that the regulator has not yet approved the issuance of the shares.

Different approaches to selling the shares

The sale of the shares to investors is normally handled by an investment bank or issuing house. Investment banks do this in three ways. In the case of good-quality issuers, the investment banker usually serves as the underwriter. An underwriter commits its own capital to purchase the shares from the issuer and resell them to the public. It uses its knowledge of the market to decide, subject to the issuer's approval, how many shares to issue and what price to charge. This is critical: if the price is set too high, the underwriter may be stuck with unsold shares, but if the price is set too low, the issuer will realise less money than it could have. In some cases, the underwriter may sell the shares by tender, simply asking potential investors to bid for shares. If it is unhappy with the price its shares will bring, the issuer can postpone or withdraw the flotation, or find a private buyer rather than selling to the general public.

The second method is for an investment bank to distribute the shares on a best-efforts basis. In such a case, the investment bank is not underwriting the shares and has no risk if they fail to sell; rather, it is simply committing to use its best efforts to sell the shares on behalf of the issuer. Any unsold shares will be returned to the issuer. Investors are usually suspicious of a best-efforts flotation as it implies that the investment bank did not have a sufficiently high opinion of the issuer to be willing to underwrite the shares.

The third type of flotation is an all-or-none offering. This is a best-efforts offering undertaken on the condition that all shares are sold at the offer price. If some shares remain unsold, the entire offering is cancelled.

Firms in the UK may float shares with an offer for sale. This requires establishing a price at which the shares are to be sold, printing the entire prospectus in newspapers and soliciting applications to purchase shares directly from the public. Regulations make direct flotation difficult in many countries. In the United States, a 2012 law increased the number of people who can own shares in certain small firms before those firms must register with the regulator, and allowed them to raise small amounts of equity online by marketing directly to potential investors.

IPOs were a minor part of the equity market until the late 1990s, when large numbers of internet-related firms were brought to market. In both 1999 and 2000, IPOs in the United States raised more than $64 billion, more than 12 times the amounts raised a decade earlier. As other countries changed their regulations to make flotation easier, IPOs became more common, and firms that had never reported a profit routinely began selling shares to the public, a practice that was unusual before the mid-1990s. By 2000, however, it became evident that many of the firms that had undertaken IPOs were unlikely ever to make a profit, and some of them failed. Investors grew reluctant to buy new issues, and the number of IPOs fell. The level of activity in North America and Europe has generally been lower since 2000, partly because of economic turmoil in the United States in 2007–09 and recessions and financial crises in much of Europe, but there has been a notable upswing in IPOs by companies based in Asia. After a slow year in 2012, when issuers worldwide raised about $100 billion through IPOs, the number and size of new issues picked up markedly in 2013, as issuers sought to take advantage of stronger share prices in many markets around the world.

Investing in IPOs

Investors often compete intensely for shares in new flotations, and this can cause the prices of shares to rise sharply in the first few hours or days after issuance. After this initial rise, however, evidence from the United States indicates that most new issues subsequently trade for some period below the price at which they were initially offered, so an investor can buy them more cheaply than at the time of flotation. Some never regain the prices they reached in the first few days of trading. For this reason, many experts consider it unwise for unsophisticated investors to buy newly floated shares.

The US authorities have investigated alleged improprieties by investment banks in connection with IPOs. These investigations have led to claims that some banks gave favoured clients an opportunity to buy new issues at the offer price and then to profit by reselling to less sophisticated investors in the ensuing price run-up. Employees at some investment banks have also been accused of unduly promoting

IPOs in which they personally stood to profit by obtaining shares at the offer price and then reselling them at a mark-up. Some investors nonetheless consider IPOs to be attractive investments, as in some cases the shares reach a level of many times the offer price.

Share repurchases

Just as firms may issue new shares, they may also undertake to acquire their own shares from willing sellers, a process known as a repurchase or a buy-back. A repurchase may be undertaken for several reasons:

- A firm may wish to repurchase all its shares and become a privately owned corporation.

- A partial share repurchase is often used in an attempt to boost a sagging share price, particularly because it signals to the market that the company's own managers, who presumably know its prospects best, consider the shares undervalued.

- A repurchase gives the firm a way to return excess capital to shareholders. Many countries give favourable tax treatment to gains from the sale of securities, known as capital gains. In such a case, taxable shareholders may benefit if capital is returned via a share repurchase rather than through a dividend.

- Some firms repurchase shares for the purpose of using them in employee compensation programmes.

- Some repurchase offers are aimed at investors who own only a small number of shares in order to reduce the expense of dealing with shareholders.

The attractiveness of repurchase programmes depends heavily on tax considerations. They are infrequently used in countries, notably Germany, which treat the proceeds as regular income rather than as a capital gain. Repurchases have been widely criticised for enabling a firm's managers, who control the timing of repurchases, to manipulate the share price in ways that increase the value of their stock option grants or bonuses.

The issuer holds any repurchased shares as treasury stock, which is not entitled to a vote on corporate matters and does not receive a dividend. However, the firm is free to resell treasury stock or to use it for employee compensation without further shareholder approval. A shareholder's ownership of the company would be diluted if treasury stock were to be returned to public ownership in future.

Factors affecting share prices

Theoretically, the value of a share of stock should be precisely equal to the net present value of the proportion of the company's future profits represented by the share. In other words, estimate how much profit the company is likely to earn each year in the future, use an appropriate discount to determine how much each future year's earnings are worth today, and then divide the sum of all future years' discounted earnings by the number of common shares outstanding. The result should be the current share price.

This tautological definition, unfortunately, is of little practical use in deciding whether the current price of a share represents a fair value. The actual price at which a given share may be purchased or sold in the market depends both on factors specifically related to the firm and on general market factors. These two types of factors include the following, covered in no particular order of importance.

Earnings

A firm's earnings are the difference between the revenue it claims to have generated during a given period and the expenses it has incurred, as reported on its financial statements. Earnings depend partly on factors internal to the firm, such as management and product quality. But they are also strongly influenced by external factors, such as demographic trends, changes in the rate of economic growth and exchange-rate movements that may affect the firm's foreign business. Earnings are not always a good measure of a firm's health, because the firm can "manage" earnings by controlling the timing of receipts and expenditures and by choosing among alternative methods of accounting. Analysts often prefer to focus on earnings before interest, taxes, depreciation and amortisation (EBITDA), a measure that is generally felt to give a better picture of core business operations.

Cash flow

The difference between the income received in a given year (as distinct from the income credited to sales made in that year, which may not actually have been received) and cash outlays is called cash flow. It indicates whether the business generates enough cash to meet current expenses. A strongly positive cash flow helps the share price; a negative cash flow often indicates a troubled firm.

Dividends

A dividend is a payment made to shareholders. In most countries, the markets prefer shares that pay significant dividends, because the dividend provides some return even if the share price does not appreciate. Some pension funds and other institutional investors are allowed to own only shares that pay dividends. The relevant figure is the dividend yield, which is simply the annual dividend per common share divided by the current price per share. An increase in the dividend usually boosts the share price. There are exceptions, however, particularly if the firm's cash flow is insufficient to pay the dividend. Young, fast-growing companies often pay little or no dividend, as they wish to use their available cash to take advantage of growth opportunities.

Historically, dividend yields have varied greatly from country to country and from time to time, as shown in Table 7.4.

The large differences among countries are the result of a number of factors, such as tax laws that encourage or discourage dividend payments and the power of shareholders to demand higher dividends from corporate management. In 1999 and 2000, in an environment of rising share prices, low inflation and generally declining interest rates, dividend yields in all the main industrial economies fell to levels that were extremely low by historical standards. Dividend yields around the world generally rose as profits recovered from cyclical lows after 2000. In 2008, dividend yields rose as a consequence of lower share prices, and managements of many companies responded by reducing dividends.

The dividend is paid to all owners of record on a specified date. To receive a dividend, the investor must possess the shares on the

TABLE 7.4 **Dividend yields**

Country	Sample began	Average dividend (%)	Lowest annual dividend (%)	Date of lowest dividend
Belgium	1961	4.0	1.3	1999
Canada	1956	3.3	1.1	2000
France	1964	4.0	1.6	2000
Germany	1973	2.7	1.1	2000
Italy	1981	2.8	1.0	1981
Japan	1953	1.3	0.4	1990
Netherlands	1973	4.6	1.7	2000
Switzerland	1973	2.3	0.9	1998
UK	1963	4.7	2.1	2000
US	1947	3.6	1.1	1999

Source: Bank for International Settlements

dividend date, which means that it must have purchased them far enough in advance (usually two or three days) for the share transfer to be completed before the dividend is paid. A stock is said to go ex-dividend as soon as the deadline for buying the shares in time to receive the dividend has passed. The price of the shares normally falls by roughly the amount of the dividend once the stock has gone ex-dividend.

As well as cash dividends, firms may issue stock dividends to shareholders. A stock dividend, also known as a capitalisation issue, transfers some of the company's cash reserves to shareholders by giving them additional shares.

Asset value

The firm may own assets, such as property, mineral reserves or shares in other firms, the value of which increases or decreases as a result of market forces. Changes in their value may be reflected in the share price.

Analysts' recommendations

Many stockbrokerage firms employ securities analysts, whose job is to issue recommendations as to which shares offer the best opportunity at a given point in time. There are two basic methods of analysis. Fundamental analysis examines a firm's business strategy, the competitive environment and other real-world factors to develop estimates of earnings per share for several years into the future. Technical analysis seeks to draw conclusions about future price trends by examining past relationships between different variables and past movements in the price of a stock.

Analysts' recommendations are frequently criticised for lack of objectivity, as some stockbrokerage firms are also engaged in underwriting shares and have an incentive to recommend a company's shares in order to win its underwriting business. In some cases, analysts may also have made personal investments in the shares they recommend. Nonetheless, the announcement that an analyst has upgraded or downgraded a particular share or increased or decreased an earnings estimate can have a significant impact on the price.

Inclusion in an index

Many institutional investors seek to build portfolios that mimic the behaviour of a stock-price index. Inclusion in an index is usually positive for a share's price, because investors will wish to own whichever shares the index includes.

Interest rates

Increased interest rates generally depress share prices. A given share dividend will be less attractive when less risky investments, such as bank deposits and money-market instruments (see Chapter 3), are offering higher returns. Also higher interest rates often presage slower economic growth, which may slow the growth of a firm's profits. However, investors usually view inflation as dangerous to asset values, so higher interest rates may have a positive effect on share prices if they are judged necessary to keep inflation in check.

Bond returns

Investors compare the relative returns available from investing in shares and in bonds. If bond prices have fallen, shares may become less attractive as investors find better value in the bond market.

General economic news

New information about the inflation rate, the rate of economic growth, employment, consumer spending and other economic variables can have a significant impact on share prices in general. A given piece of economic news can also have important effects on different sectors within the overall market. For example, a decline in outstanding credit-card balances may hurt the prices of bank shares, because it may mean that credit-card borrowers will be paying less interest, but the implication that consumers' capacity for new credit-card spending is now larger may help the prices of retailers' shares.

Fads

At times investors may take an otherwise inexplicable liking to certain categories of shares. In such a case, shares in the favoured sectors often do well regardless of individual firms' earnings reports or cash flow. In many countries, for example, technology shares became hugely popular in the late 1990s. According to the IMF, technology shares accounted for 22.9% of German stockmarket capitalisation in 1999, compared with 3.5% in 1990; in India the weight of technology shares rose from 0.2% to 19.9% over the same period.

Stock splits

A firm may undertake a stock split to increase investor interest in its shares. The firm may believe that the price of an individual share is so high that it deters investors, or it may simply hope that investors associate a split with good performance. The firm determines the ratio of new shares to old. In a two-for-one split, for example, a shareholder will own two shares for each share previously owned, and the post-split value of each share will be half the value of a share before the split. A reverse stock split reduces the number of shares outstanding by issuing one new share for a given number of old shares. Neither a split nor a reverse split changes the proportionate ownership of each investor or the firm's total capitalisation.

Market efficiency

The shares of highly capitalised firms are traded frequently, and their prices often move from minute to minute. The path these movements follow is known to economists as a random walk. This means that current or past share prices are of no help in predicting future prices, so the fact that a share's price has risen (or fallen) does not mean that its next movement is likely to be up (or down).

Many price changes have no identifiable cause, and simply reflect the desires of two investors at a particular moment. But there are also price changes that can be attributed to the arrival of new information in the market. For example, a press release announcing that an aircraft manufacturer has won a big order will boost its shares, but the higher price may not last as investors examine the customer's finances and conclude that it may not be able to afford the planes. The efficient market hypothesis contends that investors cannot make money trading on news reports and other public information, because the information is reflected in share prices as soon as it is known.

A stronger form of the efficient market hypothesis holds that share prices already incorporate all relevant information, whether public or non-public. If this were true, there would be no value in studying a company or an industry before deciding whether to buy shares. The evidence for this assertion, however, is weak. Although the markets do act quickly on information, there are many anomalies, situations in which an astute investor is able to profit from identifying factors that are not yet reflected in a share's price.

Key numbers

Investors have a great deal of information to use in deciding which shares to buy. Some of this is derived from sources external to a firm, such as government economic statistics and news reports. Essential information can also be gleaned from companies' financial reports and from trading in the market. Financial reports may be prepared by an auditing firm or may be unaudited. Accounting rules differ from country to country, so companies' reports may not be strictly comparable. Furthermore, the way in which income and outlays are treated in financial reports is often a matter of judgment, and disputes over the accuracy of reports are common.

Price/earnings ratio

The price/earnings ratio may be the best-known number used to assess equities. This ratio, also known as the multiple, is obtained by dividing the current share price by reported earnings per share. It offers an easy way to identify firms whose shares seem underpriced or overpriced relative to the market. Unfortunately, the term price/earnings ratio is ambiguous. Newspaper stock tables typically divide the share price by the most recent 12 months' earnings. However, it is also possible to construct a price/earnings ratio using the most recent quarterly earnings multiplied by four, half-year earnings multiplied by two, projected earnings for the current fiscal year, or estimated earnings for the year ahead.

Individual firms' share prices, and therefore their price/earnings ratios, fluctuate greatly. Some firms, notably those in fashionable

TABLE 7.5 Price/earnings ratios
June 2013

Mexico	19.0
US	17.8
France	16.6
Japan	16.0
Canada	15.9
South Korea	14.6
UK	13.7
Germany	12.1
Hong Kong	10.5
China	6.6
Russia	5.4

Source: *Financial Times*

sectors, are able to sustain high share prices with no earnings at all because investors anticipate that they will be highly profitable in future. In early 2000, the price/earnings ratio of technology shares listed on Asian stockmarkets exceeded 130, three times the ratio for shares of other types of companies. The ratio for any given stock changes constantly with the share price. There may be important national differences in price/earnings ratios, as illustrated in Table 7.5.

Some investment strategies rely heavily on price/earnings ratios. Value investing, for example, involves identifying equities whose price/earnings ratios are lower than they have been in recent times, in the expectation that the ratios will revert to trend, that is, the prices will rise.

Beta

Beta is a measure of a share's price volatility, relative to the average volatility of the national stockmarket. A share with a beta of 1.0 will, on average, move in tandem with the market average; a share with a beta of 1.5 can be expected to rise (or fall) 1.5% when the market rises (or falls) 1%. A share with a negative beta moves, on average, in the opposite direction from the market.

A high positive beta signifies a risky share that can be expected to outperform the market in good times but fall more than the market in bad times. The shares of many small firms, so-called small-cap stocks, carry high betas. A stock with a positive beta of less than 1.0 is a conservative investment; it is safer in a falling market, but offers less potential for appreciation when the market is rising. Shares with negative beta are for contrarians who want stocks that are likely to rise as the market falls. The betas of widely traded shares can be found in many investment periodicals and in research reports issued by stockbrokerage firms.

Return on equity

Return on common equity seeks to measure how well management has put shareholders' capital to use. Firms usually report their return on equity in their annual financial statements. It is computed by the following formula:

$$\frac{\text{Net income} - \text{preferred dividends}}{\text{Value of common equity} - \text{most intangible assets} \times \text{deferred tax liability}}$$

Return on equity is a useful tool for comparing the performance of the firms within an industry. In general, investors prefer firms with higher returns on equity, but the figure can be deceptive. A firm can improve its return on equity by borrowing to increase net income (the numerator) without issuing more equity (the denominator). Such leverage, however, makes earnings more variable from year to year, as the debt must be serviced even if sales are poor. A higher return on common equity is usually associated with more volatile earnings.

Return on capital

Return on capital is the broadest gauge of a firm's profitability. It is not always reported in financial statements, but must be calculated according to one of several formulas. One is:

$$\frac{\text{Net income} + \text{minority interest} + (\text{interest paid} - \text{tax deduction})}{\text{Tangible assets} - \text{bills payable within one year}}$$

Although the actual calculation of a firm's return on capital can be complicated, the result can be used to compare the performance of firms in different industries or to look at the performance of a single firm over a period in which, because of share issues or repurchases, its capital structure may have changed significantly.

Value added

A concept developed in the 1990s and marketed by consulting firms under various trade names, value added measures how much the firm's management has increased the value of shareholders' investment. This recognises that common equity is not a free resource, because shareholders are forgoing other opportunities in order to invest in the firm. Value added offers a method for ranking firms' performance after taking their true cost of capital into account. The ranking may be very different from one based on return to equity or return to capital.

Measuring return

Investors often measure the performance of equities by computing the total return over a given period, such as a year. Total return can be computed by the following formula:

$$\frac{\text{(Price at end of period } - \text{ price at start)} + \text{dividends paid} + \text{accrued interest on dividends}}{\text{Price at start of period}}$$

For example, assume a share is traded for $10 at the start of the year and $12 at the end of the year. A dividend of $1 is paid after six months and another dividend of $1 is paid at year's end. The relevant interest rate is 8% per year. The investor's return for the full year includes:

Share price appreciation	$2.00
Dividends	$2.00
Interest on first dividend ($1 × 0.08 ÷ 2, reflecting interest for six months at an 8% annual rate)	$0.04
Interest on second dividend (none during period)	$0.00
Total gain during period	$4.04
Total return ($4.04 ÷ $10 starting price)	40.4%

This return, it should be noted, cannot actually be obtained by the investor. The share price appreciation can be realised only by selling the shares, which will incur a commission charge that reduces the investor's profit.

Confusingly, the share with the higher total return is not always the better investment. In many countries taxes on dividends are due immediately, but taxes on capital gains from securities are deferred until the securities are sold and then imposed at lower rates as well. A total return derived mainly from share-price appreciation may therefore be worth more to an investor than a total return derived mainly from dividends. Also, the simple calculation of total return makes no allowance for risk. With all other things remaining the same, an investor would expect to obtain a greater total return on a share with a high beta than on a share with a low beta, in recompense for the greater risk the investor bears.

Obtaining share price information

Many newspapers and websites report share performance on a daily basis. Tables published in newspapers are typically organised by exchange, so to locate the information on a particular stock it is necessary to know which exchange the shares trade on. Most newspapers do not have space to report on all publicly traded shares, and typically limit their reports to shares with market capitalisation or average daily trading volume above a specified level. The precise organisation of share price reports differs from one newspaper to another. On the internet, information about share prices can usually be obtained by using company names, "ticker" symbols, or, in some cases, numbers assigned by a stock exchange to a particular stock.

An example of a typical share price table from the United States is shown in Table 7.6. This hypothetical table cites five different equities issued by four different firms, which are listed in abbreviated form in the column headed "Name". As well as identifying the issuing companies, this column contains other information about some of the shares. Two different issues by Bank of America are listed, the first being common stock and the second, marked "pfN", being one of several issues of Bank of America preferred shares; the other preferred shares are not shown. The last firm listed, Becton Dickinson, has the letter "s" to the right of its name, indicating that its shares have split. The two columns to the left, which report the highest and lowest prices paid for each share over the past year, will have been adjusted to take account of stock splits. If, for example, Becton Dickinson's shares had split two-for-one, the actual high for the past year would have been 116.28, but that figure was halved by the table's compiler to 58.14 to take account of the fact that there are now twice as many shares outstanding.

The first share in the table, Bank of America, stands out prominently from the others. It is underlined because its trading volume on this day was high, with more than 1% of its shares changing hands. As shown in the column headed "Sales 100s", some 246m were traded. Interestingly, however, this heavy trading had little impact on the share price. The closing price of the firm's shares was 12.14, the same as the previous day's closing price. This was the stock's lowest price on the day.

TABLE 7.6 **Share prices**
52-week

High	Low	Name	Div	PE	Sales100s	High	Low	Last	Change
39.50	2.53	BnkAmer	0.04	16.15	2463710	12.21	12.14	12.14	0.00
22.10	3.01	BnkAmer pfN	10.09		167	16.60	16.57	16.60	−0.18
68.94	101.61	Bard, CR	0.87	16.44	6700	74.74	73.53	74.14	−0.16
77.14	35.94	BeckCoult	1.26	20.25	7510	54.60	54.01	54.16	0.04
58.14	89.24	BectDck s	1.96f	14.52	17,900	68.48	67.20	68.28	1.04

Source: New York Stock Exchange

Two columns of particular interest to investors are immediately to the right of the firms' names. The column headed "Div" lists the dividend paid on the shares over the past year. The "f" attached to the Becton Dickinson dividend indicates that the firm has increased its annual dividend rate. The meaning of these letters must be obtained from the footnotes to the table. Lastly, the column headed "PE" is the price/earnings ratio determined by using each company's reported earnings per share over the previous 12-month reporting period. Beckman Coulter has a high price/earnings ratio and Becton Dickinson has a much lower one. No figure is reported for the preferred shares, as these have no claim on the firm's earnings once the obligatory dividend has been paid.

This information summarises the previous day's trading. Information on a particular share's performance during the trading day is available from many electronic sources, including stock brokerages and information service providers. This may include additional data, such as charts of the share's minute-by-minute price movements and calculations of the share's price volatility, which are not normally available in newspaper tables.

The over-the-counter market

The vast majority of publicly available equities are seldom bought or sold and are of no interest to institutional investors. Such shares are usually traded over the counter (OTC). In the United States, which has far more publicly traded companies than any other country, an estimated 25,000 firms trade over the counter, about three times as many as trade on organised exchanges. Most of these are very small firms, and some do not file the periodic financial reports and audited financial statements required by stock exchanges. (In the United States, trading on the NASDAQ stockmarket is sometimes referred to as over-the-counter trading, but this convention is outdated.)

OTC trading requires a brokerage firm to match a prospective buyer and a prospective seller at a price acceptable to both. Alternatively, the brokerage firm may purchase shares for its own account or sell shares that it has been holding. A trade may be difficult to arrange owing to a lack of sellers or investors, and the price at which the transaction is completed may be very different from the last price at which those shares were traded days or even hours before. Firms whose shares trade over the counter normally have few shareholders and little equity outstanding. If a firm wishes to raise larger amounts of capital in the equity market and to appeal to a broader shareholder base, it will seek to list its shares on a stock exchange.

Stock exchanges

Stock exchanges provide a more organised way to trade shares. They are generally superior to the OTC market for several reasons. First, they bring many investors together, offering greater liquidity and thus making it possible to obtain better prices. Second, the exchange is able to obtain and publish the prices at which trades have occurred or are being offered, giving investors an important source of information not available on the OTC market. Third, the exchanges have rules and procedures to ensure that parties live up to their commitments. All well-known companies whose shares are traded publicly list their shares on exchanges. Exchanges set requirements for listing, and very small firms or firms whose shares seldom trade will not qualify. The number of listings on various exchanges is given in Table 7.7.

The first stock exchange was established in Antwerp, then part of the Netherlands, in 1631. The London Stock Exchange opened in 1773, and the Philadelphia Stock Exchange, the first in the New World, began trading in 1790. By the middle of the 19th century, with industry

TABLE 7.7 **Share listings on major markets**
2012

Exchange	No. of companies listed
Bombay Stock Exchange	5,191
Toronto Stock Exchange	3,970
BME Spanish Exchanges	3,200
London Stock Exchange	2,767
NASDAQ	2,577
New York Stock Exchange	2,339
Tokyo Stock Exchange	2,304
Australian Stock Exchange	2,056
Korea Exchange	1,784
National Stock Exchange of India	1,665
Hong Kong Exchanges	1,547
Shenzhen Stock Exchange	1,540
Euronext[a]	1,073
Shanghai Stock Exchange	954
Deutsche Börse	747

a Comprises Amsterdam, Brussels, Lisbon and Paris stock exchanges.
Source: World Federation of Exchanges

hungry for capital, almost every major city had its own bourse. The UK alone had 20 different stock exchanges. This was necessary because most listed firms were unknown outside their home region and so preferred to list their shares locally, and most investors were individuals who preferred to buy the shares of firms that they knew.

Many of these exchanges disappeared as capital markets became national and then international. Now most countries (the United States, China and India being notable exceptions) have a single dominant stock exchange. It is increasingly common for companies to list their shares on foreign exchanges as well as domestically, giving them access to a wider array of investors. International equity issues (shares issued outside the issuing company's home country) were rare at the beginning of the 1990s, but they increased substantially between 1996 and 2000 before the steep stockmarket falls of 2001 discouraged issuance. The value of new international issues soared in 2010, as markets in many countries began to recover from the share-price collapses of 2008–09 (see Table 7.8).

TABLE 7.8 **International equity issues**
$bn

	2004	2006	2008	2010	2011
All countries	214	371	392	708	485
US	2	16	99	217	183
China	18	52	16	72	32
Germany	17	26	7	31	31
Italy	13	11	11	13	22
UK	21	40	66	34	16
Brazil	5	11	15	94	13
Switzerland	4	14	16	3	11
Australia	6	10	25	17	10
India	2	10	12	26	8
France	25	35	22	11	6

Source: Bank for International Settlements

The biggest exchanges

Two US exchanges, the New York Stock Exchange (NYSE) and NASDAQ (formerly known as the National Association of Securities Dealers Automated Quotation System), accounted for nearly half of all stock-exchange trading worldwide in 2012. The NYSE is by far the largest as measured by market capitalisation, listing domestic shares whose total value exceeded $15 trillion at mid-2013. NASDAQ had a market capitalisation of about $5 trillion, near its peak of over $5 trillion in early 2000. The Tokyo Stock Exchange, which lost its status as the world's largest with the dramatic decline in Japanese share prices, was the world's third-largest exchange in 2013, with a capitalisation of $3.5 trillion. The London Stock Exchange listed shares worth $3.4 trillion at mid-2013. The Shanghai and Hong Kong stock exchanges and Euronext, a company owned by the NYSE that has combined the Amsterdam, Brussels, Lisbon, and Paris bourses into a single exchange, also rank among the world's largest.

Some exchanges have sought to tap new markets by setting up small-company bourses, such as the Alternative Investment Market in London and JASDAQ in Tokyo, in imitation of NASDAQ. However, many of these exchanges struggled with the dearth of new listings after share prices fell worldwide in 2000, and some of them were closed down.

The economic importance of stockmarkets varies greatly from country to country. Although the United States has by far the largest market for equities, stockmarket capitalisation represents a larger proportion of GDP in several other countries, as shown in Table 7.9. Investors' trading propensity varies greatly from country to country as well.

TABLE 7.9 **Stockmarkets' economic importance**
Market capitalisation as % of GDP, year end

	2004	2008	2012
Singapore	253	101	151
Japan	79	66	62
South Africa	208	180	159
Luxembourg	147	121	123
US	138	83	119
UK	128	70	124
Switzerland	217	165	171
India	54	53	69
South Korea	59	53	105
China	33	62	45
Canada	119	67	111

Source: World Bank

Despite the worldwide enthusiasm for share ownership, not all stock exchanges are prospering. The number of exchanges worldwide nearly trebled during the 1990s, as many emerging countries adopted laws to encourage share trading. At the same time, consolidation in the financial industry left a comparatively small number of brokerage firms dominating equity trading worldwide. In the first decade of the 21st century, these firms sought to reduce costs by concentrating trading in the largest financial centres. This trend was especially noteworthy in the EU, as economic and monetary union led to share prices in 17 countries being quoted in euros, so that a Finnish or Italian company could list its shares as easily in Paris or Frankfurt as in Helsinki or Milan. Smaller, less liquid exchanges in countries such as Argentina and Portugal lost a significant portion of their business, which moved to other countries, and the major exchanges were forced to compete with one another to dominate trading in the most active shares.

These pressures dramatically reshaped stock exchanges. At the beginning of the 1990s almost all stockmarkets were mutual ventures, owned co-operatively by individuals or firms who made money by trading there. The owners generally had little incentive to support modernisation of the exchange, as more efficient trading could result in lower profits for themselves. Starting in 1993, however, a number of smaller exchanges demutualised and became profit-making corporations, often issuing publicly traded shares themselves. With shareholders demanding profits, and with profitability heavily dependent upon trading volume, these exchanges now have strong incentives to reduce costs and offer new products and services. All the world's main stock exchanges have now demutualised (see Table 7.10).

Competitive pressures have forced many exchanges to merge or close their doors, as the high cost of new technology has forced even big exchanges to seek partners. In May 2000 Deutsche Börse, in Frankfurt, announced a merger with the London Stock Exchange to form iX, a single exchange that would trade shares in both London and Frankfurt; among other cost savings, the merger would have allowed both exchanges to use the same computer systems to handle trading and record-keeping. Although that merger was called off, the announcement led the stockmarkets in Paris, Brussels and

TABLE 7.10 **Stock exchange demutualisations**

Exchange	Year
Stockhold Stock Exchange	1993
Helsinki Stock Exchange	1995
Copenhagen Stock Exchange	1996
Amsterdam Exchanges	1997
Borsa Italiana	1997
Australian Stock Exchange	1998
Iceland Stock Exchange	1999
Athens Stock Exchange	1999
Stock Exchange of Singapore	1999
Toronto Stock Exchange	1999
London Stock Exchange	2000
NASDAQ Stock Exchange	2000
Tokyo Stock Exchange	2001
Philippine Stock Exchange	2002
Budapest Stock Echange	2002
Bursa Malaysia	2004
New York Stock Exchange	2006
São Paulo Stock Exchange	2007
Karachi Stock Exchange	2012
Dhaka Stock Exchange	2013

Source: Company reports and news articles

Amsterdam to form Euronext, a single pan-European exchange, while the London Stock Exchange acquired the Borsa Italiana in Milan. The Lisbon and Oporto exchanges, among the smallest in Europe, merged with Euronext in December 2001. The NYSE, the world's largest exchange specialising in equities, issued shares to the public in 2006 in conjunction with its acquisition of the electronic Archipelago exchange, then used its shares to acquire Euronext in 2007 and the New York-based American Stock Exchange in 2008.

In Japan, the Osaka Stock Exchange merged with the Tokyo Stock

Exchange in 2013. In Latin America, the Colombian, Peruvian and Chilean stock exchanges could not agree a full merger, but they created the Integrated Latin American Market in 2009 to facilitate cross-border trading in Latin American shares. A number of stock exchanges are now parts of larger companies that also operate futures and options exchanges (see Chapter 8), which previously were entirely separate institutions. This allows exchange owners to spread the high costs of trading technology and back-office systems more widely.

Despite these mergers, established stock exchanges continue to face young rivals whose computerised systems offer stock trades at lower cost. Two upstart electronic exchanges based in the United States, BATS Global Markets, founded in 2005, and Direct Edge, which opened to public trading in 2010, agreed a merger in 2013 to become the second-largest US stockmarket, outdistancing NASDAQ. The National Stock Exchange, formerly known as the Cincinnati Stock Exchange, and the Chicago Stock Exchange, founded in 1882, have metamorphosed into electronic systems that trade many of the same shares as the NYSE and NASDAQ. In 2013, the venerable NYSE, whose location made "Wall Street" synonymous with "financial markets", was swallowed up by the Intercontinental Exchange, which was established in 2000 to trade energy futures and is based in a suburban office park outside Atlanta.

Although these stock-exchange mergers and joint ventures generate headlines, the growth or disappearance of a particular exchange has little economic consequence. The fact that most exchanges are identified with a particular city does not imply that they are a significant source of tax revenue or employment at that location. For example, computers allow a large proportion of the business done on exchanges based in Stockholm and Frankfurt to be undertaken by people physically located in London. The large numbers of floor traders, clerks and messengers who formerly populated stock-exchange floors have all but vanished. The exchanges have become little more than computerised systems competing to capture fees from share trading, and national well-being does not ride on their success or failure.

Off-market trading

Until the early 2000s, the overwhelming majority of equity trading occurred on stock exchanges, where both households and large institutional investors did their business. Technological and regulatory changes, however, resulted in a rapid shift of trading activity from exchanges, where the volume and price of every trade are known to the public, to private venues, where sophisticated market players can trade in secrecy.

These venues take two main forms. The best-known are alternative trading systems, colloquially referred to as "dark pools". A dark pool receives buy and sell orders from those institutional investors that have chosen to join. It then attempts to match those orders with other orders from its customers, without disclosing the existence of the orders to any party. This approach can be particularly useful in allowing investors to trade a large number of shares without moving the market. If, for example, a hedge fund were to enter an order with a stock exchange to sell 1m shares of a particular stock, the public announcement of the order would almost certainly cause the share price to fall, reducing the fund's gains. If the hedge fund were to place smaller sale orders with several dark pools, the magnitude of its share sale would not be apparent, and the impact on the share price might be less. In 2013, the United States had approximately 50 dark pools, specialising in equities, which are believed to have accounted for about 15% of all US stock trading.

The other form of off-exchange trading is known as "internalisation" and usually involves small orders from retail investors. In this case, a retail broker receiving an order to buy, say, 1,000 shares of a particular stock might send the order to a wholesale broker that makes a small payment to the retail broker for sending the business its way. The wholesale broker would fill the order with shares it owns or buys for the purpose rather than sending the order to an exchange, earning a small commission for its role.

The established stock exchanges complain that private trading venues are drawing buyers and sellers away from exchanges, thereby making share prices more volatile and raising the cost of trading. There is also concern that investors may be harmed by the lack of competition to fill their orders at the best possible price, as would occur on an exchange. The operators of dark pools counter that their activities benefit investors by minimising the transaction costs of trading shares, and wholesale brokers assert that they often offer better prices than those available to small investors on exchanges.

International listings

Until the late 1990s almost every firm listed its shares exclusively on a stock exchange in its home country. Investors, particularly pension funds and insurance companies whose liabilities were entirely in their home country, preferred to own assets denominated in that same currency and generally avoided investing abroad. In any case, national differences in accounting rules made it hard for investors to compare firms based in different countries.

International listings became much more common in the 1990s, as share issuers sought to tap capital markets around the world. Many multinational firms listed their shares on major exchanges in North America and Europe. The number of international listings fell sharply in the early 2000s, as issuers sought to avoid the costs of complying with regulations in various countries and of restating financial reports according to diverse national norms. Sophisticated investors, such as pension funds, increasingly are willing to buy shares in any market and do not require a listing in the local market. London is the most important location for international share trading.

Depositary receipts

A firm may not wish to list its shares internationally for various legal and financial reasons. Depositary receipts offer a means for firms to tap foreign capital markets without directly listing their shares abroad. The best-known securities of this sort are American depositary receipts, or ADRs, which are traded in the United States; European depositary receipts, or EDRs, which trade mainly in London; and global depositary receipts, or GDRs, which trade elsewhere. Latin American companies account for a large share of trading in ADRs, and the GDRs of Indian companies are the biggest source of GDR trading in London.

These securities come in two varieties. A sponsored ADR, EDR or GDR is set up at the behest of the share issuer, which deposits the desired number of its own shares with a bank in the country where the receipts are to be traded. The receipts themselves are technically securities issued by the bank, giving the holder a claim on the earnings and price appreciation of the shares the bank holds. An unsponsored ADR, EDR or GDR is set up on the initiative of an outside party, such as an investment bank, rather than of the firm that has issued the shares. Both sponsored and unsponsored depositary receipts trade on stock exchanges. The main difference between them is that owners of unsponsored receipts may have more difficulty obtaining financial reports and other information from the share issuer, because the issuer has not sought to issue the receipts.

In 2013, depositary receipts of approximately 2,700 companies were traded on various exchanges around the world.

Emerging markets

During the 1990s there was rapid growth in equity markets in many Latin American, Asian, African and east European countries, which are collectively known as emerging markets. There is no precise definition of this term, but it is generally applied to countries where per head incomes are lower than in Japan, Australia, the United States, Canada and western Europe, and where open capital markets are a recent development. In previous decades, many emerging-market countries had high inflation rates and were ruled by governments with a deep suspicion of capital markets. The reversal of both of these trends led to a fourfold increase in emerging-market equity issues, from $5.6 billion in 1991 to $22.8 billion in 1997, before the onset of financial crises in Asia caused issuance to slow. Much of this growth occurred in Asian countries where equity markets were negligible or non-existent before 1990, notably India and China. Most emerging markets weathered the global financial crisis of 2008 relatively well, and the growth of their equity markets continued until 2013, when slowing growth in China and Brazil made investors wary of the prospects of emerging markets in general. In 2012, an estimated $572 billion flowed into emerging markets in the form of equity investment.

FIG 7.1 **Price changes in emerging-country share indexes**
Annual % change, local currency

Source: World Federation of Exchanges

Emerging-market share prices are generally more volatile than those in more developed markets. This is because of the comparatively small capitalisation of the markets and strong investor sensitivity to potential political or economic changes. This volatility is particularly pronounced for foreign investors, because even if a particular emerging-market share rises in local currency terms, exchange-rate movements may lead to a loss in terms of the investor's currency. Figure 7.1 illustrates the volatility of stockmarkets in emerging economies.

Trading shares

A share trade begins when an investor contacts a stockbrokerage firm to place an order to buy or sell stock. There are many different types of orders, which give the broker varying amounts of discretion. The most basic is a market order or an at best instruction, which instructs the broker to buy or sell the desired number of shares at the best price presently available in the market. A limit order requires the broker to complete the transaction only at the specified price or better, with the risk that the order will never be executed because the specified price is not reached. A stop order instructs the broker to buy or sell the shares once a specified price is reached, although the actual transaction price can be above or below the specified level.

Investors may also qualify their orders in various ways. A day order is good on only one particular day and is cancelled if it is not executed. A good-till-cancelled order, also known as an open order, remains active until it is either filled or cancelled. A fill-or-kill order requires the brokerage firm to buy or sell all the shares immediately or else to cancel the entire order, and an immediate or cancel order, known as an execute or eliminate order in the UK, tells the broker to buy or sell as many shares as possible immediately and to cancel the remainder of the order.

After verifying the investor's order, the brokerage firm passes it to the computer system at the appropriate stock exchange. In some cases, a given equity may trade on several exchanges. A broker working in its client's best interest will undertake the trade wherever it can obtain the best price.

How stock exchanges work

There are vast differences in the ways that stock exchanges function.

The traditional model for a stock exchange is known as an auction market, in which shares for purchase or sale are offered to brokers on a trading floor. An auction market uses specialised brokers, known as specialists or marketmakers, who are required to ensure orderly trading in the particular shares for which they are responsible. A brokerage firm sends each buy or sell order to its floor broker, who communicates it to the specialist. Each specialist maintains a book listing the bid price for each pending offer to buy the share and the asked price or offer price for each offer to sell. Floor brokers of other firms may accept the highest bid price or the lowest offer price to complete the trade. If there is a lack of bids or an imbalance between buy and sell orders that keeps a particular share from trading, the specialists must buy or sell shares in order to keep the market functioning smoothly.

This sort of auction market used to be the norm. But computerisation has permitted the development of electronic auction markets as well. All major stock exchanges now operate primarily or exclusively through electronic auctions.

Electronic auction markets function in one of three ways. Some offer a continuous or order-driven auction, in which the highest prices being bid and lowest prices being offered are continuously updated by computers, which automatically match buy and sell orders. Call auction markets execute trades at predetermined times rather than continuously, to assure adequate liquidity in particular shares. Dealer markets may have substantial human involvement in posting the prices at which investors are prepared to buy and sell shares. One growing problem with some computerised systems is that market participants can enter buy and sell orders that they have no intention of completing so as to mislead others about current conditions. For example, a large investor seeking to sell shares might briefly enter buy orders above the current market price but then cancel them immediately without completing the trades. This could convince other market participants that demand for the shares is stronger than previously believed and cause them to bid up the price, allowing the investor to sell its shares for an above-market price. On some exchanges, such fictitious orders account for a large proportion of the buy and sell orders entered by customers.

Traditional auction markets with human brokers retain certain advantages. If an electronic system does not have marketmakers, as is sometimes the case, a buy or sell order for an unpopular stock may not find a match; this cannot occur in a market where a marketmaker is available to arrange a trade. Nevertheless, as electronic share auction systems have become more sophisticated, they have forced drastic change upon exchanges with a high-cost human infrastructure. Most exchanges have abandoned floor trading altogether because of the cost.

Competition in trading

The way in which trading is organised greatly affects the cost of buying equities. Until the mid-1970s most stock exchanges allowed their members, the brokerage firms, to charge fixed commissions for each share bought or sold. Commissions were deregulated in the United States in 1975 and in the UK in 1979. This opened the way for discount brokerages, which offer share trading by telephone and use the resultant cost savings to charge lower commissions. Since 1996 internet brokerages have handled individual transactions by personal computer at even lower cost. The fall in commissions has permitted individuals to attempt new trading strategies, aiming to take advantage of tiny changes in a share's price, that would not be feasible with higher commissions. One of these is day trading, which involves the purchase of shares with the intention to resell quickly and reap a tiny profit. A related strategy is algorithmic trading, in which frequent buy and sell orders are placed automatically by a computer based on predefined instructions.

The fact that an investor communicates electronically with a stockbroker has no bearing on the way the share trade occurs. This is generally up to the broker, which has considerable discretion in arranging the trade and in deciding where the trade will be transacted. Wherever the transaction occurs, investors will face a gap, or spread, between the price at which it can buy shares and the price at which it can sell them. In 1997 the US government alleged that the members of NASDAQ conspired to maintain wide spreads. Spreads subsequently narrowed, and the presence of high-frequency traders and competition from alternative trading systems has squeezed them further. For the most widely traded shares, such as those included in the Standard & Poor's 500 stock index, spreads are now in the range of 1.3 cents per share, far narrower than in the 1990s.

There has also been concern about payment for order flow, a practice in which a marketmaker rebates part of its spread to stockbrokerage firms that bring it business, as these payments may induce stockbrokers not to make a trade in the way most beneficial to the customer. As spreads narrow, payment for order flow is less attractive to marketmakers, as they have less opportunity to profit from the transaction.

Institutional trading

Individual investors' stockmarket trades almost always involve a small number of shares of a single security. Institutional investors, however, have different requirements, and their trades may be handled differently.

■ **Block trades** involve offers to buy or sell large amounts of stock, usually 10,000 shares or more. On a floor-based exchange, block trades are often handled off the floor by brokers who must assemble enough buyers or sellers to complete the transaction, but who must act quickly and discreetly to prevent word of the impending deal from moving prices in the market. Big trades can be difficult to complete in a single block on electronic exchanges, because posting an investor's intentions on members' screens would immediately change the price. In such a case, the trade can be broken into smaller transactions conducted over a period of time, or can be handled through dark pools to disguise the magnitude of the intended purchase or sale.

■ **Basket trades** allow investors to trade shares in several different companies as part of a single transaction. This type of trading, which is confined to a few big exchanges, is popular among investors who are attempting to mimic a particular index, and who therefore want to buy or sell some shares of each stock in the index at the same time.

■ **Program or algorithmic trades** are initiated by computers that have been programmed to identify share prices that are out of line with the prices of futures or options on those same shares. The program trader may then buy shares and sell options, or vice versa, in some combination in order to profit from what may be a tiny anomaly in prices. A large number of the orders placed by algorithmic traders are intended to "test the market" and are cancelled before they can be executed, leading to concerns that stock-exchange order books may not accurately reflect the prices at which individuals will be willing to buy and sell shares. However, as algorithmic traders generally hold shares for only a brief period and seek to end each trading day "flat", without exposure to changes in market prices, it is not clear that their activities adversely affect other investors buying and selling shares.

■ **Short sales** are transactions in which an investor (a short seller) borrows shares for a specified period and then sells them at the current market price, in the expectation that the price will be lower when it must buy shares to repay the lender. The short seller loses money if the share price does not fall as expected. In some countries, information about short positions must be reported and published. This can be important information for investors, because the existence of large short positions in a particular share means that short sellers will need to buy those shares in the market so they can repay the brokers from whom they have borrowed.

Clearing and settlement

An important function of stock exchanges is to ensure that trades are completed precisely as the parties have agreed. This involves two separate functions, clearing and settlement.

When brokers have executed a trade on an exchange, they report the details to the exchange. The exchange's clearing house reconciles the reports of all brokers involved to make sure that all parties are in agreement as to the price and the number of shares traded. Settlement then involves the transfer of the shares and money. Formerly, most exchanges operated their own clearing and settlement systems. As the cost of clearing and settlement is a significant part of the total cost of trading, however, exchanges have been under pressure to combine their systems or to engage third parties able to handle these functions more efficiently.

Settlement must occur within a time limit established by regulators. In the more advanced economies trades are settled within three days, and US, Canadian and European exchanges are seeking to make the settlement time even shorter. In less active markets, particularly in poorer countries, settlement can take a week or more. Lengthy settlement times deter investors, because they increase the chance that a transaction will not be completed and also make it difficult to resell shares quickly.

Investing on margin

Investors often purchase shares with borrowed money. Stockbrokerage firms make such loans, known as margin loans, accepting the purchased shares as collateral. Margin lending is regulated by national banking authorities, who generally insist that credit be extended for only a portion of the value of the shares purchased. An investor's initial margin is the amount of cash that must be deposited with the broker to acquire shares with a margin loan. Margin investors must also maintain a specified maintenance margin. The maintenance margin requires the owner to maintain a certain amount of equity, which is the current market value of the shares less the amount of the margin loan. If the market value of the shares falls, the amount of the investor's equity will decrease. If the amount falls below an agreed level, the lender may issue a margin call, requiring the investor to deposit additional cash. If the investor fails to meet the margin call, the lender may sell the shares and apply the proceeds against the outstanding debt. The amount of margin debt outstanding varies greatly over time. Margin borrowing is generally considered a sign of investor optimism, as margin investors can lose heavily if share prices fall.

Measuring market performance

Private information providers and exchanges have developed many measures to track the performance of equity markets. Two types of performance are particularly important to investors: those related to price, and those related to risk.

Price measures

There are two basic types of price measures:

■ **Averages,** such as the Dow Jones Industrial, Utility and Transportation Averages on the New York Stock Exchange, track the value of a specific group of shares, with adjustments for the capitalisation of each company in the average and for the inclusion of new companies to replace those that have merged or gone bankrupt.

■ **Indexes,** such as the Financial Times Stock Exchange (FTSE) 100 stock index in London, relate the current value of the shares in the index to the value during some base period, also adjusting for the deletion of some shares and the inclusion of others.

No index or average can offer a perfect picture of the market, because the shares tracked represent a non-random sample of all shares listed and each measure tracks a different set of shares. There is no single answer to a question such as: How did the Frankfurt stockmarket do in the early 1990s? The Commerzbank Index was at 1,701.2 on the last day of 1990 and 2,358.9 on the last day of 1995, a gain of 38.7%. The DAX Performance Index ended 1990 at 1,398.2 and was at 2,253.88 five years later, a gain of 61.2%. This difference reflected the composition of the indexes. The Commerzbank Index included 78 shares that accounted for about 70% of Frankfurt share trading. The DAX tracked 30 stocks that accounted for about 61% of trading.

Several newer indexes, such as the Dow Jones Euro Stoxx 50 and the Euro-Stars index of 29 euro-zone stocks, are competing to become the investment benchmark for Europe. Matters are even more confusing in New York, where several different indexes – the Standard & Poor's 500 stock index, the New York Stock Exchange Composite Index, the NASDAQ Composite Index and the Dow Jones Industrial Average (DJIA) – all tell different stories about price trends. According to the S&P 500, US stocks rose by 13.41% in 2012. The NYSE Composite, which includes some foreign companies, rose by 12.93% and the NASDAQ Composite by 15.91%, whereas the DJIA, which is composed of 30 stocks, rose by 7.26%.

There are several reasons for these differences. First, there is no statistically sound way to create an index which is truly representative of the market; each index comprises different shares, and its performance depends upon the shares included. Second, all indexes are vulnerable to selection bias. When a firm whose shares are in the index merges, becomes a privately held firm or enters bankruptcy proceedings, the sponsor of the index has great flexibility to pick a replacement. There is an incentive to select a firm whose shares are popular and widely followed, because a strong performance by that share will, in turn, stimulate interest in the index.

A third reason is the growing popularity of index or tracker funds, which seek to mimic the performance of a particular index. The manager of a tracker fund does not select particular shares, but maintains a portfolio of the same shares as are in the index being tracked, in the same proportion. The S&P 500 is a particularly popular index for trackers, increasing the demand for the shares it includes; the other two main NYSE indexes are not as widely used by fund managers.

As well as these general market indexes there are thousands of indexes developed to measure various aspects of equity trading, from bank shares listed on a particular market to emerging-market stockmarkets as a group. Table 7.11 shows the annual performance of some of the major indexes in recent years.

TABLE 7.11 **Performance of stockmarket indexes**
Annual % return, without reinvested dividends

Index	Country	2000	2004	2008	2012
FTSE 100	UK	-10.20	7.54	-31.33	5.84
S&P/TSX Composite	Canada	6.20	12.48	-35.02	4.00
CAC 40	France	-0.01	7.40	-42.68	15.23
DAX	Germany	-20.70	7.34	-40.37	29.06
FTSE/MIB	Italy	2.48	14.98	-49.53	7.84
Nikkei 225	Japan	-27.20	7.61	-42.12	22.94
AEX	Netherlands	-5.04	3.09	-52.32	9.68
SMI	Switzerland	7.47	3.74	-34.77	4.93
NASDAQ	US	39.30	8.59	-40.54	15.91
S&P 500	US	-10.14	8.99	-38.49	13.41

Source: Bloomberg

Risk measures

The risk of investing in a particular stockmarket is measured by its volatility. This term has a precise statistical meaning when applied to stockmarkets: a market's volatility is the annualised standard deviation of daily percentage changes in a selected stock price index. A market's volatility varies from time to time. The volatility of all major markets soared during the big stock price drops of October 1997 and September 1998. But some markets seem persistently less volatile than others. London has been the least volatile of the world's main markets in recent years, and the Italian exchange has been among the most volatile.

8 Futures and options markets

MANAGING RISK is one of the essential functions of financial markets. One of the biggest of these risks is time. The completion of any business transaction requires time, but if prices change during this period a potentially profitable deal may turn out to be a costly mistake. The purpose of futures and options markets is to help protect against the risks inherent in a world where prices change constantly.

The mechanisms used to obtain this protection are futures and options contracts, which are agreements to buy or sell assets in the future at certain prices or under certain conditions. Futures and options contracts come in two basic forms. This chapter deals with the standardised contracts that are traded on exchanges. Forward contracts, which are less likely to be standardised and are often traded privately rather than on exchanges, are discussed in Chapter 9, as are other derivative contracts that are used to manage risk or speculate but are not traded on exchanges.

Futures and options markets were outgrowths of commodities markets, which allow a person to acquire or sell physical stocks of minerals, grains and other long-lasting products. Commodities markets have existed for millennia. They have served the important function of setting prices for commodities, and have offered a means for those who produce a commodity to trade it for other sorts of goods. Commodities markets, however, cannot help the investor whose store of commodities loses value as the price falls, or the potential user who wants to lock in a price for the future supply of a commodity that may or may not be needed. Futures and options markets were developed to play this role.

The origin of futures and options trading is lost in history. Aristotle wrote of Thales, a Greek philosopher, who reached individual agreements with the owners of olive presses whereby, in return for a payment, he obtained the right to first use of each owner's press after harvest. These options on all his region's pressing capacity gave Thales control over the olive crop. By the late 1500s, fish dealers in Holland were buying and selling herring that had yet to be caught – the essence of a futures market. The sale of other commodities on a to-arrive basis soon followed. At a time when communications were poor and transport was unreliable, these markets allowed manufacturers to lock in the price of their raw material and assured ship owners a profit on their cargoes. Futures and options have been bought and sold on exchanges since at least the 1600s. The leap from one-off deals to standardised contracts came in 1865, when the Chicago Board of Trade began trading futures contracts in grain.

The characteristics of commodities

Commodities are physical goods, but not all physical goods are commodities. Commodities have certain characteristics that make it feasible to trade them in markets:

- They can be stored for long periods, or in some cases for unlimited periods.

- Their value depends heavily on measurable physical attributes and on the physical location of the commodities.

- Commodities with the same physical attributes and the same physical location are fungible. If a buyer has contracted to purchase oil of a certain density and sulphur content or wheat of a certain type and moisture content, it need not be concerned about which well pumped the oil or which farmer grew the wheat.

Most participants in the markets for physical commodities are producers, users, or firms that have established themselves as intermediaries between producers and users. Few investors are interested in physical commodities strictly as a financial investment, because it is usually much less costly to purchase and hold futures contracts than to purchase and store the commodities themselves.

Why trade futures and options?

Futures and options contracts, unlike bonds and shares, do not represent long-term investments with income potential. On the contrary, a futures or options contract pays no interest or dividends, and the money tied up in it is money that cannot be invested to receive interest. Futures and options investors operate from one of two fundamental motives.

Hedging

This involves the use of futures or options to offset specific risks. In April, before planting his soyabeans, an Iowan farmer might sell September futures contracts, which commit him to supply a specific quantity of soyabeans at the agreed price after harvest. The farmer, who must sell his product in the physical commodities market after harvest, thus uses futures to hedge the risk that the price of a tonne of soyabeans will fall between April and September. Conversely, a processor who hopes to purchase 10,000 tonnes of soyabeans in September may buy soyabean futures contracts in April to protect himself against the risk that the price of the physical commodity, raw soyabeans, might rise over the summer. Typically, hedgers have made a decision to take on certain types of risks and to avoid others. For example, a French oil company might determine not to trade petroleum futures, as its shareholders have deliberately chosen to take oil-related risks by investing in the firm, but it might buy euro futures to prevent a fluctuating dollar from affecting the profit it reports in euros.

Speculation

This involves trading with the intention of profiting from changes in the prices of futures or options contracts, rather than from a desire to hedge specific risks. Although speculation is often derided as an unproductive activity, it is essential to the smooth functioning of the market. By buying and selling contracts with great frequency, speculators vastly increase liquidity: the supply of money in the markets. Without the liquidity that speculators provide, the futures and options markets would be less attractive to hedgers because it would be more difficult to buy and sell contracts at favourable prices. Firms that use futures or options for hedging may also be active as speculators. In many markets, floor traders or locals, individuals trading for themselves on a full-time basis, also play a prominent role.

Futures and options exchanges

Futures and options trading takes place on organised exchanges. There are about 35 significant exchanges around the world and many smaller ones. Some exchanges that trade futures also trade shares, and most futures exchanges now deal in options. Most exchanges were once co-operatives owned by the members who traded on the exchange floor, but technological change has led to large-scale consolidation among exchanges, including those trading different types of products. Most trading is now handled by computer, and major exchanges have become shareholder-owned companies which operate in several locations to spread the cost of developing new technology. The most important futures and options exchanges, as measured by the number of contracts traded, are listed in Table 8.1.

There is intense competition among exchanges to develop new contracts and to cut costs to make existing contracts more attractive. All futures and options trades are subject to brokerage commissions, taxes and fees levied by the exchange itself. Since many trading strategies aim to exploit small price differences among contracts, even a minor change in the cost structure can have a significant effect on the volume of trading.

Traditionally, head-to-head competition among futures and options exchanges was rare; if two exchanges were to offer precisely the same contract, investors would be expected to gravitate towards the market with more liquidity – that is, with the greater volume of trading – and trading in the corresponding contract at the other exchange would wither. Technology has facilitated direct competition among exchanges in products such as currency futures and equity options. But competition more often involves contracts that are similar though not identical. The relatively new commodity contracts traded on exchanges in China and India have not supplanted contracts on

TABLE 8.1 **The leading futures and options exchanges**
2012

Exchange	No. of futures and options contracts traded (m)
CME Group,[a] US	2,890
Eurex, Germany/Switzerland/US	2,291
National Stock Exchange of India	2,010
NYSE Euronext,[b] US/UK/FR/NL/B/P	1,951
Korea Exchange	1,835
BM&F Bovespa, Brazil	1,636
Chicago Board Options Exchange, US	1,134
Nasdaq OMX Group,[c] US/DK/SV/SU	1,115
Moscow Echange	1,062
Multi Commodity Exchange of India	960

a Includes Chicago Mercantile Exchange, Chicago Board of Trade, New York Mercantile Exchange, Commodity Exchange, Kansas City Board of Trade.
b Includes New York Stock Exchange, London International Financial Futures Exchange, the former French futures exchange (MATIF), and the Amsterdam, Brussels, Lisbon and Paris bourses.
c Includes NASDAQ Options Market, Philadelphia and Boston Stock Exchanges and Nordic derivatives exchanges.
Source: Futures Industry Association

other exchanges, but provide for local delivery points to better serve the needs of manufacturers in those fast-growing economies.

An exchange may discontinue trading in an established contract if there is insufficient interest. For example, the advent of the single European currency on January 1st 1999 meant the end of contracts on 12 countries' currencies and interest rates and their replacement by far fewer contracts on euro exchange and interest rates. In 1997 the French notional bond contract, traded on the MATIF in Paris, was the fifth most active futures contract in the world, with nearly 34m contracts being traded. By 1999, with many other euro-denominated interest-rate futures available, only 6m notional bond futures were traded. Changes in user industries may cause a contract to disappear; the Tokyo Commodity Exchange's cotton yarn futures were discontinued in 2000, after annual volume fell from 2.3m in 1992 to a few thousand contracts in 1999; and the Chicago Mercantile Exchange's famed pork-belly contract was discontinued in 2011. Many newly introduced contracts are subsequently withdrawn if investor interest proves weak.

Merger pressures

Economic forces have reshaped the futures and options landscape in recent years. In 1990 Japan was home to 16 commodity exchanges, from the Maebashi Dried Cocoon Exchange to the Tokyo Commodity Exchange. After the closure of the Central Japan Commodities Exchange in 2011, only four remain. The Chinese government forced many exchanges to merge or close, reducing the number of futures and options markets from 40 in 1993 to four today. Even as mergers among exchanges have become common, existing exchanges have used their trading systems to offer new types of contracts. Some of the most significant changes are as follows:

- In 2007, the Chicago Mercantile Exchange, best known for financial futures, bought its cross-town rival, the Chicago Board of Trade, famed for trading in agricultural commodities. A year later it took control of the New York Mercantile Exchange, which trades energy futures and options, and the Commodity Exchange in New York, which specialises in metals futures and options. In 2012 it bought the Kansas City Board of Trade, which ran a futures market in hard red winter wheat, and in 2013 it opened a new exchange in London to trade currency futures and options.

- The London Stock Exchange Group has opened new contracts in electricity and wheat futures in Italy, where it owns the Milan stock exchange, and also trades stock options in several European countries.

- In Brazil, the São Paulo Stock Exchange and the Brazilian Mercantile and Futures Exchange merged in 2008.

- Deutsche Börse, owner of the former Frankfurt Stock Exchange, created the Eurex futures and options exchange in 1999 in partnership with the Swiss exchange. It added the International Securities Exchange, a US-based options exchange, in 2007 and the European Energy Exchange, which trades futures and options contracts on electricity, in 2011.

■ The Intercontinental Exchange, which started out by offering energy futures contracts in 2000, acquired the International Petroleum Exchange of London in 2001 and added the New York Cotton Exchange, the Coffee, Sugar and Cocoa Exchange and the Winnipeg Commodity Exchange in 2007. Its purchase of NYSE Euronext in 2013 gave it control of the New York Stock Exchange and the Euronext stock exchange.

■ The Hong Kong Exchanges, originally the operator of a major stock exchange, took control of the London Metal Exchange in 2013.

Such alliances and mergers were not achieved easily. Traditionally, the exchanges were co-operatives owned by the people who traded there, and who feared for their livelihoods if the contracts they handled were traded on other exchanges or with electronic systems. In many cases, members opposed both technical innovations and co-operation with other exchanges, but continuing economic and technological pressures left little choice. From the viewpoint of institutional investors, exchange mergers have the potential to lower trading costs, particularly by reducing the total amount of cash deposits, or margin, required to support their trading (see A margin of security, page 227).

Regulators in several countries have approved the creation of new, all-electronic exchanges since 2000. Some of these have been highly successful; the Multi-Commodity Exchange of India, established in 2003, ranks among the largest exchanges in the world for trading in commodities. Many of the upstart exchanges, however, have failed to gain enough trading volume to challenge the long-established exchanges.

Futures contracts

A futures contract represents a deal between two investors who may not be known to each other and are unaware of one another's motives. A futures contract is a derivative, because its price and terms are derived from an underlying asset, sometimes known as the underlying. A new contract may be created any time two investors desire to create one. Although there is a limit to the amount of copper that can be mined in a given year, there is no limit to the number of copper futures contracts that can be traded.

Types of contracts

Futures contracts can be divided into two basic categories:

- **Commodity futures** were once based exclusively upon bulk commodities, known as physicals. Recently, however, the rising demand for ways to manage risks has led to trading of non-physical contracts as well.

- **Financial futures** were first traded only in 1972. Despite initial controversy over their desirability, they have become popular as a result of the abandonment of fixed exchange rates in the major industrial countries in the 1970s and the deregulation of interest rates in subsequent years. Trading volume in financial futures now exceeds trading volume in commodity futures by a wide margin.

How futures are traded

To buy or sell futures contracts, an investor must deal with a registered broker, also known as a futures commission merchant. Many futures commission merchants are owned by large banks or securities companies that are active in other financial markets as well. The futures commission merchant maintains staff and computer systems to trade on the exchanges of which it is a member.

The customer's order gives the futures commission merchant specific directions:

- A market order, also referred to as an at-the-market order, is to be executed immediately, whatever the conditions in the market.
- A limit order is to be executed only at a specified price.
- A market-if-touched order is to be executed as soon as the market has reached a specified price, but the actual trade may be at a higher or lower price.

■ An all-or-none order must be filled in its entirety or not at all.

■ A fill-or-kill order must be filled immediately in its entirety or the order is cancelled.

In every trade the two parties take opposite positions. The buyer of the contract, who agrees to receive the commodities specified, is said to be in a long position. The French oil firm mentioned above under "Hedging", for example, would be long euros if it has agreed to receive euros at the expiry of its contract. The seller of a contract is said to be in a short position. It may not own the commodities it has agreed to deliver, but it is obliged to have them or to pay their value in cash at the expiry of the contract.

Once a trade has been completed, the participants are both obligated to the exchange rather than to each other. Either party separately may terminate its contract at any point by arranging an offset, without affecting the other party's position. If the Iowan soyabean farmer mentioned above decides in July to end his September delivery obligation, he would buy (at the price current in July) the same number of September contracts that he previously sold, and the two sets of contracts would cancel each other out. This is often referred to as liquidation of the initial contracts. If the price of the contracts purchased in July is greater than the price at which the farmer originally sold the contracts in April, he will have lost money on his futures transactions; if the price in July is less, he will have made money. Note, however, that as a hedger the farmer is concerned not about futures-market profits but about the amount he will receive for his crop. If he sells his soyabeans for a good price, he is likely to regard any loss in the futures market as a sort of insurance premium that bought him protection if soyabean prices had fallen.

Contract terms

A futures contract contains the specifications of the transaction. The specifications of all contracts in a given asset on a given exchange are identical, apart from the expiration dates. This standardisation is an important feature of futures markets as it makes contracts interchangeable, freeing traders and investors from the need to worry about unusual provisions. The specifications cover the following:

- **Contract size.** This specifies how much of the asset must be delivered under one contract. Size for commodity futures is usually specified by weight or quantity. One cocoa contract traded on the New York Board of Trade, for example, involves the obligation to sell or buy 10 tonnes of cocoa. For financial futures, the value of the underlying asset is specified in monetary terms. The buyer of one contract on British pounds on the Chicago Mercantile Exchange is contracting to purchase £62,500. Other types of contracts also must specify quantity. The seller of a UK electricity contract on the Intercontinental Exchange in London is obligated to provide 5 megawatt hours of electricity each day for one month.

- **Quality.** Contracts for commodity futures specify the physical quality of the product the seller has promised to supply. They often use industry-standard product grades. The arabica coffee contract on the BM&F Bovespa exchange in São Paulo requires evenly coloured or greenish Brazilian-grown coffee of type six or better, with a maximum of 8% wormy or bored beans, packed in new jute bags of 60kg each. Some contracts allow the seller to substitute substandard product at a reduced price. Quality standards are not relevant for most financial futures contracts, such as currencies.

- **Delivery date.** Every contract is available with a choice of delivery dates – the dates on which the parties are obliged to complete the terms of the contract. Contracts are typically identified by month, with delivery on a specified day or days of the month. Trading in a contract ceases on or before the delivery date. The Brent Crude oil futures traded on the Intercontinental Exchange, for example, have monthly delivery dates over the next year, quarterly dates for the following 12 months and half-yearly dates for the year after that. Brent trading for a given delivery month ceases on the business day immediately preceding the 15th day before the first day of the delivery month.

- **Price limits.** To facilitate smooth trading, each contract specifies the smallest allowable price movement, known as a tick or a point. The tick size of the Chicago Board of Trade's Northern

Spring Wheat contract is 1/4 cent per American bushel (2.84 hectolitres); as one contract covers 5,000 bushels, the price of a contract therefore changes in increments of $12.50 (5,000 × $0.0025). Many contracts also specify daily limits for price changes to avoid large day-to-day price swings. Chicago spring wheat futures may not rise or fall by more than 60 cents per bushel on any day.

■ **Position limits.** The exchange imposes a limit on the number of contracts a speculator may hold for a particular delivery month and a particular commodity. The purpose of position limits is to prevent a speculator from cornering the market by owning a large proportion of open contracts and thus being able to manipulate the price. Position limits do not usually apply to investors who can prove to the exchange that they are hedgers.

■ **Settlement.** Most futures transactions do not lead to the actual delivery of the underlying products. However, the contract specifies when and where delivery must be made and may provide for the alternative of cash settlement, in which the parties fulfil their obligations by making or receiving cash payments rather than exchanging goods.

Trading

There are three main methods of trading futures contracts:

■ **Continuous-auction or open-outcry trading** is conducted by floor brokers or pit brokers on the floor of the exchange. The brokers stand in a certain area of the floor or in a trading pit or ring, an enclosed area with steps or risers so that each floor broker can see and be seen by all the others in the pit. The futures commission merchant has a clerk outside each pit, who receives customers' orders by telephone. The clerk relays the orders to the firm's floor brokers with hand signals, electronic messages or on slips of paper carried into the pit by runners. The floor broker then announces the buy or sell offer in the pit, and other brokers respond with shouts or hand signals until a price is agreed. This is the form of futures trading most familiar to the public. Until recently, most of the world's main futures exchanges used open-outcry trading for at least some of their contracts. However, exchanges such as Euronext and Eurex have eliminated all open-outcry trading, and only 7% of the trading at the CME Group exchanges was conducted by open outcry in 2012. Canada's Winnipeg Commodity Exchange, which trades futures contracts on barley and canola (rapeseed), abandoned open-outcry trading in 2004, and the trading pit for hard red winter wheat at the Kansas City Board of Trade was closed in 2013.

■ **Single-price auction trading**, also known as session trading, is used especially in Japan. An exchange official opens each session of trading in a given contract by posting a provisional price for the nearest delivery month. Members then put in their buy and sell orders at that price. If sell orders outnumber buy orders, the price is lowered to attract more buy orders; if buy orders outnumber sell orders, the price is raised a fraction. When the number of buy orders is equal to the number of sell orders the price is fixed. All contracts for that delivery month are executed at the fixed price during the session. The process is repeated to set the price for the next-nearest delivery month, and so on. There are four to six sessions for each commodity each trading day.

■ **Electronic trading** is conducted through a computer system rather than on a trading floor. In most cases, exchange members have exclusive access to the system, but some exchanges allow non-members to submit buy and sell offers anonymously by computer. In either case, market participants need not be physically located in the same city, or country, as the exchange. Various systems use differing rules to match buy offers with sell offers, to post transaction prices and to inform all market participants of pending buy and sell offers. The details of these rules make a great difference to the way trading occurs and directly affect the ability of market participants to assure themselves of the best possible price.

In general, electronic systems transact contracts at much lower cost than trading pits. Yet some exchanges resisted the introduction of electronic trading. This was partly because of some members' self-interest: electronic systems reduce or eliminate the need for floor brokers, clerks and other personnel. Another reason is that open-outcry trading, in which a floor broker gains a feel for the market by observing other brokers, may have advantages for contracts that are thinly traded and for the execution of complex trading strategies. However, the competitive pressures among exchanges have become so strong that exchanges have been forced to adopt electronic trading in order to attract investors who demand the lowest possible trading cost.

Electronic systems have opened the way for after-hours trading. This is a recent innovation that allows customers to trade outside the official exchange opening hours. Prices in after-hours trading may not be as favourable as during the trading day because there is less liquidity, but investors are able to respond to late news without waiting for the following day's trading. Electronic trading of some of the most popular contracts is available 24 hours a day.

The most heavily traded futures contracts are listed in Table 8.2.

TABLE 8.2 **Leading futures contracts**
2012

Contract	Exchange	No. traded, m
US dollar/Indian rupee	National Stock Exchange of India	620
US dollar/Indian rupee	Multi-Commodity Exchange of India	551
Mini S&P 500	Chicago Mercantile Exchange	474
3-month eurodollar	Chicago Mercantile Exchange	426
US dollar/Russian rouble	Moscow Exchange	373
One-day interbank deposit	BM&F Bovespa	341
Soy meal	Dalian Commodity Exchange	326
DJ Euro Stoxx 50	Eurex	315
Euro-Bund	Eurex	184
US 10-year Treasury	Chicago Board of Trade	184

Source: Futures Industry Association

How prices are set

The method for establishing the price of a contract is set in the contract specifications. These state which currency the price is quoted in and the unit for which the price is quoted. Prices for agricultural futures traded in the United States are normally quoted in cents and, for some contracts, in fractions of a cent. Prices in most other countries and for US financial futures contracts are quoted in decimals rather than fractions.

The quoted price

The quoted price is not the price of a contract but of the specified unit. It must be multiplied by the number of units per contract to determine the price of one contract. Consider the International Petroleum Exchange's Brent Crude contract, which is priced in US dollars even though it trades in London. The quoted price is for a single barrel of oil (42 American gallons, or 159 litres). One contract provides for the future purchase or sale of 1,000 barrels of oil. If a given month's Brent Crude contract is trading at $65.00, one contract costs 1,000 × $65.00, or $65,000. A 10 cent drop in the posted price means a decrease of $100 (1,000 × $0.10) in the value of a contract.

Price movements

Prices in the markets change constantly in response to supply and demand, which are affected mainly by news from outside, although in a highly selective way. A fall in New York share prices will immediately affect trading in Standard & Poor's 500 stock index futures at the Chicago Mercantile Exchange, but may not be noticed by traders in cattle futures. Investors in commodity futures pay close attention to information that could affect the price of the underlying commodity. For example, orange juice futures will soar on reports of frost that could damage the orange crop in Brazil, and copper futures will be sensitive to statistics on construction activity. Investors in financial futures are concerned more with economic data that might signal interest-rate changes.

Limits on price movements

For some contracts, the contract specifications limit the amount that the price may rise or fall in a given day. A limit move means that the contract has fluctuated as much as allowed on that day. A contract that has risen the maximum allowable amount is said to be limit up. One that has fallen the permissible maximum is limit down. A locked market has reached its price limit, and trading may proceed only at current prices or prices closer to the previous day's settlement price.

The spot price

The reference price for any futures contract is the spot price, the amount required to go out and purchase those items today. The difference between the spot price of an asset and the price of a futures contract for the nearest delivery month is the basis or the swap rate. As a contract approaches its delivery date its price normally converges with the spot price. The reasoning is intuitive. If the price of Japanese yen to be delivered 30 days from now is far above the spot price, a buyer could purchase yen now in the spot market and put them in the bank for 30 days rather than buying a futures contract.

Term factor

Most of the time the price of a contract rises as the delivery month becomes more distant. This reflects both the greater risk of big price changes over the life of a longer-term contract and the fact that the buyer of that contract has money tied up for a longer period. If this price relationship exists, with each delivery date for a particular contract having a higher price than the previous delivery date, the market is called a normal market, or is said to be in contango. If near-term contracts cost more than more distant contracts, the market is said to be inverted or in backwardation.

Obtaining price information

The current price of a futures contract is simply the most recent price at which a contract was exchanged. Active traders and investors can subscribe to private information services. In general, though, futures exchanges treat up-to-the-minute data about prices and orders as valuable information and supply it to market participants for a fee. As prices for heavily traded contracts change constantly, individual investors are unlikely to have as much information about futures market conditions as large market participants.

Commodity futures markets

There are four main categories of commodity futures: agricultural products, metals, energy and environmental products, and transport.

Agricultural futures

Cereals were the first products on which futures contracts were traded. Now hundreds of different contracts are traded on raw and processed grains and oils, live and slaughtered animals, sugar, orange juice, coffee and inedible agricultural products such as lumber, rubber and cotton. Table 8.3 lists the agricultural contracts with the largest volume in 2012.

TABLE 8.3 **Leading agricultural commodities contracts** 2012

Contract	Exchange	No. traded (m)
Soya meal	Dalian Commodity Exchange	326
White sugar	Zhengzhou Commodity Exchange	148
Rubber	Shanghai Futures Exchange	75
Corn	Chicago Board of Trade	73
Soya oil	Dalian Commodity Exchange	69
Soyabeans	Chicago Board of Trade	52
No. 1 soyabeans	Dalian Commodity Exchange	45
Palm oil	Dalian Commodity Exchange	43
Corn	Dalian Commodity Exchange	38
Soya oil	Chicago Board of Trade	28

Source: Futures Industry Association

Until recently, global volume in agricultural futures trading was dominated by the Chicago Board of Trade, which was the first exchange to trade agricultural futures. Since the early 2000s, however, Chinese exchanges have emerged as centres for trading grains, soya products and industrial commodities. Agricultural futures trading has not consolidated at a few exchanges in the same way as trading in most other types of futures. The survival of many contracts on many exchanges is a result of two characteristics specific to farm products. First, many crops have a large number of varieties, creating demand for several separate contracts for each generic commodity. Although soyabean futures were already heavily traded at the Chicago Board of Trade and the Tokyo Grain Exchange, the latter opened a separate contract in 2000 to meet demand for non-genetically modified soya, and the Dalian Commodity Exchange opened a soyabean contract in view of heavy Chinese demand for that commodity. Second, agricultural products are processed in many locations, making it useful to have contracts with different delivery points. Thus wheat growers and users can choose among at least 18 different futures contracts (see Table 8.4).

Similarly, sugar futures trade on Euronext in Europe, the Zhengzhou Commodity Exchange in China, the Tokyo Grain Exchange in Japan, the New York Board of Trade in the United States and BM&F Bovespa in Brazil, and coffee futures are traded in London, New York, Tokyo and São Paulo. In each case, the contracts are not precise substitutes for one another, and most farmers and food processors will have a preference for the particular contract that best allows them to hedge their specific risks.

The specificity of agricultural futures has left room for specialised contracts on smaller exchanges. Thus the Euronext bread-wheat contract, which began trading in 1998, aims to exploit demand for a delivery point in Continental Europe and changes in EU agricultural policies that might lead to greater price instability within Europe. The Warenterminbörse Hannover, in Germany, now part of the RMX exchange, was established in 1998 with contracts on pork, of which Germany is Europe's largest producer and consumer, and on potatoes. The Derivatives Exchange, Malaysia, in Kuala Lumpur, has built a successful agricultural futures business on palm oil, a single commodity for which it was until recently the main trading

TABLE 8.4 **Wheat futures contracts**

Exchange	Contract traded	Delivery point
Agre	Durum Wheat	Foggia
Australian Futures Exchange	Western Australia wheat New South Wales wheat	Kwinana Track New South Wales wheat
Bolsa de Comercio de Rosario	Wheat	Rosario, Santa Fe
Chicago Board of Trade	Soft red winter wheat Northern spring wheat Hard red winter wheat	Chicago, St Louis, Toledo Chicago, St Louis, Toledo Kansas City, Hutchinson
Chicago Mercantile Exchange	Black Sea wheat	Russia, Ukraine, Romania
Johannesburg Stock Exchange	Bread milling wheat	South Africa
Mercado a Termino de Buenos Aires	Hard bread wheat	Buenos Aires, Rosario, Quequen, Ingeniero White
Minneapolis Grain Exchange	Hard red spring wheat	Minneapolis, Red Wing, Duluth
Multi Commodity Exchange of India	Wheat (standard mill quality)	Delhi, Khanna, Karnal, Kanpur, Kota, Indore
NYSE Euronext	Feed wheat Milling wheat	UK Rouen
National Commodity & Derivatives Exchange	Wheat	Delhi, Ahmedabad, Kanpur, others
National Multi-Commodity Exchange of India	Wheat	Delhi
Zhengzhou Commodity Exchange	Hard white winter wheat Strong gluten wheat	Eastern China Eastern China

Source: Exchange reports

location. The Multi-Commodity Exchange of India and the National Commodity and Derivatives Exchange have both grown rapidly amid India's economic liberalisation.

Metals futures

Precious metals, such as gold, and industrial metals, such as copper, have been traded in futures markets since the middle of the 19th

TABLE 8.5 **Leading metals contracts**
2012

Contract	Exchange	No. traded, m
Steel rebar	Shanghai Futures Exchange	181
Aluminium	London Metal Exchange	59
Copper	Shanghai Futures Exchange	57
Silver, 1kg	Multi-Commodity Exchange of India	51
Gold	New York Mercantile Exchange	44
Silver, 5kg	Multi-Commodity Exchange of India	36
Gold Petal	Multi-Commodity Exchange of India	36
Copper	London Metal Exchange	36
Copper	Multi-Commodity Exchange of India	33
Zinc	London Metal Exchange	30

Source: Exchange reports

century. Metals prices can be highly volatile. Mining companies and industrial users normally maintain large stocks of metals, and futures markets provide a means to hedge the risk that the value of these stocks will fall. Industrial users can also employ futures to stabilise the prices of key raw materials.

Trading in gold futures is quite different from trading in other metals. Although some investors in gold futures mine gold or use it in manufacturing, most gold futures trading is related to gold's traditional role as a store of value in times of inflation. Hence gold is among the most heavily traded of all metals. However, not all gold trading occurs on futures markets, as many speculators trade shares of gold-mining companies as an alternative to futures contracts.

Unlike users of agricultural products, users of metals are not concerned with local variations in quality. Although there are quality differences among ores, metals have been extracted from ore and processed to specific standards before they are traded in financial markets. As a result, metals users throughout the world employ a comparatively small number of contracts, and there is almost no local trading of metals futures. Before 2005, the London

Metal Exchange, the Tokyo Commodity Exchange and the New York Mercantile Exchange accounted for almost all futures trading in metals, but the relatively new Shanghai Futures Exchange and the Multi-Commodity Exchange of India have become important. China's rapid industrial growth has given the Shanghai exchange an important role in determining the world price of copper. Table 8.5 lists the most widely traded contracts.

Energy futures

Trading in energy-related futures products dates back to the oil crises of the 1970s and, in the United States, to the regulation-induced natural gas shortages of the same period. Futures contracts on petroleum and petroleum derivatives are popular. The amount of oil traded daily in futures markets far outstrips actual world demand for petroleum. There are also contracts based on the spread, or difference, between the prices of different petroleum products. After hurricanes damaged US refineries and production facilities in August and September 2005, energy futures contracts played an important role in helping the markets adjust to high oil and natural gas prices.

Natural gas futures have become well-established in North America, with the New York Mercantile Exchange offering three separate contracts for various delivery points in the United States and Canada. Because each contract is tied to the capacity of pipelines serving a specific location, the contracts are of little use to gas users in other countries. Many more natural gas contracts are likely to be created on various exchanges to meet local demands. The most widely traded energy futures contracts are listed in Table 8.6.

The arrival of price competition in wholesale electricity markets has led to the creation of futures contracts on electricity. The volume of trading in individual contracts is small, because each is tied to the price of power delivered to a specific location. The Sydney Futures Exchange in Australia, for example, trades separate contracts on electricity delivered to the states of New South Wales and Victoria. The first contract on electricity in the UK began trading on the International Petroleum Exchange in 2000. Electricity deregulation also stimulated development of the first coal futures contract, which began trading in 1999.

TABLE 8.6 **Leading energy contracts**
2012

Contract	Exchange	No. traded, m
Brent crude	ICE Futures Europe	147
Light sweet crude	New York Mercantile Exchange	141
Natural gas – Henry Hub	New York Mercantile Exchange	95
Gas oil	ICE Futures Europe	64
Crude oil	Multi-Commodity Exchange of India	58
Gasoline	New York Mercantile Exchange	37
No. 2 heating oil	New York Mercantile Exchange	36
West Texas crude	ICE Futures Europe	33
Natural Gas	Multi-Commodity Exchange of India	28
Natural gas swap – Henry Hub	New York Mercantile Exchange	18

Source: Exchange reports

One interesting innovation in commodity futures trading is environmental futures. A programme in the United States created tradable allowances for the emission of sulphur dioxide starting in 1995, each allowance giving the owner the right to emit 1 American ton (907kg) of sulphur dioxide during or after the specified year. The allowances are auctioned annually at the Chicago Board of Trade and are traded privately after auction. This system encourages firms to reduce emissions in the least costly way, and to use the allowances for pollution sources that would be most costly to mitigate. The main purchasers are electricity utilities and oil refiners. Some governments want to establish similar tradable permits for other categories of air emissions, particularly carbon dioxide, a gas implicated in global warming, which is emitted mainly in the burning of fossil fuels. After the EU imposed caps on industries' emissions of carbon dioxide and other so-called greenhouse gases, the International Petroleum Exchange began trading futures on the price of carbon-dioxide emission rights in April 2005.

Commodity-related futures

As the delivered price of physicals depends greatly upon the cost of transport, there is a demand to hedge freight rates. The Baltic Exchange in London, a centre for arranging bulk shipping, produces indexes of bulk maritime shipping rates, but Euronext ceased trading a futures contract on the Baltic rates index because of lack of volume. Freight futures are traded on the Norwegian Futures and Options Clearinghouse, the Singapore Exchange, the Intercontinental Exchange and the New York Mercantile Exchange.

Exchanges are also developing other non-physical contracts that may be used to hedge commodity prices. The Chicago Mercantile Exchange, for example, began offering contracts on temperatures, useful for hedging agricultural or energy prices, in 1999, and Eurex sells futures contracts designed to manage the risk of damage from hurricanes affecting the United States.

Reading commodity futures price tables

Many newspapers publish data summarising the previous day's commodity trading. Table 8.7 illustrates a typical newspaper price table for a commodity futures contract.

TABLE 8.7 **Reading a commodity futures price table**
Orange Juice (NYBOT)
15,000lb – cents/lb

Month	Open	High	Low	Settle	Change	Lifetime high	Lifetime low	Open interest
Mar 10	100.50	100.50	99.35	99.95	−0.50	127.95	96.10	17,978
May 10	100.65	100.80	99.75	100.50	−0.15	130.00	96.50	4,105
Jul 10	101.20	101.20	100.25	100.80	−0.45	132.00	99.75	2,464
Nov 10	101.75	103.25	101.75	102.40	0.15	132.75	101.75	551
Est vol 2,434		prev vol 2,976		open int 25,863: +627				

According to the heading, this table reports trading in orange juice futures on the New York Board of Trade (NYBOT).

The following line provides two essential pieces of information.

First, one contract covers 15,000lb (6,804kg) of juice. Second, prices are listed in cents per lb, equivalent to 0.454kg. A listed price must therefore be multiplied by 15,000 to obtain the price of a contract in cents, then divided by 100 to obtain the price in dollars. The first column lists the delivery months for which there has been active trading. These are not necessarily the only months available. Many contracts permit trading for delivery months several years into the future, but there is frequently little or no trading for more distant months and therefore no information to publish.

The next four columns list the price of the first trade for each delivery month on the previous day (open), the high and low prices for each delivery month, and the official closing price (settle). As there are often many trades at various prices in the final moments of trading, the settlement price does not purport to be the price of the day's final trade. It is usually a weighted average of the prices of trades immediately before the close of trading, as computed by the exchange. Note that the market is in contango.

The column headed "change" is the difference between the settlement price on this day and that on the previous trading day. May orange juice is $0.0015 per lb lower, so the value of one contract has fallen by $22.50 since the previous day. November juice is 15 hundredths of a cent higher, so a contract worth $15,337.50 at the previous close (15,000 times the price of $1.0225) is now worth $15,360 (15,000 times the price of $1.0240).

"Lifetime high" and "lifetime low" are the highest and lowest prices at which contracts for that delivery month have ever traded, and show that orange juice for future delivery in all four contract months is about 30% cheaper now than it was a few months ago. "Open interest" gives the number of contracts that are still active. Although many other contracts have been sold, in most cases the buyers have liquidated them by buying or selling offsetting contracts. According to these numbers, most trading in orange juice futures occurs within a few months of delivery. The line at the bottom lists the total number of orange juice contracts traded this day and the previous day, the total open interest in all delivery months (including those not listed in this table), and the change in the number of open contracts from the previous day.

Financial futures markets

Financial futures, a comparatively recent innovation, have become popular instruments to hedge the risks of interest-rate changes, exchange-rate movements and share-price changes. The first financial futures, traded on the Chicago Mercantile Exchange in 1972, allowed businesses to control the risks of exchange-rate changes. Hundreds of contracts now trade on exchanges around the world. Global turnover stalled in 1999, but resumed rapid growth in 2001. Worldwide turnover increased fivefold between 2000 and 2008, with especially rapid growth in Europe, where financial futures were slower to develop than in the United States. But trading has declined significantly since 2008 (see Table 8.8).

TABLE 8.8 **Turnover of exchange-traded financial futures**
$trn

	1996	2000	2004	2008	2012
All markets	269	318	832	1,547	1,160
North America	120	151	441	851	620
Europe	86	112	337	591	415
Asia, Australia, New Zealand	60	52	48	89	99
Other markets	3	3	6	16	26

Source: Bank for International Settlements

Trading volume in financial futures now dwarfs volume in commodity futures. All the world's most heavily traded futures contracts involve financial instruments.

Interest-rate futures

The most important category of financial futures allows financial institutions and bond investors to hedge the risk that changes in interest rates will affect the value of their assets. Trading in interest-rate futures accounts for over 90% of all financial futures trading.

The first interest-rate contract, introduced on the Chicago Board

FIG 8.1 **Trading volume in interest-rate futures**
Contracts traded, m

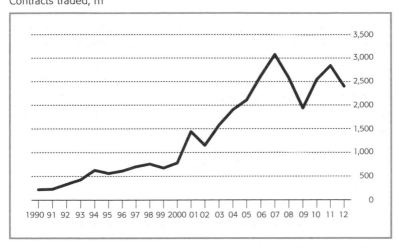

Source: Bank for International Settlements

of Trade in 1975, allowed financial institutions to hedge the risk that changes in interest rates would alter the value of their portfolios of residential mortgages. The first treasury-bill contracts traded in 1976. The success of these contracts led to the creation of financial futures exchanges in Europe during the 1980s. The 3-month Eurodollar contract at the Chicago Mercantile Exchange, tied to interest rates on dollar deposits outside the United States, has long been the most heavily traded financial futures contract. But the market is diverse, with exchanges in Australia, Canada, Malaysia, Spain and dozens of other countries trading contracts on local-currency interest rates. Figure 8.1 traces the growth of the market.

Initially, interest-rate futures were used mainly to hedge changes in long-term interest rates. More recently, contracts on short-term rates have become popular and now account for more than half of all trading in interest-rate futures. Although hedgers use interest-rate futures to limit their losses if rates change, many speculators have found interest-rate futures an efficient way to bet on anticipated interest-rate changes without owning bonds.

To understand how interest-rate futures are used, consider a

Treasury bond contract on the Chicago Board of Trade. The contract is based on a bond with a face value of $100,000 and a nominal interest rate, or coupon, of 6%, and the quoted price is per $1,000. In June 2009 such a bond was trading at a price of about 114, so purchasing a single bond would have cost $114,000 (1.14 × $100,000). Assume that an investor expected long-term interest rates in June 2010 to be lower than in June 2009. It could have purchased a bond for $114,000 and held it for a year, or it could have acquired one bond futures contract for June 2010 delivery, priced at 110.50, by making a down payment of $4,320. Now suppose that a fall in interest rates had caused the price of the bond to rise 1%. The bond would be worth $115,140, and the June 2010 bond future, on its expiration, would be priced at 115.14. The owner of the bond would have:

$1,140 in capital appreciation (1% of the price paid)
+ $6,000 in interest (representing payments of 6% on a $100,000 coupon for 12 months)
= $7,140 total profit
6.26% return on the initial investment

The owner of the futures contract would have:

$4,640 in capital appreciation [(115.14 − 110.50) × 1,000]
− $259.20 forgone interest on the $4,320 down payment at 6% for 12 months
= $4,380.80 total profit
101.4% return on the initial investment

Hence in a rising market the investor in interest-rate futures is able to earn a far better return than an investor in the underlying interest-rate-sensitive securities. Conversely, however, the futures investor in this example would have a much greater loss than the bond investor if interest rates were to fall.

Currency futures

Although exchange-rate contracts are the oldest financial futures, their popularity has remained modest (see Figure 8.2). There are two reasons for this. First, much currency hedging is now done with the use of derivatives contracts that are not traded on exchanges. These contracts

FIG 8.2 **Trading in currency futures**
Number of contracts, m

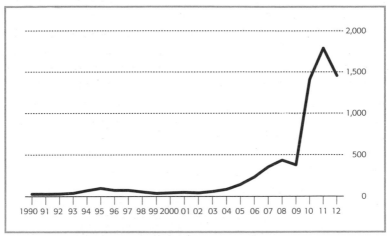

Source: Bank for International Settlements

are discussed in Chapter 9. Second, the stabilisation of exchange rates among 12 European countries in advance of the creation of a single currency, followed by the launch of the euro on January 1st 1999 and the subsequent participation of additional countries, eliminated the demand for contracts on the exchange rates among countries in the euro zone.

Much currency futures trading now takes place on markets in emerging economies. Contracts on the exchange rate between the dollar and the Indian rupee, traded on both the National Stock Exchange of India and the Multi-Commodity Exchange of India, have become the most heavily traded futures contracts in the world. Futures on the exchange rate of the dollar and the Russian rouble and the dollar and the Brazilian real are also heavily traded. Many smaller futures exchanges around the world trade contracts on the exchange rate between the local currency and the dollar or the euro.

Stock-index futures

Contracts on the future level of a particular share index have proven enormously popular among portfolio managers. Their growth has

FIG 8.3 **Stock Index futures trading**
Contracts traded, m

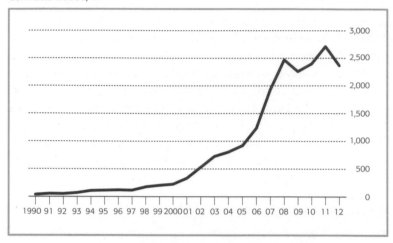

Source: Bank for International Settlements

gone hand in hand with the growth of tracker or index equity funds (discussed in Chapter 6) as they offer a nearly exact hedge for a share portfolio that is constructed to mimic the index. Figure 8.3 shows the growth of the index futures market.

The most popular stock-index futures are those on the Standard & Poor's 500 Index in the United States, the Dow Jones/Euro Stoxx 50 index and the Nikkei 225 index of Japanese stocks. Other important contracts are based on the DAX-30 in Germany, the CAC-40 in France, the FTSE Index in London, the NASDAQ 100 Index in the United States, the Ibovespa in Brazil, the KOSPI in South Korea and the Australian All-Ordinaries Index. A futures contract on the most famous stockmarket indicator of all, the Dow Jones Industrial Average of 30 shares on the New York Stock Exchange, began trading only in 1997 because the index's owner previously opposed its use in futures trading. Stock-index futures are also traded on many smaller exchanges. The Australian Stock Exchange, for example, offers contracts on the ASX 50 and ASX 200 share indexes, and the Oslo Stock Exchange trades futures on its OBX share-price index.

Share-price futures

Many stock exchanges trade futures contracts on the prices of individual shares. A contract based on the future share price of China Telecom, for example, trades on the Hong Kong Futures Exchange. Although many similar contracts exist, few are notably successful as in most cases trading in the underlying equity is not lively enough to sustain interest in a futures contract. Futures on individual shares were permitted in the United States only in 2000; their introduction was delayed for many years because of opposition from stock exchanges, which did not welcome a competing product, as well as fears that speculators could trade share-price futures to circumvent limits on borrowing to buy shares.

Other financial futures

Exchanges have experimented with many different types of contracts to increase demand for futures trading. A contract on corn yields, offered on the Chicago Board of Trade, is based on the US Department of Agriculture's estimates of yields per acre (0.4ha) and allowed farmers and crop insurance companies to hedge the risk of a poor harvest; however, the contract was abandoned because of a lack of interest. Other insurance-related futures contracts are under discussion in the United States and Europe. A futures contract based on the US consumer-price index was abandoned for want of interest in 1988, but more recently futures contracts on inflation-indexed US Treasury bonds have filled a similar role. The Chicago Mercantile Exchange has traded the first contracts on residential property prices, based on the S&P/Case Shiller Home Price Index; the contract is valued at $250 times the index, so loses $250 in value when the index falls by one point. Eurex introduced contracts on UK retail, office and industrial property price indexes in 2011.

Reading financial futures price tables

Price tables for financial futures can be harder to understand than those for commodity futures, because the basis for determining prices is not always clear. Table 8.9, for example, reports futures trading on the Deutsche Aktienindex (DAX), an index of German shares, which is traded on the Eurex exchange. On this trading day investors were more optimistic about the future course of German share prices. To understand the impact upon futures prices, however, it is necessary to consult the contract specifications published by the exchange, which do not accompany the published table. These reveal that the contract is valued at €25 per DAX index point. At this day's closing price, one June DAX contract would cost (5,039 × €25), or €125,975.

TABLE 8.9 **DAX (Eurex)**

Month	Open	High	Low	Settle	Prev close	Change
June 09	5,039.50	5,046.50	5,039.00	5,042.00	5,039.00	+3.00
Sept 09	5,045.00	5,051.50	5,043.50	5,051.50	5,045.00	+6.50
Dec 09	5,050.50	5,062.00	5,049.00	5,059.00	5,049.50	+9.50

The DAX contract obviously cannot be delivered in a physical sense, but must be settled in cash. Suppose that a June DAX contract were to trade at the closing price, and that both the buyer and the seller were to hold the contract until the delivery date – in this case, according to the contract specifications, the third Friday of June. Suppose further that the DAX index on that date were to close at 5,100. The seller of the futures contract, who is short the DAX, would have a loss of [(5,100 − 5,039) × 25], or €1,525, and the buyer of the contract would have a gain of equal amount.

Clearance and settlement

Initiating a futures transaction requires two parties, a buyer and a seller. No trade is possible unless both parties agree to the terms. Once the bargain has been struck, however, the parties have no further responsibilities to one another. The exchange itself acts in place of the buyer for every seller and in place of the seller for all buyers. This facilitates trading in two important ways. First, either party to the original transaction is free to terminate its obligations by taking an offsetting position, without the consent of the other party. Second, no investor needs to worry about the reliability or solvency of any other investor. The exchange guarantees that those whose contracts gain in value receive their money and collect the sums owed by owners of money-losing positions. The organisation that accomplishes this is the exchange's clearing house.

The first step in the clearing house's work is clearing, the process of determining precisely what trades have occurred. This was difficult when most trading occurred on an exchange floor and each floor broker had to record the details of each transaction, including the commodity, quantity, delivery month, price and the broker on the other side of the transaction, immediately after each trade. Exchange employees had to key the information from the floor brokers into a computer, and the two futures commission merchants whose floor brokers made the trade then had to reconcile the data with the reports of the clerks who took and confirmed the customers' orders. The process frequently resulted in "out trades", about which the two futures commission merchants had conflicting information.

The clearing process is far easier on electronic exchanges, because all the relevant information is available on the exchange's trading system at the time the trade occurs. There is thus no opportunity for incorrect information or data-entry errors to enter the system except when brokers enter mistaken bids through typing errors. Trades can often be cleared shortly after they are agreed.

Once the clearing process has been completed, the clearing house and the banking system can proceed with settlement, the process of matching payments with futures-market positions. Settlement is a far more complex process on futures exchanges than on stockmarkets, because of the exchange's role in ensuring that market participants live up to their commitments.

A margin of security

Before buying or selling a futures contract, an investor is required to deposit a down payment, known as a performance bond or initial margin, with the futures commission merchant. If the futures commission merchant is a clearing member of the exchange, it must, in turn, place a variation margin or settlement variation on deposit with the clearing house. If it is not a clearing member, the futures commission merchant must maintain an account with a clearing member, which takes financial responsibility for its trades.

The minimum initial margin required of an investor is set by the exchange, although the futures commission merchant can require a larger amount. The exchange also sets a lesser maintenance margin or variation margin, the minimum the investor is required to have on deposit at all times. The amounts depend on the contract and on whether the investor is a hedger or a speculator. In 2013, for example, the initial margin required of a speculator in the Chicago Mercantile Exchange live cattle contract was $1,350 per contract and the maintenance margin was $1,000, at a time when the value of one contract was about $60,000. Margin requirements are often lower if an investor has bought and sold different months of the same contract, so that some positions are likely to increase in value if others decrease. The idea is that the investor should always have sufficient margin on deposit to cover potential losses.

Marking to market

As part of the settlement process following each day's trading at most exchanges, the futures commission merchant recalculates the margin required of each investor. Each investor's contracts are marked to market, or revalued based on the latest settlement price. If an investor's holdings have lost value, money from the investor's account is transferred into the accounts of investors whose holdings have gained in value. Each clearing member's entire customer portfolio is marked to market in the same way. If the total value of all its customers' contracts declines, the clearing member must pay an additional variation margin to the clearing house. Conversely, money is transferred from the clearing house into the accounts of clearing members, futures commission merchants and individual customers whose contracts have gained in value.

Margin calls

In this way, every participant in trading at the exchange is forced to recognise all gains or losses after each day's trading. The clearing house itself, at least in theory, is protected from loss because each clearing member is responsible for keeping its own customers' accounts in balance. The initial margin keeps an individual investor from running up large unrecognised losses and then defaulting on payment. If the amount in a customer's account falls below the maintenance margin, the futures commission merchant issues a margin call, demanding that the investor immediately deposit enough funds to meet the initial margin. The futures commission merchant will liquidate the investor's contracts if the funds are not forthcoming. Conversely, if the amount in the account rises above the initial margin, the investor may withdraw the excess, use it as margin for other futures trades, or simply leave it on deposit.

Even then ...

This system, unfortunately, is not foolproof. Clearing members are often subsidiaries of diversified financial firms, and it is possible that the financial problems of its parent could cause a clearing member to collapse. The clearing member is supposed to keep investors' funds strictly segregated from its own trading accounts so there will be no loss to investors should the firm collapse, but firms in financial distress may be tempted to violate this rule. This occurred in 2011, when MF Global, a US firm, filed for bankruptcy protection after its trading strategy failed; the company was revealed to have used customer funds to bolster its position, although almost all of that money was eventually recovered. Despite their shortcomings, exchange clearing houses have generally worked well. The biggest scandal in exchange-traded futures was the $2.6 billion loss suffered by Sumitomo, a Japanese trading company, in 1996. This sum was lost as a result of improper trading on the London Metal Exchange, one of the few exchanges that did not require investors to meet variation margins with cash on a daily basis. It appears that exchange rules and the clearing-house structure protected futures-market investors from loss in the October 2005 bankruptcy of Refco, which owned one of the largest US futures brokerages.

Cross-margining

Some exchanges have begun to allow cross-margining, in which investors are effectively allowed to use a single account to trade on more than one exchange. Gains in contracts on one exchange may then be used to offset losses on another exchange in determining the amount of margin required, generally reducing the amount of money the investor needs to keep on deposit. The ability to offer cross-margining is one of the main factors encouraging mergers and co-operative agreements among exchanges.

Delivery

As a contract approaches its delivery date, the issue of physical delivery must be resolved. For the buyer of a futures contract, physical delivery means taking possession of the underlying assets; for the seller, it means providing those assets. The specifications of some contracts, particularly financial futures, do not permit physical delivery, and even when it is possible investors rarely desire it. Only 1–2% of all futures contracts lead to physical delivery. Most futures investors choose cash settlement, either before or on expiry, and receive the current market value of the underlying assets rather than the assets themselves.

If the seller of an expiring contract wishes to deliver the commodity, it must provide the exchange with notice of intention to deliver several days before the contract expires. The commodity must be transported to and unloaded at a delivery point acceptable under the contract specifications, at the seller's expense. Exchanges maintain approved warehouses for this purpose.

If the buyer of a futures contract wishes to take physical delivery, it must notify the exchange at the time of contract expiry. Even in the rare event that both the buyer and the seller of a contract want physical delivery, the buyer will not receive the particular goods delivered by the seller. Instead, the exchange will determine the order in which buyers may take possession of commodities that have been delivered to it.

Trading strategies

Investors in the futures markets often pursue complex strategies involving the trading of different futures contracts simultaneously. The following are among the best-known strategies for futures trading:

■ **Basis trading.** Also known as exchange of futures for physicals, this involves the simultaneous purchase of the asset underlying a futures contract and the sale of an offsetting contract in the futures market, or vice versa. An investor who has bought the physicals and sold the futures is said to be long the basis; one who has bought futures and sold physicals is short the basis. The aim of the strategy is to profit from changes in the relationship between the spot price of the physicals and the price of the futures contracts.

■ **Dynamic hedging.** This involves constant changes in a futures position in response to changes in the price of the underlying asset and the rate at which the price of the underlying asset is changing.

■ **Index arbitrage.** When someone seeks to capitalise on moment-to-moment changes in the price relationship between a share index and the futures contract on that index, by simultaneously buying the shares in the index and selling the futures, or vice versa.

■ **Spreads.** A spread is a position constructed in the expectation that the relationship between two prices will change. There are many varieties. An intra-commodity spread involves contracts in two different commodities with approximately the same delivery date and could be used to speculate, for example, that cattle prices will rise more quickly than hog prices over the next three months. An international spread might bet that the difference between petroleum futures prices in New York and in London will widen or narrow. A quality differential spread concerns the price difference between two qualities of the same commodity, such as the northern spring wheat traded in Chicago and the hard red spring wheat traded in Minneapolis.

- **Straddles.** A straddle is a type of spread that involves purchasing a contract for one delivery month while selling a contract for another delivery month of the same commodity, thereby betting on a change in the relationship between short-term and longer-term prices. A bear spread is a straddle arranged with the intention of profiting from an expected price decline but limiting the potential loss if the expectation proves wrong. This is accomplished by selling a nearby delivery month and buying a more distant month. A bull spread is the reverse operation, designed to profit from a rise in prices while limiting the potential loss by buying contracts for a nearby delivery month and selling a more distant month.

- **Strips.** A strip, also called a calendar strip, is the simultaneous purchase or sale of futures positions in consecutive months.

Measuring performance

The prices of particular physical commodities may vary greatly over time. In general, however, the prices of many physical commodities rise or fall in response to general economic conditions. When world economic growth is strong, there is greater demand for metals, timber, petroleum and other products used in construction or manufacturing. The prices of various petroleum futures contracts rose sharply in the first half of 2008, then fell through early 2009 as the world economy weakened, while the prices of cocoa, sugar and grain contracts held fairly steady.

Several indexes attempt to track the movement of commodities prices overall. The best known are those published by *The Economist*, the *Journal of Commerce* and Goldman Sachs, an investment bank, as well as the Reuters/Jeffries Commodities Research Bureau Index. Investors who wish to speculate on or hedge against movements in the average price of commodities can trade futures contracts on the Goldman Sachs Commodity Index (GSCI) at the Chicago Mercantile Exchange.

The performance of futures contracts over time cannot be measured in an aggregate way. In an individual case, one investor's profit from having purchased a contract will be offset by another investor's loss from having sold the contract. Besides, investors who use futures contracts to hedge are concerned not about the performance of the contract itself, but about the performance of their overall investment, including the asset hedged. If it reduced the investor's risk, a futures contract that lost money is frequently deemed to have been a worthwhile investment.

Exchange-traded options

Until the 1970s there were no option markets. Although some speculators arranged option trades privately, regulators regarded option trading as a dubious and even dangerous activity, intended mainly to defraud innocent investors. This characterisation was not far from the mark, as option trading was completely unregulated. It came of age only in 1973, when officials in the United States approved a plan by the Chicago Board of Trade, a futures exchange, to launch an options exchange. The Chicago Board Options Exchange (CBOE) began by offering options on the shares of 16 companies.

Since then, as investors have increasingly turned to financial markets to help manage risk, option trading has become hugely popular. The face value of contracts traded on option exchanges worldwide rose from $52 trillion in 1996 to $666 trillion in 2008 before declining to $409 trillion in 2012.

Underlying every option

The world's many option exchanges compete to offer contracts that will be attractive to investors. Every option is based on the price of some instrument that is not traded in the options market. This instrument is known as the underlying. Each contract has a precisely defined underlying, a standard size and a variety of expiration dates, typically monthly or quarterly.

Puts, calls – the long and the short of it

Although the exchange sets the ground rules for each contract, an option is created only when two parties, a buyer and a writer, strike a deal. The buyer pays the writer a premium, determined by market forces, in return for the rights inherent in the option. These rights take one of two basic forms. A put option entitles the buyer to sell the underlying at an agreed price, known as the strike price, for a specific period of time. A call option gives the buyer the right to purchase the underlying at the strike price. In other words, the buyer of a put, who is said to be long the put, expects the price of the underlying to fall by a given amount, and the writer, who is short the put, thinks that the price of the underlying will fall less or not at all. Conversely, the buyer of a call anticipates that the price of the underlying will rise above the strike price and the writer thinks it will not.

Winners and losers

If the price of the underlying changes as the buyer expects – that is, if the price falls below the strike price (in the case of a put) or rises above the strike price (in the case of a call) – the option is said to be in the money. Otherwise, the option is out of the money. If oil is trading at $90 per barrel, for example, a call option at 95 is out of the money and not worth exercising, as it is less costly to purchase the oil in the open market than to purchase it at the strike price; if the oil price rises to $100 per barrel, however, the option will be in the money and will almost certainly be exercised. Note, however, that an in-the-money option is not necessarily profitable for the buyer or unprofitable for the writer. The buyer has paid a premium to the writer, and unless the difference between the strike price and the market price of the underlying exceeds the premium, it is the writer, not the buyer, who comes out ahead.

Types of options

The underlying may be almost anything that is actively traded in a market where the current price is continuously available and indisputable. For this reason, options markets often operate on the same schedule as the markets where the underlying instruments are traded, and close when the underlying stops trading. The most widely traded types of options are described below.

Equity options

An equity option entitles the owner to buy or sell a certain number of common shares (100 is standard in most countries) in a particular company. An equity option is not a security of the company on whose shares the options are being traded; the company itself does not issue the options and receives no money for them, and the owner of the options does not receive dividends or vote on company business. If an option is eventually exercised, the owner will end up acquiring or selling the underlying shares. Equity options offer a far more economical way to speculate on share prices than purchasing the underlying shares. They may also be used to hedge positions, as when an investor owns shares and purchases a put option so as to be assured of a price at which the shares may be sold.

Index options

An index option is based on an index of prices in some market other than options. Share-price indexes are most popular, but any index will suffice as long as its value is continuously determined in a market. Thus options are traded on the Goldman Sachs Commodity Index (Chicago Mercantile Exchange), a US municipal bond index (Chicago Board of Trade), the Reuters/Commodity Research Board Index (New York Board of Trade) and the South Korean stockmarket index (Korea Futures Exchange). Each option is based on the index times a multiple. The Chicago Mercantile Exchange's option on the Standard & Poor's 500 stock index, for example, is valued at $250 times the index. This means that if the S&P is at 1,300, one contract has a nominal value of $250 \times 1,300 = \$325,000$. The nominal value, although large, has little practical importance; a market participant stands to lose or gain only the gap between the strike price and the market price of the underlying. If an investor purchases an S&P 1,300 call and the index reaches 1,305, the owner's gain and the writer's loss from the price change will be 5 points $\times$ $250/point, or $1,250. Unlike options on individual equities, an index option cannot be settled by delivery, as the index cannot be purchased. The owner of the profitable call would therefore receive a cash payment rather than stock, and the writer would make a cash payment rather than handing over shares.

Worldwide turnover in stockmarket index options reached $167 trillion in 2011 and $97 trillion in 2012, compared with less than $19 trillion in 2000. Trading in stock index options in India and China has been growing quickly, although the Futures Industry Association observed that volume in Indian stock index options has been driven by incentives offered by the exchanges and may not be sustained. Table 8.10 shows the most heavily traded contracts.

TABLE 8.10 **Leading stock index options contracts**
2012

Contract	Exchange	No. traded, m
Kospi 200 Stock Index	Korea Exchange	1,575
S&P CNX Nifty	National Stock Exchange of India	803
SPDR S&P 500	multiple	586
Euro Stoxx 50	Eurex	280
S&P 500	Chicago Board Options Exchange	174
Sensex	Bombay Stock Exchange	148
iShares Russell 2000	multiple	125
Powershares QQQ ETC	multiple	114
VIX	Chicago Board Options Exchange	110
Taiex	Taiwan Futures Exchange	108

Interest-rate options

These come in two varieties:

- **Bond options** are based on the price of a government bond, which moves inversely to interest rates. Their nominal value is set equal to the current market value of bonds with a specified par value; the Bund option traded on Eurex is based upon a German government bond with a face value of €100,000.

- **Yield options** are based on an interest rate itself, but because interest rates are typically low the nominal value of a yield option is often set by deducting the interest rate from 100. Thus the nominal value of one option on Euro Libor, a short-term interbank interest rate, is equal to €1m × (100 − the rate), and the nominal value falls as the interest rate rises.

Interest-rate options offer a less costly way to speculate on interest-rate movements than the purchase of bonds. An investor who owns bonds can use interest-rate options to protect against a loss in value, and one who has chosen not to buy bonds can use options to avoid forgoing profits should bond prices rise. Interest-rate options are usually settled in cash. Worldwide turnover in interest-rate options peaked at $522 trillion in 2008 and reached $309 trillion in 2012, compared with $47.4 trillion in 2000.

Commodity options

Options are traded on many commodities, from greasy wool (Sydney Futures Exchange) to gas oil (ICE Futures Europe). If the underlying commodity is continuously traded, for example gold, the option may be based directly on the commodity's price. Most commodities, however, do not trade continuously in markets where there is a single posted price. It is therefore necessary to base most commodity option contracts on futures-market prices, as these are posted and trade continuously. For example, as actual bags of Brazilian coffee may change hands irregularly and in private, the arabica coffee option on the Bolsa de Mercadorias & Futuros in Brazil is based on the market price of arabica futures rather than the price of actual coffee. Commodity option contracts can usually be settled either in cash or with an exchange of the underlying commodity. An estimated 57m commodity option contracts were outstanding worldwide in 2013.

Currency options

Currency options are based on the exchange rate between two currencies. Their nominal value is the amount of one currency required to purchase a given amount of the other; thus the nominal value of one Canadian dollar option on the NASDAQ OMX, formerly the Philadelphia Stock Exchange, is the amount of US dollars required to purchase C$50,000. The price of an option, however, may be expressed differently. NASDAQ OMX's Canadian dollar options are priced in US cents per Canadian dollar. To sort through this confusion,

FIG 8.4 **Exchange traded options**
Contracts traded, m

Sources: Bank for International Settlements; Futures Industry Association

assume that an investor owned a C$96 option and the Canadian dollar strengthened to 97. The owner could exercise the call and earn:

$$[(US\$0.97 - US\$0.96) \div C\$1] \times C\$50,000 = US\$500$$

As well as options on currencies, some exchanges trade option contracts based on exchange-rate futures. In general, however, interest in exchange-traded currency options has been weak as market participants have favoured over-the-counter derivatives instead. Although they account for about 5% of the number of options contracts traded on exchanges worldwide, currencies represent only a tiny share of the value of option contracts.

Figure 8.4 shows the worldwide trading volume in the main types of options.

New types of options

Growing competition from the over-the-counter market has made option exchanges introduce two important types of new products:

- **LEAPS,** an acronym for long-term equity participation securities, are simply a form of long-term option. Whereas regular options usually expire within a 12-month period, leaps may have expiration dates up to three years in the future.

- **Flex options** are a way for traders to customise the contracts they trade to meet the needs of big institutional users. Usually, this involves setting an expiration date other than the ones that are standard for the option, or setting a strike price between two prices offered on the exchange, or both.

Gains and losses

On balance, an option contract produces no net gain or loss. Rather, one party's gain is necessarily equal to the other party's loss. The premium represents the maximum loss for the buyer and the maximum gain for the writer. A put owner's maximum gain – and writer's maximum loss – occurs when the underlying loses all value. There is theoretically no limit to the potential profit of a call owner or the loss of a call writer, as the price of the underlying can increase without limit. To limit their losses, some investors prefer to write calls only when they already own the underlying security – so-called covered calls – rather than riskier uncovered or "naked" calls.

To see how this works, consider options in Pfizer, a drugs manufacturer whose shares are listed on the New York Stock Exchange. One day in 2009, when Pfizer shares traded at $15.59, the September 2009 Pfizer 16.00 put option traded on the Chicago Board Options Exchange at $1.01. That is, in return for a premium of $101 ($1.01 per share × 100 shares) the buyer obtained the right to sell 100 shares of Pfizer at $16.00 on or before the third Friday in September, the expiration date, and the writer committed itself to purchase shares at that price. Had Pfizer shares risen above 16.00 over the period, the put option would have expired worthless, leaving the writer with a $101 profit. Had the shares fallen to $15.50, the buyer of the put option could have earned $50 by purchasing 100 Pfizer shares on the stockmarket and selling, or putting, them for $16.00. Counting the initial $101 premium, however, the buyer would have suffered a net loss of $51. The breakeven point, at which neither the buyer nor

the writer would have made a profit, was $16.00 − $1.01 = $14.99.
At any share price below $14.99, the put would have returned a profit to the buyer of the option. The buyer's maximum profit would have occurred had Pfizer shares lost all value. The shares would then have been obtained for $0 and put at $16.00, thus earning a profit of

$$[100\ (\$16) - 100\ (\$0)] - 100\ (\$1.01) = \$1,499$$

and the writer would have lost the identical amount.

Styles

Options are traded in three basic styles:

- **American-style options** can be exercised at any time before their expiration date. The owner of an American-style call, for example, can exercise the option whenever the price of the underlying shares exceeds the strike price.

- **European-style options**, in contrast, can be exercised only at or near the expiration date. If the price of a share were to rise briefly above the strike price but then fall back before the expiration date, the owner of an American-style call could exercise it at a profit, but the owner of a European-style call could not. The exchange determines whether its option contracts will be American or European style, although some exchanges trade both simultaneously.

- **Capped options** have a predetermined cap price, which is above the strike price for a call and below the strike price for a put. The option is automatically exercised when the underlying closes at or above (for a call) or at or below (for a put) the cap price.

Expiration dates

The date on which an option contract expires is set by the exchange. Most contracts have four expiration dates a year, the number being limited to create as much trading volume as possible in each contract. The exchange usually staggers the expiration dates of various options to keep overall trading volume fairly constant through the year. Some contracts with heavy trading have monthly expiration dates.

Triple-witching days

In the case of equity-index options, contract expiration dates are often marked by heavy trading of options and shares. Several times a year equity options, equity-index options and equity-index futures expire at the same time. These Fridays have become known as triple-witching days. During the 1980s triple-witching days were marked by heavy trading and sharp price movements near the close of stockmarket trading, but this phenomenon has become far less severe in recent years.

Motivations for options trading

Investors choose to trade options for one of five main reasons:

- **Risk management.** Options can allow the user to reduce or eliminate certain kinds of risks while retaining others. An engineering company signing a contract to supply automotive components at a fixed price might purchase calls on aluminium on the London Metal Exchange, thus locking in the price of an important raw material without using its capital to amass a stockpile of aluminium.

- **Hedging.** An option contract can be used to reduce or eliminate the risk that an asset will lose value. For example, an institutional investor with a large holding of German government bonds, known as Bunds, might buy Bund puts on the Eurex exchange. The puts would allow the investor to continue to own the bonds, profiting from interest payments and possible price appreciation, while protecting against a severe price drop.

- **Leveraged speculation.** Many investors favour options because a given amount of money can be employed to make a greater bet on the price of the underlying. Consider, for example, an investor that expects British share prices to rise. Purchasing each of the 100 shares in the Financial Times Stock Exchange Index (the FTSE 100) would require a large amount of cash. Investors in options, however, are required to pay only the premium, not the value of the underlying. Thus, for the same amount of money needed to buy a few shares of each firm in the FTSE, the investor could acquire enough FTSE options to earn a much larger profit if the index rises. (Of course, the owner of the options, unlike a shareholder, would receive no dividends, and would profit only if the stock index reached the specified level before the expiry of the options.)

■ **Arbitrage.** Arbitrageurs seek to profit from discrepancies in prices in different markets. Options arbitrageurs watch for changes in an option's premium or in the price of its underlying, and buy when one seems out of line with the other. Price discrepancies are usually short-lived, so an arbitrageur may open a position by purchasing an option and then close the position by selling the option within a matter of minutes.

■ **Income.** Many large investors write options that are covered by holdings in their portfolios to obtain additional income. For example, an investor owning thousands of shares in Deutsche Bank, valued at €47 per share, might write Deutsche Bank 55 calls. If the bank's shares do not reach the strike price, the investor receives a premium; if they do reach the strike price, the investor must sell the shares on which it has written options but will still enjoy €8 per share of price appreciation plus the premium. Thus writing covered options is a low-risk, income-oriented strategy, unlike writing uncovered options, which can be risky.

Option exchanges

Dozens of exchanges around the world trade option contracts. In some cases, stock exchanges also trade option contracts; in some cases, futures contracts and option contracts are traded on the same exchange; in other cases, an exchange may specialise almost exclusively in options. In almost every country there are option contracts based on the local stockmarket index and on the exchange rate of the local currency. The contract on the South Korean stock index, traded on the Korea Exchange, is by far the most widely traded option contract in the world.

Competition and the cost of technology have forced many option

TABLE 8.11 **Competition in options: QQQ trading**

Exchange	May 2009		May 2013	
	Contracts traded	Market share	Contracts traded	Market share, %
Chicago Board Options Exchange	1,314,883	34	3,650,322	19
International Securities Exchange	758,606	20	3,895,438	20
Philadelphia Stock Exchange	445,655	12	2,646,080	14
NASDAQ	379,449	10	1,538,036	8
NYSE Arca (formerly Pacific Exchange)	372,355	10	2,209,750	11
Boston Options Exchange	310,563	8	222,042	1
American Stock Exchange	240,097	7	3,111,946	16
BATS			719,194	4
C2 (CBOE)			1,153,062	6
MIAX			40,082	0
NOBO (Nasdaq OMX Group)			288,266	1

Source: Options Clearing Corporation

exchanges to merge, to join forces with equity or futures exchanges or to form alliances. The Intercontinental Exchange, which acquired NYSE Euronext in 2013, has brought options trading in European interest rates and US and European energy futures under a single roof and also controls the former American Stock Exchange and Pacific Stock Exchange, both of which were early leaders in equity options trading. The NASDAQ OMX Group acquired the Philadelphia Stock Exchange, which specialised in options, in 2005. Canadian financial exchanges agreed in 1999 to centralise option trading in Montreal, and the Swiss and German exchanges merged. The South Korean stock and futures exchanges merged in 2005. The big financial firms, which are present on all the main exchanges, strongly favour such consolidation to reduce their costs.

In the past, a particular option was typically traded on a single exchange. Exchanges are increasingly competing head-to-head. Options on euro interest rates, only slightly different from one another, trade in London, Frankfurt, Paris, Madrid and elsewhere, and several European exchanges have been developing commodity option contracts to compete with those traded on US exchanges. In the United States, regulators have forced the option exchanges to abandon the practice of trading each equity option on only one exchange; options on the Russell 2000, an index of small-company stocks, trade on the New York Stock Exchange's ARCA options exchange, the Chicago Board Options Exchange, Eurex's International Securities Exchange, NASDAQ OMX Group's Philadelphia Stock Exchange, the Boston Options Exchange (controlled by the Toronto Stock Exchange) and the Pacific Exchange. The heavily traded option contract on NASDAQ 100 stock index tracking shares, known as the QQQ option, initiated on the American Stock Exchange in 1999, now trades on 11 exchanges, and the entry of new exchanges has reduced the market shares of some established exchanges (see Table 8.11).

How options are traded

Options can be traded either by open outcry or electronically. Open-outcry trading, which is now uncommon, occurs on an exchange floor, where traders gather in a pit or ring. A ring may be devoted to a single contract or to several different ones, depending upon the volume. In either case, puts and calls for all the available expiration months and all available strike prices are traded simultaneously, and traders quote the premium they would charge for a particular expiration month and strike price. On an electronic trading system, bids and offers are submitted over computer links, and the computer system matches up buyers and writers.

Obtaining price information

Price information about option contracts is readily available from electronic information systems and on websites operated by the exchanges. Option prices can change quickly, however, and investors who are not privy to the most recent information about bids and offers are at a distinct disadvantage.

Table 8.12 reports on trading in options on the shares of Intel Corporation. The previous day's closing share price, in the left-hand column, was $28.55. The second column gives the various strike prices available on that option. The exchange normally creates new strike prices at regular intervals, so if Intel shares were to fall significantly there would be new prices added at 22.50 and 20. As indicated by the column headed "Exp.", almost all of the trading was for options expiring in March or April. Although market participants are permitted to trade options expiring up to nine months ahead, trading for distant months is typically light or non-existent.

TABLE 8.12 **Understanding an option price table**

Option/ Strike	Exp.	Call		Put	
		Vol.	Last	Vol.	Last
Intel	25.00	Jul	−136	5.60	1,946	1.75
28.55	25.00	Oct	−11	6.50	1,480	2.35
28.55	27.50	Mar	−592	1.95	2,995	0.85
28.55	27.50	Apr	170	3.00	3,569	1.75
28.55	30.00	Mar	7,003	0.60	7,245	2.10
28.55	30.00	Apr	4,842	1.55	26,479	2.90
28.55	30.00	Jul	3,975	2.80	2,625	3.90
28.55	32.50	Mar	3,800	0.20	30,159	4.00
28.55	32.50	Apr	5,345	0.75	28,140	4.50
28.55	35.00	Mar	3,410	0.05	267	6.30

Just before the close of trading on this date, a March Intel 30 call could have been purchased for a premium of $0.60. Prices and premiums are given per share; the buyer of such a call would have paid $60.00 for the right to buy 100 Intel shares at $30 each. This was a popular option: 7,003 March 30 calls were purchased on this day. As is normally the case, options at strike prices more distant from the current market price, at $32.50 and $35.00, were far cheaper than options close to the money. The number of calls traded above the current price was greater than the number of puts traded below the strike price, indicating that investors were generally expecting Intel shares to move higher before March.

Factors affecting option prices

Unlike bond and equity traders, option traders are not concerned with fundamentals, such as industry structure or the earnings of a particular firm. Rather, option-market participants focus on the relationship between the value of an option, as expressed by the premium, and the price of the underlying asset. One reason option markets were slow to develop is that it was difficult to know what constituted fair value. The value depends heavily on the likelihood that the option will be exercised, but not until 1973, with the publication of the Black-Scholes option-pricing model, did it become possible to attach precise quantitative estimates to this likelihood. Several pricing models, including refined versions of Black-Scholes, are now in widespread use. As a result, option trading has become a highly mathematical affair in which traders rely on massive amounts of data and intensive computer modelling to identify particular options that are attractively priced.

The main variables option traders use to evaluate prices are described below.

Intrinsic value

The intrinsic value of an option is simply the extent to which the option is in the money. If a company's shares are trading at 110, the 105 call has an intrinsic value of 5, because immediately upon purchase the call could be exercised for a profit of $5 per share. The premium must be greater than the intrinsic value or the writer will have no incentive to sell an option. If an option is presently out of the money, its intrinsic value is zero.

Time value

The longer the time until an option expires, the greater is the likelihood that the purchaser will be able to exercise the option. This time value is reflected in the option's price. In Table 8.12, for example, March Intel 30 puts traded at 2.10, whereas July Intel 30 puts were trading at 3.90. The substantial price difference, equal to $1.80 per share, is the time value the market places on the additional four months before expiration of the July put. Market professionals devote great effort to calculating the rate of time decay, denoted by the Greek letter θ (theta), which is the rate at which an option loses value from one day to the next. As an option approaches its expiration date, its time value approximates zero.

Volatility

Volatility refers to the frequency and magnitude of changes in the price of the underlying. It can be measured in a number of different ways, of which the most common is the standard deviation of daily price changes over a given period of time. To see why volatility matters so much for the price of an option, consider two different shares trading at $12. If one frequently rises or falls by $2 in a single day and the other rarely moves by more than 50 cents, there is a far greater probability that the more volatile share will reach any given strike price, and all options on that share will therefore have higher premiums than options on the other share.

One of the difficult issues options traders must face is deciding how much history to incorporate in their analyses of volatility. One firm might offer to write a given option for a lower premium than another firm because it looks at the volatility of the underlying asset over a longer period of time. Of course, it may well be that both firms' estimates prove wrong, as future volatility may prove to be very different from past volatility. The expected volatility of any option also has a term structure that can be calculated; the volatility of a particular call expiring two months hence would probably not be identical to the volatility of that same call expiring in five months' time. Students of the market can derive a firm's expectation of the future, known as implied volatility, from the premiums it quotes.

Delta

Represented by the Greek letter δ, delta is the change in the value of an option that is associated with a given change in the price of the underlying asset. If a 1% change in the price of the underlying currency or stockmarket index is associated with a 1% change in the value of the option, the option would have a delta of 1.00. The delta of a put option is the negative of the delta of a call option on the same underlying. Delta is not constant, but changes as the price of the underlying changes. With all other things remaining the same, an option with a low delta will have a lower premium than one with a high delta, because a change in the price of the underlying will have little effect on the option's value.

Gamma

Represented by the Greek letter γ, gamma is the rate at which an option's delta changes as the price of the underlying asset changes. Gamma is calculated as the change in delta divided by the change in the price of the underlying. A positive gamma means that a small change in the price of the underlying will cause a larger change in the value of the option than delta alone would predict. A negative gamma means that the rate of change in delta gets smaller as delta gets further away from the starting point.

Rho

Represented by the Greek letter ρ, rho is the expected change in an option's price in response to a percentage-point change in the risk-free interest rate – normally the interest rate on government bonds.

Vega

Also known by the Greek letter kappa (κ), vega refers to the change in an option's price, expressed in currency terms, in response to a percentage point change in volatility. A high vega, other things remaining the same, would make an option more costly.

Hedging strategies

Most options-market trading occurs as part of investors' broader strategies, often involving multiple types of financial instruments. The simplest strategy is a basic hedge, in which an investor purchases an asset and simultaneously buys a put option on that asset, guaranteeing a price at which the asset can be sold if its market price drops. Many strategies are far more complex.

Covering yourself

Writing covered calls or puts is a risk-minimising strategy. Covered means that the writer of the options already owns the underlying. To write a covered put, the writer would have to have a short position in the underlying, having borrowed the asset and then sold it in the expectation that the price would fall before it needed to replace the asset it had borrowed. Suppose, for example, that the writer sells short a share that is trading at $50 and must repay the share three months hence. The writer might then sell puts on the same shares with a strike price of $45. If the share price drops below $45, the writer may lose money on the put but make money by purchasing the shares it shorted at a much lower price. If the share price drops below $50 but stays above $45, the writer earns a premium on the put, which cannot be exercised, as well as making money on the short sale. If the share price rises modestly, the writer will lose money on the short sale of shares, but may earn enough from the premium on the unexercised put to cover that loss. Only a large increase in the share price would cause the writer to lose money. Similarly, writing covered calls involves writing calls on assets the writer owns, or is long on.

Baring all

The opposite strategy is to write naked calls or puts. Naked means that the writer has neither a short nor a long position in the underlying. Naked options offer the potential for higher returns than covered options, as the writer is spared the expense of investing in the underlying. However, writing naked options is a risky activity. The potential loss for the writer of a naked put is the difference between the nominal value of the option at the strike price and zero. The potential loss for the writer of a naked call is unlimited, because, at least in principle, there is no upper limit governing how high the price of an asset can climb.

Straddling

A straddle positions the investor to benefit either from high price volatility or from low price volatility. A buyer who is said to have a long straddle simultaneously takes put and call options expiring at the same time at the same strike price. For example, if the DAX is now trading at 5,085, an investor might purchase both a May 5,100 DAX put and a May 5,100 DAX call. The straddle would pay off if the DAX either falls or rises substantially. On the downside, for the straddle to be profitable the DAX would have to fall far enough below 5,100 that the investor's gain would more than cover its premiums. On the upside, the DAX would have to exceed 5,100 by a wide enough margin to pay the premiums. At any DAX value between those two points the investor would lose, even though one of the two options would be in the money. However, the writer who is said to have a short straddle profits as long as the DAX remains between those two points; the writer loses only if the index becomes more volatile than anticipated, marking a larger loss or a larger decline.

Spreading

A spread position involves two options on the same underlying, similar to a straddle, except that the put and the call expire at different times or have different strike prices.

Turbo charging

A turbo option involves the purchase of two options with different strike prices on the same side of the market, such as calls at both 55 and 60 or puts at both 40 and 35. This strategy enables the investor to earn dramatically higher returns if the price of the underlying moves far into the money.

Dynamic hedging

Dynamic hedging involves continuously realigning a hedge as the price of the underlying changes. It is widely used by large institutional investors. One of the most popular variants is delta hedging, which attempts to balance an entire portfolio of investments so that its delta is zero. The hedge is said to be dynamic because as the stocks and/or bonds in the portfolio change in value, the options position must also be changed to maintain a delta of zero. The investor must therefore continuously buy or sell options or securities. Critics charge that dynamic hedging destabilises financial markets. Keeping delta at zero often requires the investor to sell the underlying asset at a time when its price is falling or to buy when the price is rising, making market swings sharper. Portfolio insurance, a dynamic hedging strategy that purported to protect against falls in the value of stock portfolios, was briefly popular in the 1980s until a key assumption underlying the strategy – that it would always be possible to purchase new options as share prices changed – proved incorrect.

Clearing and settlement

Each option exchange operates or authorises a clearing house, a financial institution set up to ensure that all parties live up to their commitments. Once a trade has been completed, exchange rules normally require the buyer to deposit enough money with an options broker to pay the entire premium; the writer will receive the premium payment through its broker. Each broker, in turn, has an account with the clearing house, and must have enough money on deposit at the end of each day to cover the cost of the transactions it has handled. Settlement occurs when the money from buyer and writer passes through the clearing house.

Once the trade is made, there is no further connection between the buyer and the writer. Instead, the exchange itself steps in as the counterparty for each trade, removing any risk that the owner of a profitable position will fail to collect from the owner of a losing position. In most cases, the exchange's clearing house requires that each option position be marked to market each day. This means that any change in the option's market price is reflected as an increase or decrease in the value of the customer's position, and the customer will be asked to deposit additional funds if the position has lost value. If the customer fails to comply, its positions will be liquidated. The buyer of an exchange-traded option thus has no need to worry about the reliability or creditworthiness of the writer.

Terminating options

An option can be terminated in several ways. The most common is by selling or buying an offsetting option. For example, the owner of a March 1.60 sterling put on NASDAQ OMX PHLX in Philadelphia would write a March 1.60 sterling put; the offsetting positions would be closed out, with the investor recording a gain or a loss depending upon whether the put it wrote had a higher premium than the one it bought. Similarly, an investor who is short a call would close out the position by buying the identical call.

Another way to terminate an option is by exercising it. The owner of an American-style option may exercise it whenever it is in the money, but is not obliged to; the owner of an equity call at 55 may exercise as soon as the shares reach 55, or may hold on to the option in the hope that the stock will go even higher (and take the risk that it will fall back below 55, taking the option out of the money). Depending on the contract, the exchange will settle with the investor in cash or by exchanging the underlying. The exchange may force an investor with an opposing contract to settle. The owner of a Ford Motor Company put, for example, might wish to exercise the put, but the exchange will not want to own those shares. It will therefore select the writer of a similar Ford Motor Company put, usually at random, and require the writer to accept and pay for the shares.

Alternatively, the option can be held to expiration. Some option contracts, including all index contracts, are settled at expiration for cash, with the holder of a money-losing position paying the exchange, and the exchange in turn paying the holder of a profitable position. Many equity and commodity options, however, are settled with the exchange of the underlying. Investors often wish to close out contracts before expiration to avoid other costs, such as stockbrokerage commissions and commodity storage fees, which they may incur if they hold the option until expiration.

9 Derivatives markets

THE FASTEST-GROWING PART of the financial markets in recent years has been the over-the-counter market for derivatives. Over-the-counter derivatives are transactions negotiated privately between two parties, known as counterparties, without the intermediation of an exchange. In general, one of the parties to a derivatives transaction is a dealer, such as a bank or investment bank, and the other is a user, such as a non-financial corporation, an investment fund, a government agency, or an insurance company.

The term derivatives refers to a large number of financial instruments, the value of which is based on, or derived from, the prices of securities, commodities, money or other external variables. They come in hundreds of varieties. For all their diversity, however, they fall into two basic categories:

■ **Forwards** are contracts that set a price for something to be delivered in the future.

■ **Options** are contracts that allow, but do not require, one or both parties to obtain certain benefits under certain conditions. The calculation of an option contract's value must take into account the possibility that this option will be exercised.

Over-the-counter derivatives are often customised to meet an investor's requirements. This provides flexibility, with respect to the underlying, the size of the contract and the expiration date, which is not available with exchange-traded products. Additionally, over-the-counter derivatives may be based on any underlying asset on which the parties agree, whereas exchange-traded contracts are available

FIG 9.1 **Notional value of over-the-counter derivatives**
$trn

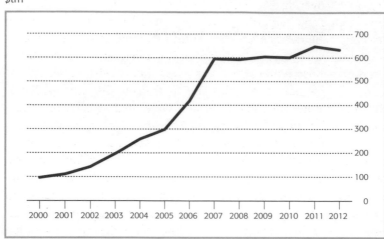

Source: Bank for International Settlements

only for certain underlying assets. Most over-the-counter derivatives involve some element of optionality, such that the price depends heavily on the value attached to the option. Many of the same mathematical procedures used to determine the value of options are therefore employed in the derivatives market as well.

As recently as the late 1980s, the market for over-the-counter derivatives barely existed. The business burgeoned in the 1990s as investors discovered that derivatives could be used to manage risk or, if desired, to increase risk in the hope of earning a higher return. Derivatives trading has also been controversial, because of both the difficulty of explaining how it works and the fact that some users have suffered large and highly publicised losses. Additionally, derivatives can allow banks and companies to take risks that are not clearly disclosed on financial statements, and can provide a means of circumventing regulations that restrict investments by insurance companies, government agencies and other entities.

The derivatives market may appear to be huge. The notional principal, or face value, of outstanding over-the-counter derivatives was $633 trillion at the end of 2012 (see Figure 9.1). But estimates of notional value seriously exaggerate the market's size. A currency derivative covering $1m-worth of euros has a notional principal of $1m, but the counterparties' potential gain or loss depends upon the amount of the euro's fluctuation against the dollar, not the notional value. The banks that are most active in the derivatives market have positions whose notional value is many times their capital, but as many of these positions cancel one another out the amount that a bank could potentially lose from derivatives trading is far less than the notional value of its derivatives. The gross market value of over-the-counter derivatives outstanding at the end of 2012 was $25 trillion. However, their net value – the amount that would have had to change hands had all the contracts been liquidated – was about $3.6 trillion, according to the International Swaps and Derivatives Association, an industry group. This amounted to 0.6% of the nominal value outstanding. Table 9.1 provides a snapshot of the derivatives market.

TABLE 9.1 **The derivatives market at December 2012**

Type	Notional value outstanding, $bn	Gross value outstanding, $bn
Foreign-exchange contracts	67,358	2,304
Interest-rate contracts	489,703	18,833
Equity-linked contracts	6,251	605
Commodity contracts	2,587	358
Credit default swaps	25,069	848
Unallocated	41,611	1,792

Note: Net values based on survey findings that net exposure = 0.6% of notional value.
Sources: Bank for International Settlements; International Swaps and Derivatives Association

The risks of derivatives

Over-the-counter derivatives pose certain risks which are less significant for derivatives traded on exchanges.

Counterparty risk

For all exchange-traded options, the exchange itself becomes the counterparty to every transaction once the initial trade has been completed, and it ensures the payment of all obligations. This is not so in the over-the-counter market, where derivatives are normally traded between two businesses. If the seller of a derivative becomes insolvent, the buyer may not be able to collect the money it is owed. Participants in the derivatives market pay close attention to the creditworthiness of their counterparties and may refuse to do business with entities whose credit standing is less than first-class. Approximately 70% of derivatives contracts are secured by collateral, offering protection to one counterparty in the event that the other defaults.

Price risk

A derivatives dealer often customises its product to meet the needs of a specific user. This is unlike exchange-traded options, whose size, underlying and expiration date are all standardised. Customisation has advantages; for example, a firm expecting to receive a foreign-currency payment might seek a currency derivative that expires on the precise day the payment is due, rather than buying an option that expires several days earlier. But customised derivatives also have disadvantages. In particular, a user wishing to sell out its position may be unable to obtain a good price, as there may be few others interested in that particular derivative.

Legal risk

Where options are traded on exchanges, there are likely to be laws that clearly set out the rights and obligations of the various parties. The legal situation is often murkier with regard to over-the-counter derivatives. In recent years, for example, several sophisticated corporate investors have brought lawsuits claiming that they were induced to buy derivatives so complex that even they could not fully understand them. In other cases, transactions entered into by government entities have been voided by courts on the grounds that the entity was not empowered to undertake such a transaction.

Settlement risk

The exchange makes sure that the parties to an option transaction comply with their obligations within strict time limits. This is not the case in the over-the-counter market. Central banks in the biggest economies have been trying to speed up the process of settling claims and paying for derivative transactions, but participants are still exposed to the risk that transactions will not be completed promptly. A particular concern is netting, the process by which all the positions between two counterparties can be set off against each other. Without netting, it is possible that party A will have to make good on its obligations to party B, even though party B is unable to make good on its own obligations to party A. It is not clear whether netting can be legally enforced in all countries, leaving the possibility that a market participant will suffer losses despite having profitable positions.

Types of derivatives

Forwards

Forwards are the simplest variety of derivative contract. A forward contract is an agreement to set a price now for something to be delivered in the future. One type of forward, a futures contract, is traded in standardised form on exchanges (as discussed in Chapter 8). Over-the-counter forward contracts are similar to futures, but can be designed with the specific size and expiration date the user desires. A particular advantage of forwards is long maturity. Most futures contracts are highly liquid only in near-term maturities, so they are not useful for a customer concerned about exchange rates or commodities prices two or three years hence, whereas a forward contract can be arranged to mature further into the future. A forward contract need not involve any option features. Financial regulators have been pushing to have more forward contracts traded on exchanges, rather than over the counter, to provide greater protection against the failure of a market participant and thereby strengthen the financial system.

Interest-rate swaps

An interest-rate swap is a contract between two parties to exchange interest-payment obligations. Most often, this involves an exchange of fixed-rate for floating-rate obligations. For example, firm A, which obtained a floating-rate bank loan because fixed-rate loans were unattractively priced, may prefer a fixed payment that can be covered by a fixed stream of income, but firm B might prefer to exchange its fixed-rate obligation for a floating rate to benefit from an anticipated fall in interest rates. In a simple swap, firm A might pay $30,000 to exchange its obligation to make payments for two years on a $1m notional amount at 1% above the London inter-bank offered rate (Libor) for firm B's obligation to pay interest on $1m at a fixed 7% rate. The notional amounts themselves do not change hands, so neither party is responsible for paying off the other's loan.

The value of an interest-rate swap obviously depends upon the behaviour of market rates. If rates were to fall, the swap position held by firm B would increase in value, as it would be required to make smaller payments over the next two years; and firm A's fixed-rate

FIG 9.2 **Notional principal of single-currency interest-rate derivatives**
$trn

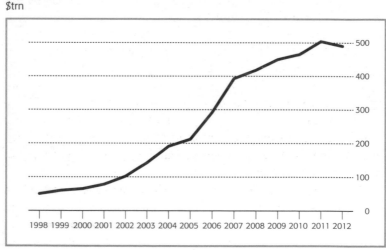

Source: Bank for International Settlements

position would lose value because the rate is now far above what the market would dictate. However, if rates were to rise, firm A's side of the swap would be worth more than firm B's.

Interest-rate swaps are by far the most common variety of derivatives contract, accounting for more than 70% of the notional value of all outstanding contracts. Financial institutions are the main end users, for purposes such as hedging mortgage portfolios and bond holdings, and own 90% of all contracts. Approximately three-quarters of all single-currency interest-rate swaps are denominated in euros or dollars, with yen and sterling accounting for most of the remainder; all other currencies combined make up less than 9% of the market. Figure 9.2 shows the rapid growth of interest-rate swaps.

Currency swaps

Currency swaps involve exchanging streams of interest payments in two different currencies. If interest rates are lower in the euro zone than in the UK, for example, a British company needing sterling might find it cheaper to borrow in euros and then swap into sterling. The value of this position will depend upon what happens to the exchange rate between the two currencies concerned during the life of the derivative. In most cases, the counterparties to a currency swap also agree to exchange their principal, at a predetermined exchange rate, when the derivative matures.

The market for currency swaps is much smaller than that for interest-rate swaps. The notional value of currency swaps used by financial institutions, for example, is barely 5% of the notional value of those same institutions' interest rate swaps. The overall market has grown relatively slowly, but demand for long-term swaps has grown much more rapidly than the market overall, suggesting that users have found currency swaps to be useful in hedging long-term exposures. Even so, 70% of currency swaps outstanding in 2013 had maturities of less than seven days.

Figure 9.3 shows the notional value of currency swaps outstanding. As each swap involves two different currencies, the total value of swaps outstanding is only half of the sum of the value of swaps in each currency. Five out of six swaps involve the US dollar, with the

FIG 9.3 **Notional principal of currency derivatives**
$trn

Source: Bank for International Settlements

euro and yen being the other main currencies involved. The average size of a currency swap exceeds $30m.

Interest-rate options

This category involves a large variety of derivatives with different types of optionality. A cap is an option contract in which the buyer pays a fee to set a maximum interest rate on a floating-rate loan. A floor is the converse, involving a minimum interest rate. A customer can purchase both a cap and a floor to arrange a collar, which effectively allows the interest rate to fluctuate only within a predetermined range. It is also possible to arrange options on caps and floors. A swaption is an option that gives the owner the right to enter into an interest-rate swap, as either the fixed-rate payer or the floating-rate payer, at a predetermined rate. A spread option is based on the difference between two interest rates in the same currency rather than on the absolute level of rates; such an option might be used to protect an investor in long-term bonds, for example, against the risk that the yield curve will steepen and the bonds will lose value relative to short-term bonds. A difference or "diff" option is based on differences in interest rates on comparable instruments in different currencies.

Interest-rate options can also be built into fixed-income products, making them respond to interest-rate changes in ways different from normal securities. Inverse floaters (also called reverse floaters) are interest-bearing notes whose interest rate is determined by subtracting an index from a fixed rate, giving a formula such as 10% minus six-month Libor; the investor thus receives less interest (and the value of its position falls) when interest rates rise, in contrast to most floating-rate securities. Multiple-index floaters have interest rates that are based on the difference between two rates, and step-up coupon notes have interest rates that increase if the security has not been called by a certain date.

Commodity derivatives

Commodity derivatives function much as commodity options, allowing the buyer to lock in a price for the commodity in return for a premium payment. Commodity options can also be combined with other sorts of options into multi-asset options. For example, an airline might feel that it could withstand higher fuel costs at most times, but not at a time of economic slowdown, which depresses air travel. The airline might therefore purchase a derivative that would entitle it to purchase aviation fuel at a specified price whenever a key interest rate is above 7% (at which point the economy is presumably slowing), but not at other times.

Trading in commodity derivatives is small relative to trading in interest-rate and currency derivatives. At the end of 2012, the notional value of all commodity derivatives outstanding was $2.6 trillion. Gold accounted for nearly one-fifth of this amount. The notional value of outstanding commodity derivatives fell by half between 2008 and early 2013, in part because market participants may have felt that new production of oil and natural gas in North America reduced the risk of a spike in energy prices.

Equity derivatives

Over-the-counter equity derivatives are traded in many different ways. Synthetic equity is a derivative designed to mimic the risks and rewards of an investment in shares or in an equity index. For example, a US firm wishing to speculate on European telephone-company shares could arrange a call option on a synthetic basket whose value is determined by the share prices of individual telephone companies. Synthetic equity can be used, among other purposes, to permit an investor such as a pension fund to take a position that it could not take by purchasing equities, owing to legal restrictions on its equity holdings. Step-down options on shares or equity indexes provide for the strike price to be adjusted downwards either at a specific date or if the price of the underlying falls to a predetermined level. Total return swaps are interest-rate swaps in which the non-floating-rate side is based on the total return of an equity index.

The market for over-the-counter equity derivatives has grown much more slowly than that for other types of derivatives. Investor demand in this area has been met by the rapid increase in equity-options trading on exchanges. Furthermore, one of the important

FIG 9.4 **Notional principal of equity-linked derivatives**
$trn

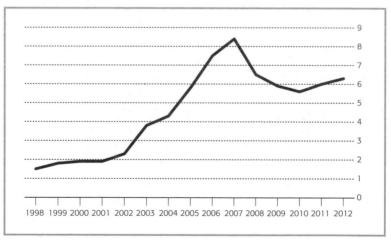

Source: Bank for International Settlements

attractions of interest-rate and exchange-rate derivatives is the ability to customise derivatives contracts to provide precise hedges for pending business transactions. Equity-linked derivatives are less useful in this respect, as few obligations depend upon the level of share prices at a particular point in time. Figure 9.4 shows the outstanding value of equity-linked derivatives.

Credit derivatives

Credit derivatives are a comparatively new development, providing a way to transfer credit risk, the risk that a debtor will fail to make payments as scheduled. The instrument used for this purpose is a credit default swap. Credit default swaps provide for the seller to pay the holder the amount of forgone payments in the event of certain "credit events" which cause a particular loan or bond not to be serviced on time.

A credit default swap is a contract in which two parties agree to exchange the risk that a borrower will default on its bonds or loans. The seller of the swap receives a fee, or premium, from the buyer. In return, the seller will compensate the buyer if there is a "credit event", such as the borrower failing to pay its obligations on time or filing for bankruptcy, as happened with General Motors in June 2009. Selling "protection" on a particular name, such as a company or a government agency, is thus similar to owning that entity's bonds, in that the seller of protection is exposed to the risk of default. Buying protection is analogous to holding a short position in a bond – that is, agreeing to sell a bond the investor does not own, in the expectation that the bond can be purchased in the future at a lower price.

Credit default swaps on a given name are usually priced similarly to that name's bonds, and the price can change frequently as investors reassess the likelihood of a credit event. If no credit event occurs, the seller of protection profits from the premium it received from the buyer. If a credit event does occur, the seller must compensate the buyer by paying the difference between the full face value of the securities and their market value after the credit event, which is invariably less than face value but often much more than zero. The precise amount of the seller's loss in that case depends on the value of the bonds after the credit event. If, for example, the troubled company has substantial unencumbered assets that can be sold to satisfy creditors, the defaulted bonds might trade at 60–70% of face value, leaving the seller of protection to make up the difference. If, however, the troubled company is likely to be dissolved, the defaulted bonds may trade at a low price, and the seller of protection will have much larger losses.

One virtue of credit default swaps is that investors are able to express views on an issuer even if it has few bonds outstanding. Suppose, for example, that an investor wishes to speculate on the improving health of the restaurant industry by purchasing the bonds of a highly leveraged restaurant operator. It may be the case that none of the present owners of that company's bonds wishes to sell, so the investor cannot execute its strategy in the cash bond market. The investor could accomplish the same end by selling a credit default swap on the name. If the company's earnings do improve, the likelihood of a credit event would diminish, allowing the investor to profit from the company's improved creditworthiness. Credit default swaps allow an unlimited number of investors to position themselves in that way so long as they can find counterparties willing to take the opposing position; the amount of bonds outstanding or available for sale is not relevant. Without credit default swaps, only those investors owning the company's bonds or loans could take such positions.

The outstanding amount of credit default swaps has grown rapidly since they were developed in the late 1990s (see Table 9.2). Initially reserved only for a small number of corporate issuers, default swaps are now written on the debt of many smaller companies, of emerging-market governments, and of a variety of governmental and quasi-governmental agencies around the world. Short-term credit default swaps are relatively uncommon, perhaps reflecting the likelihood that market participants have fairly similar views of an issuer's default risk over a 12-month time horizon.

Credit default swaps have been controversial for a variety of reasons. One concern is that the failure of a major dealer could cause systemic risk to the financial system. Counterparty risk assumed large proportions in 2008, when American International Group (AIG), an insurance company that was a major seller of credit derivatives,

TABLE 9.2 **Credit default swaps outstanding**

	$trn
2001	0.9
2002	2.2
2003	2.8
2004	8.4
2005	17.1
2006	34.4
2007	62.2
2008	38.6
2009	32.7
2010	29.9
2011	28.6
2012	25.1

Source: International Swaps and Derivatives Association

experienced large losses as a result of the defaults of firms on whose bonds it had sold protection. US authorities intervened to support the company lest its inability to fulfil its contracts should cause large losses at other financial institutions. The event led to calls for credit derivatives to be traded on an exchange that could require participants to post additional margin if their positions lost value.

A second concern about credit derivatives concerns the potential for conflict of interest. Consider the case of a hedge fund that owns equity in a company and purchases protection on the company's bonds. In such a situation, the investor might profit by using its power as a stockholder to drive the company into bankruptcy; although the value of its equity might be wiped out, the payout on the credit default swaps might more than make up that loss. In such a scenario, the investor's interest might be directly contrary to the interests of other shareholders, who are usually best served if the company can continue to operate without filing for bankruptcy protection.

The market's response to large-scale issuer defaults has also been a concern. Credit events, such as the bankruptcies of Lehman Brothers, an investment bank, in 2008 and Nortel Networks, a major telecoms company, in 2009, tested the market's ability to resolve claims and force sellers of protection on the affected bonds to live up to their commitments. Recent improvements in operating procedures enabled dealers to address the situation, and the buyers of protection generally received their payments without difficulty.

As an alternative to credit default swaps, some investors trade swaps based on the difference between the price of a particular bond and an appropriate benchmark. If a given ten-year corporate bond loses substantial value relative to a group of top-rated ten-year corporate bonds, its credit standing is presumed to have been impaired in some way and the swap would cover part or all of the owner's loss, even if the company does not default on its debts.

Synthetic securities

Structured securities are fixed-income instruments and need not involve derivatives. However, in the early years of the 21st century there was rapid growth in "synthetic" securities, which may involve a mixture of "hard" assets, such as bonds and mortgages, and derivatives of various sorts. Such securities may contain derivatives, such as swaps. A simple example might be a synthetic floating-rate note, which uses a combination of a fixed-rate bond and an interest-rate swap to provide the investor with a variable rate of interest without ownership of a variable-rate security. But synthetic securities have become far more complex, with a single security containing a wide variety of derivatives as well as equity or credit instruments.

Synthetic securities offer an investor a means of mimicking the return on a security that is not actually available in the marketplace. In some cases, it may be less costly to obtain a particular exposure synthetically than by purchasing all the underlying instruments, with their attendant trading costs. However, synthetic securities also pose risks. They may be difficult to value, as each may be unique and the underlying assets incorporated into the security may themselves not be traded at any given time. And they may perform unpredictably, as

TABLE 9.3 **Issuance of fully and partially synthetic securities**

	Partially synthetic, $bn	Fully synthetic, $bn
2004	118	36
2005	206	44
2006	410	67
2007	340	48
2008	44	1
2009	3	0
2010	8	0
2011	30	0
2012	58	0

Source: Securities Industry and Financial Markets Association

the values of the derivative components may change in unanticipated ways.

One example of such a security is a credit-linked note, intended to mimic an asset-backed security. In a standard asset-backed security, the sponsor, such as a bank, will sell a package of loans or other assets to a special-purpose entity, which raises money by selling notes to investors, who in turn receive the payments on the underlying assets. In a credit-linked note, however, the special-purpose entity sells credit protection to the owner of the assets, which in turn makes premium payments to the special-purpose entity. The investors receive the premium payments as well as any interest on the money held by the special-purpose entity, but do not have a claim on the underlying assets.

The construction of synthetic securities often involves borrowed money, or leverage. This can magnify investors' gains or losses when the value of the underlying assets changes. In 2007–08, amid the US housing-market collapse, many synthetic securities containing both credit default swaps and mortgage-backed securities performed poorly, causing large losses to investors. This was a significant contributor to the troubles of the financial system, as many securities of this sort were owned by banks. Investor interest in fully synthetic securities did not recover after the crisis, although collateralised debt obligations with synthetic features remain common. Table 9.3 shows the rapid change in this market.

Special features used in derivatives

Many derivatives of all types use multipliers as ways of increasing leverage. An interest-rate swap, for example, may provide that the party agreeing to pay a floating rate will pay not Libor plus two percentage points but rather the square of Libor minus 5%. Under this arrangement, if floating rates drop, Libor^2 − 5% will plummet and the owner's payments will diminish rapidly. However, a small increase in floating rates could cause a sharp increase in Libor^2 − 5%, and the owner of the floating rate position could owe significantly higher interest payments. Many of the large reported losses on derivatives transactions have come about because of multipliers of this sort embedded in the derivatives.

Another common arrangement in derivatives is a path-dependent option. Unlike a regular option, which pays off only if it is in the money at expiration (in the case of a European-style option) or when exercised before expiration (in the case of an American-style option), a path-dependent option has a pay-off that depends on its behaviour throughout its life. A simple path-dependent currency derivative might pay off only if the euro trades above $1.20 for seven of the 14 days before expiration. A more complex variant could conceivably require that the euro trades above $1.15 on July 1st, above $1.175 on October 1st and above $1.20 on January 1st; unless all three of these conditions are met, the exchange rate will not have followed the agreed path and the owner will not receive a payment.

Pricing derivatives

As with exchange-traded options, the prices of over-the-counter derivatives are determined mainly by mathematical models. The factors affecting prices are much the same: the level of risk-free interest rates, the volatility of the underlying, expected changes in the price of the underlying and time to expiration.

Imagine a simple interest-rate swap, in which a manufacturing company wishes to exchange payments on $1m of debt floating at Libor +3% for a fixed payment and an insurance company wishes to swap a 7% fixed-rate payment on $1m of principal for a floating rate. Before engaging in such a transaction each party, whether on its own or with the help of outside advisers, must develop a view of the likely course of interest rates over the relevant period. If they both judge that rates are likely to drop significantly, they may agree that over time the holder of the floating-rate position will probably pay less than the holder of the fixed position, so the insurer should pay a premium to the manufacturer in order to obtain the position it expects to be less costly. If they both think that interest rates will rise, they may agree that the manufacturer should pay a premium to the insurer for the opportunity to lock in a fixed rate. The precise amount of premium one party demands and the other agrees to pay will depend upon their estimates of the probable pay-offs until the derivative expires.

For "plain vanilla" derivatives, such as a simple swap, there is a large and liquid market and little disagreement about pricing. For more complicated derivatives premiums can be harder to calculate. In some cases, the premium can be determined by disaggregating one derivative product into several simpler ones and summing the prices. Many customers, even sophisticated companies, have difficulty reckoning a fair price for highly complex derivatives. They often rely on the pricing models of their bankers, which can lead to upset if, as often happens, the derivative does not perform precisely as the model expected. Many users are required to account for their derivative positions at current market value at the end of each quarter, booking a gain or a loss if the instrument has changed in value. Values, which are best described by the price at which the instrument could be sold, are often provided by banks, and unanticipated price drops can force owners to book losses.

The price a bank or other dealer will charge for a particular derivative will depend partly on the structure of the many derivative positions on the dealer's books. Dealers generally seek to minimise the risks of derivatives by hedging their own positions. They can hedge a derivative by buying an offsetting derivative from another dealer or by arranging a transaction with another customer. A dealer may offer a favourable price for a derivative contract which exposes it to loss if oil prices rise if it already holds a derivative exposing it to loss if oil prices fall, as the combination of the two positions would leave it in a neutral position with regard to oil-price changes. A customer whose proposed transaction would increase the dealer's risks might be offered a much less attractive price.

Settling derivatives trades

Trades in the over-the-counter derivatives market are settled through the banking system, according to standards established by each country's banking authorities. Central bankers, under the aegis of the Bank for International Settlements in Basel, Switzerland, have made a concerted effort to reduce the time within which the parties to a derivatives transaction must exchange contracts and money. Given the magnitude of derivatives positions, the failure of a major bank with many unsettled trades could cause the immediate failure of the banks with which it has been trading. Market forces have mitigated this risk to some extent, as banks are increasingly reluctant to trade with other banks whose creditworthiness they distrust; other banks' concern about the creditworthiness of Lehman Brothers and Bear Stearns in 2008, for example, made them reluctant to engage in derivatives trades with those institutions and contributed to their ultimate collapse.

Despite advances in trading infrastructure, banking experts still consider unsettled derivatives trades to be one of the main factors that could threaten the stability of the world's banking system, and regulators continue to push banks to settle trades more quickly. This is a particular concern with respect to credit default swaps. At the end of 2012, some 11% of outstanding credit default swap contracts had not been fully processed by a clearing house, raising the risk that a counterparty to such a contract might fail to fulfil its obligations.

Derivatives disasters

Derivatives have made it possible for firms and government agencies to manage their risks to an extent unimaginable only a decade ago. But derivatives are far from riskless and were described in 2003 by Warren Buffett, a well-known American investor, as "financial weapons of mass destruction". Used carelessly, they can increase risks in ways that users often fail to understand. As individual derivatives can be complex and difficult to comprehend, they have been blamed for a series of highly publicised financial disasters. In some cases, the dealers have been accused of selling products that were not suited to the users' needs. In others, the problem has been not with the instruments themselves, but with the financial controls of the organisation trading or using them.

Metallgesellschaft, a large German company with a big oil-trading operation, reported a \$1.9 billion loss in 1993 on its positions in oil futures and swaps. The company was seeking to hedge contracts to supply petroleum, heating oil and other products to customers. But its hedge, like most hedges, was not perfect, and decreases in oil prices caused its derivative position to lose value more rapidly than its contracts to deliver oil in future gained value. The company's directors may have compounded the loss by ordering that the hedge be unwound, or sold off, before it was scheduled to expire.

Procter & Gamble, a multinational consumer-products company, and Gibson Greetings, a manufacturer of greeting cards, announced huge losses from derivatives trading in April 1994. Both companies had purchased highly levered derivatives known as ratio swaps, based on formulas such as:

$$\text{Net payment} - 5.5\% = \frac{\text{Libor}^2}{6\%}$$

If the resulting number is positive, the dealer must make a payment to the user. As interest rates rose early in 1994, however, the numerator rose geometrically, drastically increasing the users' losses. Procter & Gamble admitted to losing \$157m, and Gibson's loss was about \$20m. Both firms recovered part of their losses from the dealer, Bankers Trust Company. In both cases, the firms' derivative investments were made in violation of their own investment policies.

Orange County, California, suffered a loss ultimately reckoned to be \$1.69 billion after the county's treasurer borrowed through repurchase agreements in order to speculate on lower interest rates. In the end, about \$8 billion of a fund totalling \$20 billion was invested in interest-sensitive derivatives such as inverse floaters, which magnify the gains or losses from interest-rate changes. These derivatives were designed to stop paying interest if market interest rates rose beyond a certain point. This large position was unhedged, and when the Federal Reserve raised interest rates six times within a nine-month period in 1994 the value of the fund's assets collapsed.

Derivatives played a role in the financial crisis that crippled Thailand in the summer of 1997. Many investors misjudged the country's situation because the Thai central bank reported holding large foreign currency reserves. The central bank did not report that most of these reserves were committed to forward contracts intended to support the currency, the baht. Once the baht's market value fell, the bank suffered huge losses on its derivatives and its reserves were wiped out. A year later several US and European banks reported significant derivatives losses in Russia after a sharp fall in the country's currency led to the failure of several banks and caused local counterparties to derivatives trades to default.

A different type of derivative, credit default swaps, played a significant role in the financial crisis that followed the 2007 collapse of the US housing market. Banks had sold complex securities incorporating credit default swaps on mortgage-backed securities, a previously untested type of derivative. As the underlying home mortgages went into default in increasing numbers, the banks and insurance companies that had written the credit default swaps were forced to make good investors' losses. Credit default swaps were an important cause of the near failure of AIG, one of the world's largest insurers, and contributed to large losses at several other financial institutions.

Accounting risks

Many problems such as these can be attributed to inadequate financial controls on the part of firms using derivatives. But the difficulty of applying strict and consistent accounting standards to derivatives positions makes it difficult for investors to assess a company's condition. Furthermore, derivatives may provide a means for users to avoid restrictions on their activities. For example, a firm which has stated that it will not purchase foreign equities could purchase a derivative that mimics the behaviour of foreign equities, exposing the firm and its investors to the same risks as if they did own foreign equities. Inadequate disclosure often makes it difficult for investors to determine whether a particular firm is using derivatives to circumvent limits on its activity.

Regulatory issues

The failures of numerous major financial institutions in the US, the UK and Continental Europe in 2008 have led to much discussion about changes to financial regulations affecting derivatives. Changes under consideration include requiring that some types of derivative instruments be traded on exchanges, rather than over the counter. Exchange trading would reduce banks' profits from derivatives, but it would also reduce the likelihood that the failure of one institution would cause losses at other institutions as a result of the failed institution's inability to fulfil obligations to derivatives counterparties.

Index

Page numbers in *italics* indicate figures; those in **bold** type indicate tables.

accounting rules 171–172, 186
adjustable bonds 87
Africa: currency trading 28
after-hours trading 209
Agricultural Bank of China 160
agricultural equipment, loans on 129
agricultural finance agencies 58
aircraft, loans on 128–129
algorithmic trading 12–13, 18, 191, 192
all-or-none orders 205
All-Ordinaries Index (Australia) 224
Alternative Investment Market, London 181
alternative trading systems *see* dark pools
Altria Group 160
American depositary receipts (ADRs) 186, 187
American International Group (AIG) 264–265, 272
American Stock Exchange 183, 243, 244
American-style options 240
Amsterdam 154
   bourse 181
analysts, securities 169
annuities 12
Antwerp Stock Exchange 178
arbitrage 3, 92, 242
ARCA options exchange 244
Archipelago exchange 183
Argentina
   bonds 73, 110, 144, 145
   financial crisis in (2001–02) 34, 106, 107, 145
   international debt securities 144

stock exchange loss of business 182
   unemployment in 34
Aristotle 197–198
Asia
   asset-backed securities 113
   currency trading 28
   emerging markets 187
   financial crisis in (1998) 5, 106
   high-yield markets 101
   initial public offerings (IPOs) 160
   price/earnings ratio of technology shares 173
   and securitisation 116
Asia-Pacific region: bond issuance 77
asset value 168
asset-backed securities 156–157, 267
   basics of 131
   buying 135
   and CDOs 116–117
   defined 75
   floating-rate 133
   home-equity 128
   issuance of 116, 117
   measuring performance 135–136
   mortgage-backed securities 112
   non-mortgage securities 112, **112**
   novel types of 129–130
   private-sector debt market 76
   risk 8, 111–112
   trading 115–116
assets
   income from 3
   interest-bearing 21
   trading 115
   valuation 2
ASX 50 share index 224
ASX 200 share index 224
at best instruction 188
at-the-market orders 204
auction markets 189–190
auctions, bond sale 7–80

Australia
auto-loan securities 128
banks' bond issuance 126
securitisation 126
Australian Stock Exchange 225
automotive loans 113, 117, 128–129
Autostrade 139

balance-of-payments
crises 33, 36
deficits 33, 38, 138
surplus 38
Banco do Brasil 161
bands 35–36
bank certificates of deposit 44, 50
bank deposits 169
Bank for International Settlements 5,
43, 46, 270
Bank of America 176
Bank of Canada 65, 66
Bank of England: Central
Moneymarkets Office 62–63
Bank of Japan 62, 68
Bank of Venice 70
bankers' acceptances 55, 63
Bankers Trust Company 271–272
banking
banking crises (1990s) 6
and bond markets 78
certificates of deposit 44
clearing organisations 29
commercial banks 15, 44
and commercial paper 54
consolidation 15, 18
credit lines 54
currency dealing 24
disintermediation 44
forced mergers due to insolvency 15
foreign banks set up offices in
London 139
gross position 29
interbank loans 58–59
and intermediation 47
lending 4, 6
liberalisation 15
as a main source of credit 44
market share 13, 44
net position 29
overnight loans 59
and price quotations 39–40
and repos 60, 61
securitisation 115, 126
short-term demand deposits 44
speculators 23
underwriting risk 134–135

bankruptcy 49, 54, 74, 194, 195, 229,
265
barrier options 20
base rate 65
basic hedge 248
basis trading 231
basket trades 192
BATS Global Markets electronic
exchange 184
bear spread 232
Bear Stearns 270
Beckman Coulter 178
Becton Dickinson 178
"below investment grade" 64, **90**, 91,
101, 102, 103, 106, 144
benchmark index 108
betas 173, 175
Big Mac Index 38
Black-Scholes option-pricing model
246
block trades 192
BM&F Bovespa exchange, São Paulo
206, 213
Bogotá exchange 25
Bolsa de Mercadorias & Futuros, Brazil
25, 26, 237
bond funds 50
bond futures 76
bond indexes *see under* bond markets
bond insurance 100
Bond Issue Arrangement Committee
(Japan) 76
bond issuers 46
bond markets 5–6, 70–110
the biggest national markets 76–77
bond futures 76
bond indexes 108–110
benchmark 108
index shortcomings 109–110
weighted 108–109
the changing nature of the market
81–84
electronic trading 82–84
secondary dealing 82–83
settlement 84
and countries with less active
money markets 46–47
defined 46
domestic and international 140
emerging-market bonds 83, 105–107,
106
enhancing security 99–100
bond insurance 100
covenants 99
sinking funds 100

exchange rates and bond prices and
returns 94–95, **95**
high-yield debt (or junk) 101–103,
102
inflation and returns on bonds 94
interest rates and bond prices
92–93, 93
international markets 103–105, 104
Eurobonds 104
foreign bonds 103–104
interpreting the price of a bond
91–92
investing 3
the issuers 73
corporations 75–76
lower levels of government 74–75
national governments 73–74
securitisation vehicles 75–76
issuing bonds 77–80
selling direct 81
setting the interest rate 80–81
swaps 79–80
underwriters and dealers 78–79
no more coupons 81
properties of bonds 87–89
coupon 88
current yield 88
duration 89
maturity 87–88
yield to maturity 88
ratings of risk 89–91, **90**
repurchase agreements 100–101
and rise in interest rates (2013) 8
robust activity (2000–2001) 6
spreads 98–99
types of bonds 84–87
adjustable bonds 87
callable bonds 85
convertible bonds 86
non-refundable bonds 85
perpetual debentures 85
putable bonds 85
straight bonds 85
STRIPS 86
structured securities 87
zero-coupon bonds 86
why issue bonds? 72–73
avoiding short-term financial
constraints 73
controlling risk 72–73
matching revenue and expenses
72
minimising financing costs 72
promoting intergenerational
equity 72

the yield curve 95–98, 97
bond options 236
bond returns 170
bonds
acceleration provision 91
adjustable 87
below-investment-grade 101, 102,
103, 144
book-entry 81
bulldog 104
callable 85, 87
capital-indexed 87
convertible 86, 87, 159
corporate 75, 76, 82, 83, 92, 99, 101,
106, 107
defined 70
dim sum 104
domestic **4**, **5**, 75, 77, 105, 107, 148,
153
emerging-market 105–107, 106,
144–146
equity-linked 147
euro 152
exchange rates and bond prices and
returns 94–95, **95**
fallen angels 102, 103
fixed-rate 111, 147, 148, 266
floating-rate 87, 147
foreign 103–104, 153
and foreign-exchange trading 21, 22
general-obligation 74
global 149
and globalisation 16
government 71, 82, 83, 98–99, 106,
152, 248
high-yield 101–103, 102
indebtedness of banks 6
inflation-indexed 87
interest rates and bond prices
92–93, 93
interest-indexed 87
international bond issues 140, 141,
149–150
issuing see under bond markets
large-scale purchases of 7
long-term 56, 93, 98, 101, 108, 148,
260
"marked to market" 82
maturities 142
mortgage 113, 118
municipal 74, 83, 100
non-refundable 85
paper 81
properties of 87–89
coupon 88

current yield 88
  duration 89
  maturity 87–88
  yield to maturity 88
putable 85, 87
raising capital 3
registered 81
revenue 74
rising stars 102–103
samurai 104
selling 156
  sale on best-efforts basis 150
  sale on fixed-price re-offer basis
    149–150
short-term (notes) 70, 260
sovereign 73, 108
special-purpose 74–75
step-up 87, 91
straight 85
transactions 5
US dollar 152
variable-rate 87
warrant 87
Yankee 104, 138
zero-coupon 86, 87
book-entry bonds 81
Borsa Italiana, Milan 183
Boston Options Exchange 244
bought deal 150
Bowie, David 129–130
Brazil
  bonds 71, 73, 74, 106
  currency options contracts 25
  debt crisis (1999) 57
  emerging markets 187
  floating rates 37
  longer-term financing 57
Brazilian Mercantile and Futures
  Exchange 202
"breaking the buck" 49
Brent Crude oil futures 206
Bretton Woods system 18, 33, 138
brokerage commissions 200
brokerage firms 15, 178, 182, 188, 189,
  190
Brussels
  and introduction of the euro 27–28
  stock exchange 181, 182–183
Buffett, Warren 270–271
bulk commodities (physicals) 204
bull spread 232
bulldog bonds 104
Bundesanleihen (Bunds) 73, 99, 241
business plans 156
buy orders 208

buy-outs, leveraged 101

CAC-40 index 224
calendar strip 232
call auction markets 190
call options 234, 240, 244, 247–248, 262
  naked 249
call premium 85
call rate 67
callable bonds 85, 87
Canada
  asset-backed commercial paper 131
  auto-loan securities 128
  bankers' acceptances 55
  commercial paper 53
  discount rate 65
  option trading 243
  provincial bonds 74
  reduced government debt (1990s)
    57
  securitisation 123–124
  short-term borrowing 56
Canada Mortgage and Housing
  Corporation 123–124
cancel order 189
capital
  cross-border flow of 103, 153
  equity 157
  long-term 3, 7
  raising 3, 13
  short-term 44, 47
  working 3
capital gains 165, 175
  defined 9
capital markets
  financing 3–4, **6**
  foreign 186
  open 187
  and stock exchanges 179
capital-indexed bonds 87
capitalisation
  company 194
  German stockmarket 170
  market 176, 180, **181**, 188
  and stock splits 170–171
  stockmarket 181
capitalisation issue (stock dividend)
  168
capped options 240, 260
car purchase: raising capital 3
carbon dioxide emissions 217
cash flow
  and asset-backed commercial paper
    130
  and bonds 81

defined 167
expected 134
and fixed-rate bonds 111
irregular 45
negative 167
positive 167
cash management 62
central banks
  and bond markets 84
  and the crawling peg 36–37
  and gold standard 32
  and inflation 34, 38
  interest rates 65–66
  intervention by 23, 39
  keeping the exchange rate stable
    34, 35
  managing floating rates 38–39
  monetary policy 64–65
  and money markets 45, 49
  open-market operations 65–66
  stripping government bonds 86
  survey of currency-trading activity
    27
  and Thailand's financial crisis 272
Central Japan Commodities Exchange
  202
Central Moneymarkets Office, Bank
  of England 62–63
certificates of deposit (CDs) see time
  deposits
change 14–16
  consolidation 15
  deregulation 15
  globalisation 15–16
  liberalisation 15
  technology 14
cheque-writing accounts 44
Chicago Board Options Exchange
  (CBOE) 233, 239, 244
Chicago Board of Trade 1, 198, 202,
  213, 217, 220–221, 222, 225, 233, 235
  Northern Spring Wheat contract
    206–207
Chicago Mercantile Exchange 19, 24,
  25–26, **25**, 202, 206, 210, 221, 225,
  228, 232, 235
Chicago Stock Exchange 184
Chilean Stock Exchange 184
China
  agricultural futures 213
  bond market 71, 77, 105, 106
  commodies exchanges 202
  commodity contracts 200–201
  emerging markets 187
  pegs and baskets 36

rapid industrial growth 216
and securitisation 116, 126
stock exchanges 179
trade in stock index options 236
Chinese Telecom 225
clearing 103, 226–227, 251
clearing houses 62–63, 227, 228, 229,
  251, 270
clearing members 227, 228–229
clearing organisations 29
closed-end funds 10
CMBS (commercial mortgage-backed
  securities) 119–120
CME Group, US **25**, 208
co-operative agreements 230
coal futures contracts 216
Coffee, Sugar and Cocoa Exchange
  203
collars 20, 260
collateralised debt obligation (CDO)
  116, 117, **117**
collateralised mortgage obligations
  (CMOs) 131–132, 133
Colombian Stock Exchange 184
commercial mortgage-backed
  securities (CMBS) 118, 119–120
commercial paper 50, 52–55, **53**, 62, 63,
  64, 66, 83
  asset-backed 130–131
  short-term 141, 142, 143, **143**
Commerzbank Index 195
commissions 190, 191
commodities
  characteristics of 198
  contracts 200–201
  futures 204, 218–219, **218**
  markets 197
  options 237, 252
  storage fees 252
  traders 2
common stock (ordinary shares) 158
companies
  acquisitions of 107
  bankers' acceptances 55
  bankruptcy 54
  bond issuance 6
  capitalisation of 194
  and commercial paper 52, 53, 54
  corporate bonds 75
  domestic 15
  emerging-market 107
  financial distress 45
  foreign direct investment in 22
  and globalisation 15–16
  insurance 10, **11**, 12

investment 10, 11, 15, 44, 45, 50
local 13
competition
among futures and options
exchanges 200
increased 14
and option exchanges 242–243, **243**
price 220
computers
abundant computing power 14
and algorithmic trading 12, 18, 192
book-entry bonds 81
electronic auction markets 189–190
futures and options trading 200
"high-frequency" trading 18
replacing face-to-face dealing 1
scanning markets for price
anomalies 31
and stock exchanges 182, 184, 189
swaps trading 149
consolidation 15, 18
construction equipment, loans on
129
consumer spending, and a rise in the
prime rate 68
continuous auction trading 207–208
contracts
commodity 200–201
derivative 26, 222–223
energy futures 203, 216, 217, **217**
enforcing 14
financial futures 210
forward 20, 25, 31, 76, **148**, 197, 253,
257, 272
futures 19, 20, 22, 198, 203, 205–207,
216, 231, 257
index 252
interest-rate options 76
options 22
convertible bonds 86, 87, 159
convertible preferred stock 159
convexity 93
corporate bonds 75, 76
indexes 136
costs
regulatory 14
trading 14, 19
counterparties 253, 255, 256, 257, 259,
264, 272, 273
coupon 88
covenants 99
covered calls 239, 249
covered interest arbitrage 30–31
covered interest parity 31
crawling peg 36–37

credit, regulating the amount of 64–65
credit cards
balances 170
purchases 3
securities 127–128
credit crisis (from 2007), and risk-
management products 8–9
credit events 263–264, 266
credit markets 7
credit ratings 54, 63–64, **64**, 91, 101,
106, 110, 144, 145
credit risk 133–134
credit-linked notes 267
creditworthiness 63, 66, 99, 119, 256,
264, 270
cross-border finance 4–5
cross-margining 230
currencies
bands 35, 36
comparing currency valuations
37–38
destabilisation 33
emerging-market 28, 107
favourite 26–28, **27, 28**
floating 35, 36
risk 105, 107
settlement 28–29
strengthening/weakening against
those of other countries 30
currency
coinage 17
and exchange rates 18, 23
government intervention 23
growth in currency trading 18, 22
no longer linked to gold 18
paper money 18
risk management 3
sovereign wealth funds 23
spot transactions 19
value of 17
currency board 33–34
currency cross-rates 41, **42**
currency indexes 42
currency markets 21–22
and algorithmic trading 12
foreign currency 13
gearing up 21–22
currency options 237–238, **238**
contracts 25–26
currency-price tables 40, **41**
currency swaps **24**, 26, 259–260, 260
current yield 88
current-account imbalances 32
Czech Republic: trade-weighted
exchange rate 42

Daiwa Bond Index 109
Dalian Commodity Exchange 213
dark pools 185, 186, 192
DAX (Deutsche Aktienindex) 225–226, **226**, 250
  Performance Index 195
DAX-30 index 224
day order 189
day trading 191
dealer markets 190
dealers, and bonds 79, 82, 86, 101
debentures 85
  perpetual (irredeemable) 85
debt
  credit-card 128
  emerging-market 105–106
  margin 194
  mezzanine 75
  restructuring 74
  senior 75
  sovereign 105
  subordinated 75
debt-to-equity ratio (gearing) 157
delivery 230, 231, 232, 235
delta 247–248
  hedging 250
demand and supply 150
demutualisations 182, **183**
Denmark
  pegs to the euro 33
  and securitisation 113, 118, 124
depositary receipts 186–187
Depository Trust Company, New York 63
depression
  and gold standard 32–33
  Great Depression 52
  and interest rates 34
deregulation 15, 44, 47–48, 52, 216
derivatives 8
  barrier options and collars 20
  currency 255
  customised 256
  defined 20
  exchange-rate 26
  foreign-exchange swaps 20, 21, 25
  forward contracts 20, 25
  forward rate agreements 20
  futures contracts 203–204
  hedging 269
  over-the-counter 238, 253–257, 254, 262, 270
  "plain vanilla" 269
  risk management 3
  trading in 4

Derivatives Exchange, Malaysia 213
derivatives markets 20–21, 21, 22, 29, 253–273
  accounting risks 272–273
  categories of derivatives 253
  credit events 263–264
  derivatives disasters 270–272
  notional value 254–255, **255**
  pricing derivatives 268
  regulatory issues 273
  risks of derivatives 255–257
    counterparty risk 256
    legal risk 256
    price risk 256
    settlement risk 257
  settling derivative trades 270
  special features used in derivatives 268
  types of derivatives 257–268
    commodity derivatives 261
    credit derivatives 263–266, **265**
    currency swaps 259–260, 260
    equity derivatives 262–263, 262
    forwards 257
    interest-rate options 260–261
    interest-rate swaps 258–259, 258
    synthetic securities 266–268, **267**
Detroit, Michigan, bond investors' losses 74
Deutsche Bank 242
Deutsche Börse 182, 202–203
Deutsche Telecom 160
devaluation 33, 36
  and the crawling peg 37
  and exchange-rate bands 36
  and the gold standard 32
  and the IMF 33
  Mexico devalues the peso 145
development banks 58
difference ("diff") options 260–261
dim sum bonds 104
Direct Edge electronic exchange 184
discount brokerages 191
discount rate 65, 89
disintermediation 44
dispute settlement 14
dividends 167–168
  yields 167, **168**
dollar: displaced by euro as main currency of bond issuance 106, 143
Dow Jones Euro Stoxx 50 index 195, 224
Dow Jones Industrial Average (DJIA) 194, 195, 224

Dow Jones Transportation Average 194
Dow Jones Utility Average 19
duration, bond 89
Dutch East India Company 154

earnings, firm's 166
earnings before interest, taxes, depreciation and amortisation (EBITDA) 166
earnings per share 177
East Asia, 1997 crisis 35
economic growth 37, 64, 65, 67, 129, 166, 169, 170
economies of scale 15
Economist, The 232
    Big Mac Index 38
education lending agencies 58
efficient market hypothesis 171
electricity
    deregulation 216
    utilities 217
electronic information systems, and price quotations 39–40
electronic trading 208–209
    auction markets 189–190
    bond markets 82–84
eliminate order 189
emerging markets
    bonds 71, 83, 105–107, 106, 145–146
    borrowers, biggest 146, **146**
    companies 107
    countries 187–188, *188*
        government debt 57
        treasury-bill issuance 56, 57
    currencies 28
    debt 106
    portfolios 110
employers
    and pension funds 12
    shares in 9
employment 94
entertainment securitisations 129–130
equities **4, 5, 6**
    a cross-border financing source 5
    foreign 272–273
    and individual investing 9–10
    the origins of 154–155, **155, 156**
equity funds 50
equity market capitalisation 155, **155**
equity markets 120–196
    activity slows (2000–2001) 6
    balancing act 157
    clearing and settlement 193
    competition in trading 190–191

depositary receipts 186–188
    emerging markets 187–188, *188*
equity 157
factors affecting share prices 166–174
    analysts' recommendations 169
    asset value 168
    beta 173
    bond returns 170
    cash flow 167
    dividends 167–168, **168**
    earnings 166
    fads 170
    general economic news 170
    inclusion in an index 169
    interest rates 169
    key numbers 171–172
    market efficiency 171
    price/earnings ratio 172–173, **172**
    return on capital 174
    return on equity 173–174
    stock splits 170–171
    value added 174
flotation process 162–166
    different approaches to selling shares 163–164
    investing in IPOs 164–165
    share repurchases 165–166
how stock exchanges work 189–190
institutional trading 191–193
    basket trades 192
    block trades 192
    program or algorithmic trades 192
    short sales 192–193
international listings 186
investing on margin 193–194
measuring market performance 194–196
    price measures 194–196, **196**
    risk measures 196
measuring return 175
obtaining share price information 176–177, **177**
off-market trading 185–186
origin of equities 154–155, **155, 156**
over-the-counter market 177–178
raising capital 155–158
    balancing act 157
    equity 157
    loans 156–157
    venture capital 157–158
stock exchanges 178–184, **179, 180**
    the biggest exchanges 180–184, **181, 183**

trading shares 188–189
types of equity 158–162
  common stock or ordinary
    shares 158–159
  convertible preferred stock 159
  flotation 160–161, **161**
  issuing shares 159–160
  preferred stock 159–160
  private offering 161–162
  secondary offering 162
  warrants 159
  venture capital 157–158
equity options 235, 252
equity-index options 241
Estonia
  currency pegged to the euro 34
  the euro adopted as its currency 34
Eurex 202, 208, 218, 225, 226, **226**, 236,
  241, 244
Euribor 59
euro, the
  and commercial paper 54
  dollar/euro trades 27
  and exchange-market activity 18
  and issuance of international
    securities 141, **142**
  launch of (January 1999) 18, 27–28,
    141, 223
  and reduction of trading in
    European centres 27–28
  replaces dollar as main currency of
    bond issuance 106, 143
Euro Libor 236–237
Euro-Stars index of 29 euro-zone
  stocks 195
Eurobonds 104, 139, 153
Euroclear, Brussels 63
Eurodollar paper 141
Eurodollars 137, 221
Eurokiwis 141
Euromarkets 137–139, 141, 149, 153
Euronext 181, 182–183, 203, 208, 213,
  243
Europe
  asset-backed commercial paper 131
  asset-backed securities 113
  auto-loan securities 128
  bond insurance 100
  CMBS issuance 120
  corporate-bond market 77
  credit-card securities 128
  financial meltdown (2008–13) 5
  high-yield markets 101
  large government deficits (from
    2008) 57

mortgage securities 123
repo market 62
  and securitisation 116, **127**
  venture capital 158
European Central Bank (ECB) 65,
  66–67
European depositary receipts (EDRs)
  186, 187
European Energy Exchange 203
European Exchange Rate Mechanism
  35–36
European Investment Bank, bond
  issuers 144
European Union
  and bond interest 153
  debt securities trading in 83
  Euronext bread-wheat contract 213
  government bonds 99
  reduced government debt (1990s)
    57
  share prices quoted in euros 182
European-style options 240
Euroyen 141
ex-dividend stock 168
exchange of futures for physicals 231
exchange rates
  abandonment of fixed exchange
    rates 204
  bond prices and returns 94–95, **95**
  covered interest arbitrage 30–31
  covered interest parity 31
  and currency trading 18, 23
  determined by market forces 18
  exchange-rate crises (1990s) 6
  forward 30
  the fundamental price in any
    economy 17
  and futures market 19
  government intervention 23, 107
  managing *see under* foreign-
    exchange markets
  and real interest rates 30
  stabilisation of 223
  trade-weighted 42–43, 43
  volatile 2, 30
  why they change 30–31
execute order 189
expiration dates 240
exporters 22
extension risk 134

Facebook 161
fallen angels 102, 103
Fannie Mae 74, 118, 118–119, 121, 122,
  125, 126

Farmer Macs 122–123
farmers, early
    and a basic financial market 2
    volatile exchange rates 2
Federal Agricultural Mortgage Credit
    Corporation (FAMCC) 122–123
Federal Home Loan Bank System 58
Federal Home Loan Mortgage
    Corporation (FHLMC) 122
Federal National Mortgage
    Association (FNMA) 118, 121
Federal Reserve Board 121, 131
fill-or-kill orders 189, 205
film distribution companies 129
financial crises
    Asia and Russia (1998) 5
    Europe financial meltdown (2008–
        13) 5, 141, 143
    and credit markets 7
    United States financial meltdown
        (2008–09) 5
    United States recession (2001) 5
    worldwide 45–46, 52, 53, 101, 107,
        113–114, 187, 232
financial futures 204
financial industry, consolidation in
    182
financial institutions, failures of 7
financial markets
    attributes of larger markets 13–14
    forces of change 14–16
        consolidation 15
        deregulation 15
        globalisation 15–16
        liberalisation 15
        technology 14
    growth in 1990s 6
    historic 1–2
    investors 9–13
        algorithmic traders 12–13
        hedge funds 11–12
        insurance companies 12
        mutual funds 10, **11**
        pension funds 12
        other institutions 13
    rise of the formal markets 13–14
    roles of 2–3
    size of 3–6, **4**, **5**
        cross-border measure 4–5
        international breakdown 5–6, **6**
        turn-of-the-century slowdown 6–9
financial meltdowns
    Europe (2008–13) 5
    United States (2008–09) 5
financial reports 171–172, 186

Financial Times Stock Exchange
    (FTSE) 224, 242
    100 stock index 194, 241
Fitch 63–64, **64**, 90
fixed-rate systems
    Bretton Woods 33
    gold standard 32–33
    pegs 33–34
    shortcomings 34–35
flex options 239
floating rates 37, 125
    managing 38–39
floor trading 189, 190, 192
floors 260
flotation 160–161, **161**
    all-or-nothing offering 163
    best-efforts basis 163
    investment banker as underwriter
        163
flotation process *see under* equity
    markets
follow-on offering 162
Ford Motor Company 252
foreign direct investment 22
foreign-exchange markets 17–43
    average daily turnover 17
    comparing currency valuations
        37–38
        indications of overshooting 38
    currency markets and related
        markets 21–22
        gearing up 21–22
    fall in trading at turn of the century
        7
    favourite currencies 27–28, **27**, **28**
    growth of trading 18
    Herstatt risk 29
    history 17–18
    how currencies are traded 19–21
        the derivatives market 20–21, 21
        the futures market 19
        the options market 20
        the spot market 19
    main trading locations 23–26, **24**, **25**
    managing exchange rates 32–37
        fixed-rate shortcomings 34–35
        fixed-rate systems 32–34
        floating rates 37
        semi-fixed systems 35–37
    managing floating rates 38–39
    obtaining price information 39–42
        cross-rates 41, **42**
        currency indexes 42
        forward rates 40, **41**
    the players 22–23

exporters and importers 22
governments 23
investors 22
speculators 23
role of 17
settlement 28–29
trade-weighted exchange rate 42–43,
43
why exchange rates change 30–31
covered interest arbitrage 30–31
covered interest parity 31
real interest rates 30
foreign-exchange swaps 20, 21, **24**, 25
forward contracts (forwards) 20, 25, 31,
76, **148**, 197, 253, 257, 272
forward exchange rate 30
forward markets 31, 39
forward rate agreements 20
forward rates 31, 40, **41**
forward transactions **24**
France
and bond markets 76–77, 95
French notional bond contract 201
longer-term debt 56
Obligations assimilable du trésor
(OATs) 73
short-term debt 56
Frankfurt stockmarket 195
Freddie Macs 74, 122
fund managers
hedge funds 11–12
mutual funds and unit trusts 10
and NYSE indexes 196
fundamental analysis 169
futures
agricultural 210, 212–214, **212**, **214**
cattle 210
coffee 210, 213
commodity 204, 210
copper 210
currency 20, 24–25, 202, 222–223,
223
energy 216–217, **217**
environmental 217
financial 202, 204, 210, 220–225
gold 215
interest-rate 220–222, 221
metal 202, 214–216, **215**
natural gas 216, **217**
orange juice 210, 218, **218**
risk management 3
share-price 235
stock-index 223–224, 224
sugar 213
trading in 4

futures and options markets 197–252
the characteristics of commodities
198
clearance and settlement 226–227,
251–252
terminating options 251–252
commodity futures market 212–218
agricultural futures 212–214, **212**,
214
commodity-related futures 218
energy futures 216–217, **217**
metals futures 214–216, **215**
contract terms 205–207
contract size 206
delivery date 206
position limits 207
price limits 206–207
quality 206
settlement 207
delivery 230
exchange-traded options 233–239
commodity options 237
currency options 237–238, **238**
equity options 235
index options 235–236, **236**
interest-rate options 236–237
new types of options 238–239
puts and calls 233–234
underlying every option 233
winners and losers 234
expiration dates 240
factors affecting option prices
246–248
gamma 248
rho 248
vega 248
volatility 247–248
financial futures markets 220–225
currency futures 222–223, 223
interest-rate futures 220–221, 221
share-price futures 225
stock-index futures 223–224, 224
other financial futures 225, **226**
futures contracts 203–204
futures and options exchanges
200–202, 201
gains and losses 239–240
hedging strategies 248
baring all 249
covering yourself 249
dynamic hedging 250–251
spreading 250
straddling 249–250
turbo charging 250
how futures are traded 204–205

how options are traded 244
how prices are set 210
    limits on price movements 211
    price movements 210
    quoted price 210
    spot price 211
    term factor 211
margin of security 227–230
    cross-margining 230
    margin calls 228–229
    marking to market 228
measuring performance 232–233
merger pressures 202–203
motivations for options trading
        241–242
    arbitrage 242
    hedging 241
    income 242
    leveraged speculation 241–243
    risk management 241
obtaining price information 211–212,
    244–245, **245**
option exchanges 242–244, **243**
reading commodity futures price
    tables 218–219, **218**
reading financial futures price
    tables 225–226, **226**
styles 240
    American-style options 240
    capped options 240
    European-style options 240
trading 207–209
    continuous-auction or open-
        outcry trading 207–208
    electronic trading 208–209, **209**
    single-price auction trading 208
trading strategies 231–232
    basic trading 231
    dynamic hedging 231
    index arbitrage 231
    spreads 231
    straddles 232
    strips 232
triple-witching dates 241
types of contracts
    commodity futures 204
    financial futures 204
why trade futures and options?
        199–200
    hedging 199
    speculation 199–200
futures commission merchants 204,
    227–228
futures contracts 19, 20, 25, 62, 198
futures exchanges 184

Futures Industry Association 236
futures market 19

gamma 248
GE Capital 152
gearing 157
    gearing up 21–22
    see also leverage
General Motors 161, 263
general-obligation bonds 74
Generally Accepted Accounting
    Principles (GAAP) 162
Germany
    bond markets 76, 105
    Bundesanleihen (Bunds) 73, 99, 241
    and commercial paper 54
    long-term borrowing 56
    money-market funds 48
    Pfandbriefe 124–125, 135, 153
    pork contracts 213
    share repurchase programmes 165
    technology shares 170
    yield curve 96, 97
Gibson Greetings 271
gilts 73
Ginnie Mae 121–122, 125, 126
global depositary receipts (GDRs)
    186, 187
global warming 217
globalisation 15–16
gold standard 32–33, 138
Goldman Sachs 232
Goldman Sachs Commodity Index
    (GSCI) 232, 235
good-till-cancelled order 189
government agency notes 58, 63
Government National Mortgage
    Association (GNMA) 121–122
governments
    and bond issue 73–74, 76, 80
    bond issuers 144
    budget deficits 70–71
    economic statistics 171
    and exchange-rate management
        32, 107
    and globalisation 15–16
    increased budget deficits to combat
        recession 57
    intervention 23, 39
    managing floating rates 38–39
    rating short-term government debt
        64
    sovereign wealth funds 23
    treasury bills 55–57
Great Depression 52

Greece: government bonds 99
greenhouse gases 217
gross position 29
guarantees, securitisation 114

"hard" assets 266
hard call protection 86
hedge funds 11–12, 185, 265
    speculation 18, 23
hedging 62, 199, 221, 232, 233, 235, 259, 271
    basic hedge 248
    currency 222
    delta 250
    derivatives 269
    dynamic 231, 250–251
    and option contracts 241
    strategies 248
Herstatt risk 29
high-frequency trading 10, 12–13, 18, 23
home purchase, raising capital 3
home-equity loans 68, 117, 128
Hong Kong
    currency pegged to US dollar 34
    foreign bonds 104
Hong Kong Futures Exchange 225
Hong Kong Stock Exchanges 181, 203
housing finance corporations 58
Hypothekenpfandbriefe 124

Ibovespa (Brazil) 224
ICE Futures **25**
ICE Futures Europe 237
illiquid markets 13, 136, 150
IMF *see* International Monetary Fund
immediate order 189
implied volatility 247
importers 22
index arbitrage 231
index equity funds 224
index funds 195
index options 235–236, **236**
indexes
    performance **196**
    price measures 194–195
    stock-price 169
India
    commodity contracts 200–201
    currency options contracts 25
    depositary receipts 186
    economic liberalisation 214
    emerging markets 187
    sale of bonds and short-term paper 144
    and securitisation 116

stock exchanges 179
technology shares 170
trade in stock index options 236
"indications of interest" 80
Indonesia
    1997 crisis 35
    currency pegs 107
industrial capacity utilisation 94
inflation
    and central banks 34, 38, 65–66
    and covered interest arbitrage 30, 31
    effects of 7
    and foreign-exchange markets 17
    high 7, 52
    and higher interest rates 169
    and interest-indexed bonds 8
    low 7, 167
    managing 64–65
    and real interest rates 30
    and returns on bonds 94
    and the three-month rate 68
    and yield curve 96
inflation-indexed bonds 87
informal markets 13
information service providers 177
initial margin 227, 228, 229
initial public offerings (IPOs) 160–161, **161**, 164
    investing in 164–165
innovation
    adjusting to constant innovation 14
    encouraged 115
    and risk management 8
insolvency, of major banks and investment banks 15
institutional investors 50
institutional trading *see under* equity markets
insurance companies 10, **11**, 12, 91, 186, 254
insurance underwriting 4
Integrated Latin American Market 184
Intel Corporation 244–245, 246
Inter-American Development Bank 60
interbank loans 58–59, 63
interbank markets 23
Intercontinental Exchange 184, 203, 206, 243
interest equalisation tax 138, 139
interest rates
    on bank deposits 9–10
    benchmark 99
    on bond investments 9–10
    on a bond issue 79–80
    and bond prices 92–93, 93

central bank 65–66
deregulation of 204
determined by market forces 44–45
euro 243
fall in 48, 106
fixed 128
floating 128, 148
and foreign-exchange markets 17
long-term 48, 56, 66, 71, 101
low-interest-rate environment 6, 77
lowering 34
nominal 94
and prices 50–51, **51**
real 30, 38, 40
rise in 8, 33–34, 36, 59, 64, 99, 108,
    146, 147, 169
short-term 38, 48, 51, 52, 56, 62,
    66–69, 87, 96
interest-rate options 236–237, 260–261
    contracts 76
intergenerational equity 72
intermediation 47
internalisation 185
international agency paper 60, 63
International Capital Markets
    Association (ICMA) 151
international equity issues 179–180,
    180
international fixed income markets
    137–153
    bond issuance 140, 149–150
    Euromarkets, a brief history of
        137–139
        back in business 138–139
        market surge 138
    global bonds 149
    the international bond market
        today 139, 140, 141–142, **142**
    the issuers 144–146, **145, 146**
    looking ahead 153
    money-market instruments 142–143,
        143
    obtaining price information 151–152,
        152
    swaps market 147–149, **148**
    towards international standards 151
    trading 150
    types of instruments 146–147
        equity-linked bonds 147
        fixed-rate bonds 147
        floating-rate bonds 147
international listings 186
International Monetary Fund (IMF)
    lending to members 33
    and share fads 170

special drawing rights (SDRs) 33
International Petroleum Exchange,
    London 203, 216, 217
    Brent Crude contract 210
international portfolio investment 22
International Securities Exchange
    203–204, 244
international spread 231
International Swaps and Derivatives
    Association 255
internet
    and bond sales 80
    brokerages 191
    and share prices 176
intervention 23, 39
intra-commodity spread 231
intrinsic value 246
inverse (reverse) floaters 261, 271–272
inverted market 211
investment
    algorithmic traders 12–13
    bond 9
    capital gains 9
    foreign direct 22
    and foreign-exchange markets 17
    hedge funds 11–12
    individual 9–10, 15
    institutional 10–13, **11**, 15, 18
    insurance companies 12
    international portfolio 22
    mutual funds 10
    overnight investments 50
    pension funds 12
    role of financial markets 3
    yield 9
investment banks
    and bond indexes 108
    and bonds 78, 80, 86, 149
    distribution of shares on best-
        efforts basis 163
    indexes of performance of asset-
        backed securities 136
    insolvency 15
    and IPOs 164–165
    and repos 61
    and securitisation 113, 119–120
    speculators 23
investment companies 10, 11, 15, 44,
    45, 50
Investment Company Institute 48
investment funds **11**, 23, 47, 253
investment managers 108
investment trusts 10, 50
investor protection/regulation 14
Ireland, and securitisation 123

irredeemable debentures 85
Italy
    government bonds 99
    local government bonds 74
    and securitisation 116
    volatile stock exchange 196
    iX (proposed single exchange) 182

Japan
    bankers' cartel 76
    Bond Issue Arrangement
        Committee 76
    bonds 73, 74
    commodity exchanges 202
    cross-border share and bond
        transactions 5
    discount rate 65
    economy 67
    foreign bonds 104
    gensaki market (repos with
        Japanese government bonds) 62
    government bonds (JPGs) 73
    high-yield markets 101
    institutional investors 10
    liberalisation 15
    long-term bonds 56
    money-market funds 48
    overnight rates 67–68, 67
    and securitisation 116, 125–126
    share price decline 180
    short-term securities 56
    stock exchange merger (2013)
        183–184
    and trade in government securities
        84
    weighted indexes 109
    yield curve 96, 97
Japan Housing Finance Agency 126
Japanese yen, dollar/yen trades 27
JASDAQ (Tokyo) 181
Johannesburg SE 25
joint ventures 184
Journal of Commerce 232
JP Morgan Emerging Market Bond
    Index Plus (EMBI+) 109
junk bonds 101

Kansas City Board of Trade 202,
    208
Kennedy, President John 138
Keynes, John Maynard 154
Korea Exchange 25, 242
Korean Futures Exchange 235
KOSPI (South Korea) 224
Kuwait, pegs and baskets 36

labour unions 12
Latin America
    depositary receipts 186
    emerging markets 187
    and exchange-rate problems 145
    stock exchanges 184
LEAPS (long-term equity participation
    securities) 239
legal procedures
    enforcing contracts 14
    settling disputes 14
Lehman Brothers 84, 270
lending, reduction in 6, 7
lesser maintenance margin 228
letters of credit 130
leverage 21–22, 72, 101, 174, 267
    see also gearing
leveraged speculation 241
liberalisation 15
Libor *see* London inter-bank offered
    rate
life insurance companies 119–120
life insurance policies 12, 129
limit down 211
limit move 211
limit orders 188–189, 204
limit up 211
liquidation of the initial contracts 205
liquidity 13–14
    and after-hours trading 209
    and futures and options exchanges
        200
    futures contracts 257
    lack of 65
    of main bond markets 105
    meeting short-run liquidity needs
        45
    and money markets 46, 47
    and repos 60
    short-term liquidity transactions 44
    and speculation 199–200
    and stock exchanges 178
Lisbon Stock Exchange 181, 183
listing particulars/prospectus 162
loans
    automotive 113, 117, 128–129, 133
    and averting bankruptcy 54
    bank 72, 139, 156, 258
    and bankers' acceptances 55
    central bank loan rates 65
    and commercial paper 53
    credit-card 68, 133, 134
    domestic 4
    floating-rate 59, 258
    home-equity 68, 117, 128

interbank 58–59, 139
international bank **4**, 5–6, **5**
mortgage 68
overnight 59
repayment 35
repo 61
short-term 59, 139
small business 129
student 129, 130
subprime 128
syndicated **6**, 16
uncollateralised 66
unsecured 59
local government notes 58, 63
local governments 58
locked market 211
London
  currency trading 24, 27, **28**
  foreign banks set up offices 139
  most important location for
    international share trading 186
London inter-bank offered rate (Libor)
  59, 133, 258, 261, 268
London Metal Exchange 203, 215–216,
  229, 241
London Stock Exchange 2, 150, 178,
  180–183, 196
London Stock Exchange Group 202
long position 205
Luxembourg Stock Exchange 150

Maebashi Dried Cocoon Exchange
  202
maintenance margin 194, 229
managed float 35–37
  bands 35–36
  the crawling peg 36–37
  pegs and baskets 36
  target zones 36
manufactured-housing securities 129
margin calls 194, 228–229
margin loan 194
marginal lending rate 65
market efficiency 171
market in backwardation 211
market in contango 211, 219
market orders 188, 204
market performance, measuring
  194–196
  price measures 194–196
    averages 194
    indexes 194
market-if-touched orders 204
marketmakers 189, 191
marking to market 228

matched book trading 61
matched sale-purchase transactions 65
MATIF, Paris 201
maturity, bond 87–88
medium-term notes 141, 142
mergers
  among commodity exchanges
    292–293
  and cross-margining 230
  forced 15
Metallgesellschaft 271
MexDer **25**
Mexico
  abandons its crawling peg 37
  bond markets 71
  bond sales abroad 144
  debt crisis (1995) 57
  devalues the peso 145
  floating rates 37
  trade-weighted exchange rate 42
MF Global 229
MICeZ/RTS, Russia **25**
Milan stock exchange 202
Monetary Control Act (1980) (US) 44
monetary policy
  and the ECB 66
  and money markets 64–65
money changers, street-corner 2
money markets 44–69
  credit ratings and the money
    market 63–64, **64**
    tier importance 64
  defined 44, 46
  and foreign-exchange trading 21
  "freezing" of 45–46
  futures and the money markets 62
  how trading occurs 62–63
  interest rates and prices 50–51
  investing 3
  investing in money markets 47–50
    individual sweep accounts 50
    institutional investors 50
    money-market funds 47–48, **48**
    stable value 49–50
  money markets and monetary
    policy 64–66
    central bank interest rates 65–66
  repos 60–62
  types of instruments 51–60, **51**
    bankers' acceptances 55
    commercial paper 50, 52–55, **53**
    government agency notes 58
    interbank loans 58–59
    international agency paper 60
    local government notes 58

time deposits 59–60
treasury bills 55–57, **57**
watching short-term interest rates
66–69
overnight rates 67–68, 67
the prime rate 68
spreads 66–67
UK mortgage rates 69
what money markets do 46
money-market funds 47–48, 48, 50, 52
money-market instruments 142–143,
143
moneychangers 19
Moody's Investor Services 63–64, **64**,
90
mortgage-backed securities *see under*
securitisation
mortgages
adjustable-rate mortgage loans 68
agricultural 123
commercial 116
fixed-rate 125, 134
office-building 114
primary mortgage market 118
secondary mortgage market 118, 123
UK mortgage rates 69, 125
US home mortgages go into default
272
Moscow Narodny Bank 137
Multi-Commodity Exchange of India
203, 214, 216, 223
multinational corporations 144, 186
multiple-index floaters 261
mutual funds 10, 50, 82, 131, 136
mutual ventures 182

naked calls 249
naked puts 249
NASDAQ 178, 180, 181, 184, 191
NASDAQ 100 Index 224, 244
NASDAQ Composite Index 195
NASDAQ OMX PHLX (previously
Philadelphia Stock Exchange) 26,
237, 243, 244, 252
National Association of Securities
Dealers Automated Quotation
System (later NASDAQ) 180
National Commodity and Derivatives
Exchange 214
national debt-management offices 86
National Home Loans 125
National Housing Act (Canada) 123
National Stock Exchange (formerly
known as Cincinnati Stock
Exchange) 184

National Stock Exchange of India 25,
26, 223
net position 29
net value 255
Netherlands, and commercial paper
54
netting 26, 257
New York, currency trading 24
New York Board of Trade (NYBOT)
206, 213, 218, 235
New York Cotton Exchange 203
New York Mercantile Exchange 202,
216
New York Stock Exchange (NYSE) 1,
180–184, 194, 203, 225, 239
ARCA options exchange 244
New York Stock Exchange Composite
Index 195
NHA MBS 123
Nikkei 225 index 224
Nikko Bond Performance Index 109
Nomura Bond Performance Index 109
non-mortgage securities *see under*
securitisation
non-refundable bonds 85
normal market 211
notional principal 254
notional value 254–255, 261

Obligations assimilable du trésor
(OATs) 73
OBX share-price index 224
Oeffentliche Pfandbriefe 124
off-market trading 185–186
offer document 77–78
official statement (bond issuance)
77–78
oil market 13
oil refiners 217
"open interest" 219
open order 189
open repos 61
open-market operations 65–66
open-outcry trading 207–208, 209
Oporto stock exchange 183
option traders 246
optionality factory 132–133
options 253
American-style 240
barrier 20
bond 236
capped 240, 260
commodity 237, 252
currency 20, 25–26, 202, 237–238, 238
difference ("diff") 260–261

equity 235, 244, 252
equity-index 241
European-style 240
exchange-traded 20, 251, 256
flex 239
global foreign-exchange market
    turnover **24**
index 235–236, **236**
interest-rate 236–237, 260–261
metal 202
multi-asset 261
naked 249
path-dependent 268
price information 244–245, **245**
risk management 3
spread 260
step-down 262
and structured securities 87
trading 244
yield 236–237
see also call options; put options
    and under futures and options
    markets
options contracts 22
    currency 25–26
options exchanges 184, 242–244, **243**
options markets 20, 233, 234, 246
Organisation for Economic Co-
    operation and Development
    (OECD) 10
originator, the 118, 119
Osaka Stock Exchange 183–184
Oslo Stock Exchange 225
"out trades" 227
over-the-counter, derivatives 238
over-the-counter transactions 82,
    177–178
    currency options 26
    international bonds 150
overleveraged (highly geared) firms
    157
overnight loans 59
overnight rates 67, 67
overnight repos 61, 100

Pacific Exchange 244
par value 85, 88
Paris
    and introduction of the euro 27–28
    stock exchange 181, 182–183
pass-throughs 119, 121, 122, 124
path-dependent option 268
pay-as-you-go schemes 8
payment for order flow 191
payment-in-kind (PIK) 102

pegs 33–35, 107
    and baskets 36
    the crawling peg 36–37
pension funds **11**, 12, 50, 82, 91, 167,
    186
pensions
    old age pension (UK) 7
    pay-as-you-go schemes 7–8
    pre-funded individual pensions
        8, 12
    private pension schemes 8
    social security programme (US) 7
People's Bank of China 126
per-share value 49
performance bond 227
perpetual debentures 85
Peruvian stock exchange 184
PetroChina 160
Pfandbriefe 124–125, 135, 153
Pfizer 239–240
Philadelphia Stock Exchange (later
    NASDAQ OMX PHLX) 26, 178, 243,
    244
Philip Morris International 160–161
physicals (bulk commodities) 204, 231
Pittsburgh, Pennsylvania 80
planned amortisation class (Z tranche)
    133
points (smallest allowable price
    movements) 207
pork-belly contract 202
portfolio insurance 251
portfolio managers 110, 223
Portugal, stock exchanges 182, 183
position limits 207
pound sterling, minor role in London
    market 27
preferred stock 158–159
    convertible 159
prepayment risk 134
price discovery 2
price setting 2
price/earnings ratio ('the multiple')
    172–173, **172**
price/yield curve 93, 93
prices
    agricultural 218
    arbitrage 3
    bond 91, 91–95, 93, 106, 170
    commodity 94, 232
    domestic currency 39
    energy 218, 261
    international market price
        information 151–152, **152**
    "lifetime high" 219

"lifetime low" 219
and low inflation 7
market 2, 192, 235
metals 215
natural gas 216
obtaining price information 39–40,
    244–245, **245**
oil 216, 234, 271
option 244–245
price analyses of various products
    in different countries 38
price movements 210–211
price transparency 84
the quoted price 210
settlement 219
share 5, 10, 175, 241, 251
    collapses of 2008–09 180
    factors affecting *see under* equity
        markets
    obtaining information 176–177,
        177
    worldwide fall (2000) 181
shares, emerging-market 188
stabilising domestic 37
volatility 106, 145
pricing (of fixed-rated asset-backed
securities) *see under* securitisation
prime rate 68
private offering 161–162
private pension schemes 8
privatisation 160
Procter & Gamble 271
program trades 192
property insurance policies 129
prospectus (bond issuance) 77–78
"protection" 263–264
public-sector debt 75
purchasing power parity 38
put options 234, 235, 239, 240, 241,
    244, 246
    naked 249
putable bonds 85, 87

QQQ option 244
QQQ trading **243**
qualified institutional buyers (QIBs)
    150
quality differential spread 231

rail cars, loans on 129
raising capital 3
random walk 171
rating agencies 89–91, 99, 105, 109, 118,
    134, 144, 145
ratio swaps 271

real interest rates 30
real-time settlement 63
recession
    countries enter recession (2001) 107
    and "freezing" of money markets
        45–46
    and gold standard 32
    United States (2001) 5
red herring 162
redundancies 73
Refco 229
reliability 14
REMICs (real estate mortgage
    investment conduits) 120
repo rate 60, 66–67
repurchase agreements (repos) 60–62,
    65, 66, 100–101, 271
reserves
    foreign-currency 74
    gold 138
Resolution Trust Corporation 119
return on capital 174
return on equity 173–174
Reuters, and price quotations 39–40
Reuters/Commodity Research Board
    Index 235
Reuters/Jeffries Commodities
    Research Bureau Index 232
revenue bonds 74
reverse repos 61, 100, 101
reverse stock splits 170–171
rho 248
rising stars 102–103
risk management 3, 8–9, 197, 233, 241
risk measures 196
risk(s)
    accounting 272–273
    attaching a price to risk 3
    and bond markets 71, 72
    and commercial paper 54–55
    counterparty 63, 256, 264
    credit 133–134
    currency 105, 107
    exchange-rate 20
    extension 134
    and hedging 199, 221
    and high-yield issuers 101
    legal 256
    prepayment 134
    price 256
    ratings on bond issuance risk 89–91,
        90
    of recording artists 115
    redistribution of 8
    reinvestment 86

risk aversion of money-market
investors 45
servicing 135
settlement 257
synthetic securities 268–269
trading 3
underwriting 134–135
RMX exchange 213
Roche Holding 149
Rome, and introduction of the euro
27–28
Russell 2000 index 244
Russia
bonds 73, 106, 107, 110
exchange-rate problems 145
financial crisis in (1998) 5, 57, 107,
272
Russian exchange 25

S&P/Case Shiller Home Price Index
225
Sallie Mae 129
samurai bonds 104
São Paulo Stock Exchange, Brazil 24,
202
savings, retirement 10, 12
school authorities 58
secondary dealing 82
secondary markets 99, 118, 120, 122,
129, 150
secondary offering 162
securities
acquired by investment trusts 10
agency 120–123, **120**
and algorithmic trading 12
asset-backed *see* asset-backed
securities
available information about 14
commercial mortgage-backed
(CMBS) 119–120
credit-card 127–128
debt **71**, 76, 80, 83, 139, 141, 145
euro-dominated 141
fixed-income 71, 135
floating-rate 261
and foreign-exchange trading 21
government 67, 84, 96, 97, 98, 142,
150
long-term equity participation
(LEAPS) 239
longer-term 46, 125
manufactured-housing 129
money-market 47, 49, 50–51, 58, 61
mortgage-backed *see under*
securitisation

non-mortgage *see under*
securitisation
prices 12, 13
registration of new 52
in retirement accounts 9
sale of 4, 5, 65
short-term 49, 50, 56, 143
structured 87, 131–132
synthetic 266–268, **267**
underlying interest-rate-sensitive
222
US Treasury 68
securities analysts 169
Securities and Exchange Commission
52
securities markets, size of 139, 139, 141
securities regulator 162
securitisation 7, 111–136
asset-backed commercial paper
130–131
buying asset-backed securities 135
categories of asset-backed securities
112
defined 113, 156–157
market development 116–118, 117,
117
measuring performance 135–136
mortgage securities outside the
United States 123–126, **123**
Australia 126
Canada 123–124
China 126
Denmark 124
Germany 124–125
Japan 125–126
UK 125
other parts of Europe 125
mortgage-backed securities 118–120,
123, 124, 267
CMBS 118, 119–120
Fannie Mae led the way 118–119
pass-through certificates 119
REMICs 120
spreads on 133–134
non-mortgage securities 126–130, **127**
automotive loans 128–129
credit-card securities 127–128
home-equity loans 128
manufactured-housing securities
129
student loans 129, 130
assorted others 129–130
pricing 133–135
asset characteristics 134
credit risk 133–134

extension risk 134
prepayment risk 134
rating 134
servicing risk 135
underwriting risk 134–135
the process 113
securitisation process 113–114
recourse to guarantees 114
structured finance 131–133
the optionality factor 132–133
of unsound loans 113–114
US agency securities 120–123, **120**
Fannie Maes 121
Farmer Macs 122–123
Freddie Macs 122
Ginnie Maes 121–122
why securitise? 114–116
security
enhancing 99–100
bond insurance 100
covenants 99
sinking funds 100
sell orders 208
semi-fixed systems 35–37
bands 35–36
the crawling basket 36–37
the crawling peg 36–37
pegs and baskets 36
target zones 36
semi-sovereigns 74, 75
servicing risk 135
session trading 208
settlement 28–29, 193, 207, 227, 251
Shanghai Futures Exchange 216
Shanghai Stock Exchange 181
share-price indexes 235
shareholders' funds 114
shares
different approaches to selling
163–164
early shareholder-owned
enterprises 154
in employers 9
factors affecting prices see under
equity markets
fads 170
and foreign-exchange markets 22
gilt-edged 73
and globalisation 16
indexes of 109, *188*
issuing 159–160
market value 194
negotiable share certificates 154
obtaining share price information
176–177, **177**

ordinary (common stock) 158
raising capital 3, 13
selling 13
share repurchases 165–166
technology 170, 172
trading 188–189
the value of share turnover 155, **156**
shipping containers, loans on 129
short sales 192–193
short-term demand deposits 44
short-term euronotes 142
short-term notes 62, 67
Singapore
foreign bonds 104
over-the-counter currency options
26
pegs and baskets 36
single European currency 35, 77, 99,
142, 201, 223
single-price auction trading 208
sinking funds 100
small businesses, bank lending to 4,
156
small-cap stocks 173
South Korea
1997 crisis 35
bond markets 77, 110
currency pegs 107
exchange-rate problems 145
floating rates 37
liberalisation 15
merger of stock and futures
exchanges 243
South Korean stock index 235, 242
sovereign ceiling 105
sovereign wealth funds 23
sovereigns 73–74, 75
Spain
bonds 74
and commercial paper 54
government bonds 99
mortgage-backed securities 133–134
and securitisation 123
special drawing rights (SDRs) 33
special-purpose bonds 74–75
specialists 189
speculation 199–200, 232
leveraged 241
speculators 23
sports securitisations 130
spot market 19, 21, 21, 24, **24**, 29, 31
spot price 211
spot rates 40
spot transactions **24**
spread option 260

spreading 250
spreads 13, 24, 40, 47, 66–67, 92, 98–99,
    133–134, 191, 231
stabilisation programmes 144
stable value 49–50
Standard & Poor's (S&P) 63–64, **64**,
    90, 103
    500 stock index 191, 195–196, 210,
        224, 235
step-down options 262
step-up bonds 87, 91
step-up coupon notes 261
stock brokerages 177
stock dividend (capitalisation issue)
    168
stock exchanges 178–184
    the biggest exchanges 180–184, **181,
        183**
    demutualisations 182, **183**
    how they work 189–190
    London 2
    National Stock Exchange of India 25
    New York 1
    order books 192
    Philadelphia (now NASDAQ OMX
        PHLX) 26
    Russian exchange 25, 26
    secondary dealing 82
    securities traded 135
    selling shares 13
stock markets
    crash of 2008–09 9
    investing 3
    rise in (2012–13) 8
    volatility 196
stock price
    indexes 169
    stock price drops (October 1997 and
        September 1998) 196
stock splits 170–171
stockbrokerage commissions 252
stop order 189
straddles/straddling 232, 249–250
straight bonds 85
strike price 234, 242, 244, 244–245
strips 232
STRIPS (separately registered interest
    and principal of securities) 86, 132
structured securities 87, 131–132
    the optionality factor 132–133
Student Loan Marketing Association
    (SLMA) 129
student loans 129, 130
subprime loans 128
sulphur dioxide emissions 217

Sumitomo 229
support tranche 132–133
surety bonds 130
swap spreads 148
swaps 79, 147
    credit default 263–265, **265**, 267, 270,
        272
    currency **24**, 26, 259–260, 260
    fixed-for-floating 147–148
    foreign-exchange 20, 21, **24**, 25
    interest-rate 148, **148**, 258–259, 258,
        266, 268
    ratio 271
swaps market 147–149, **148**
swaption 260
sweep accounts 50
Switzerland, sale of bonds and short-
    term paper 144
Sydney Futures Exchange 221, 237
syndicates 78, 149–150
synthetic securities 266–268, **267**

Taiwan, and securitisation 116
target zones 36
taxation 14
    and bond issuance 81
    interest equalisation tax 138, 139
    receipts 58
    revenue generated by formal
        markets 13
    tax anticipation notes 58
    tax increases 73
    tax laws and dividend payments
        167
    withholding tax 153
technical analysis 169
Tel Aviv exchange 25
telecommunications 14
Tennessee Valley Authority 58
term factor 211
term repos 61
Thailand
    1997 crisis 35, 272
    currency pegs 107
    exchange-rate problems 145
Thales 198
three-month rate 67, 68
"ticker" symbols 176
ticks (smallest allowable price
    movements) 207
time deposits (certificates of deposit)
    59–60, 64, 142
time value 246–247
toggle provisions 102
Tokyo, currency trading 24

Tokyo Commodity Exchange 201–202, 216
Tokyo Grain Exchange 213
Tokyo Stock Exchange 180, 184
Toronto Stock Exchange 244
tracker funds 195–196, 224
trade-weighted exchange rates 42–43, 43
trading locations 23–26, **24, 25**
tranches 132–133, 149
transparency 14
transport commissions 58
treasuries, national, intervention by 23
treasury bills (t-bills) 23, 55–57, **57,** 63
treasury stock 165–166
triple-witching days 241
Turkey
    financial crisis in 106
    international debt securities 144
two-for-one splits 170

UK
    bond market 105
    collapse of housing market (2008) 125
    and commercial paper 54
    commissions deregulated 190
    consolidation in 15
    credit-card securities 128
    foreign bonds 104
    high-yield markets 101
    institutional investors 10
    money-market funds 48
    mortgage rates 69
    old-age pensions 7
    over-the-counter currency options 26
    share flotation 163
    short-term treasury debt 56
    and spreads 66
    venture capital 158
    yield curve 96, 97
uncovered ("naked") calls 239
underleveraged firms 157
underlying 204, 233, 234, 242
    commodities/products 207, 210
    exchanging 252
    spreading 250
    volatility 247
underlying assets 204, 206, 231, 247, 248
underlying equity 225
underlying interest-rate-sensitive securities 222
underwriters
    and bond issuance 78–79

setting interest rate on a bond issue 79
    and share sales 163
    underwriting risk 134–135
unemployment
    in Argentina 34
    and interest-rate policy 39
    in United States 129
unit trusts 10
United Arab Emirates, auto-loan securities 128
United States
    agency securities 120–123, **120**
    asset-backed commercial paper 131
    auto-loan securities 128
    balance-of-payments deficit 138
    bankers' acceptances 55
    bond insurance 100
    bond markets 70, **71,** 73–74, 76, **77,** 78, 101, 105
    bond regulations 150
    CMBS issuance 120
    and commercial paper 52, 53, **53,** 54, 64
    commissions deregulated 190
    consolidation in 15
    credit-card securities 127–128
    currency options contracts 25
    dark pools 185
    deregulation by 47–48, 52
    discount rate 65
    economic growth 129
    economic turmoil (2007–09) 164
    financial meltdown (2008–09) 5
    foreign bonds 104
    global bonds 149
    housing-market collapse 267, 272
    individual investment 9
    initial public offerings (IPOs) 160, **161,** 164
    institutional investors 10
    interest rates 6
    large government deficit (from 2008) 57
    largest market for equities 181
    manufactured-housing securities 129
    mortgage securities 113, 136
    national debt 56
    over-the-counter currency options 26
    over-the-counter trading 177–178
    prime rate 68
    private-sector debt securities 76
    recession (2001) 5

red herring 162
reduced government debt (1990s)
57
registration of new securities 52
REMICs 120
repo market 61
rescue of Fannie Mae and Freddie
Mac 74
sale of bonds and short-term paper
144
and securitisation 116, **127**
settlement time 194
share flotation 163
shift of short-term capital into
investment funds 47
social security programme 7
and spreads 66
stock exchanges 179
stockbrokers prohibited from
setting uniform commissions for
share trading 15
time deposits 60
and trade in government securities
84
trading on NASDAQ stockmarket
178
unemployment 129
venture capital 158
yield curve 96, 97
US consumer-price index 225
US Department of Agriculture 123, 225
US dollar
dollar/euro trades 27
dollar/yen trades 27
effect of euro's introduction 28
US Federal Reserve 49, 66, 272
US municipal bond indexes 235
US Treasury
bills 56
bonds (Treasuries) 8, 73, 80, 92, 98,
103, 104, 222, 225
and Farmer Macs 123
securities 68

value added 174

value in vesting 173
variable-rate bonds 87
variation margin 228
vega 248
venture capital 157–158
Veterans Administration 122
volatility 106, 173, 177, 188, 196, 247,
248, 249, 268

wages
increases 94
reductions 73
Walt Disney Co, The 129
Warenterminbörse Hannover 213
warrant bonds 87
warrants 159
weighted average maturity 134
weighted index 108–109
wheat futures contracts 213, **214**
Winnipeg Commodity Exchange 203,
208
World Bank
bond issuers 144
global bonds 149
international agency paper 60
price analyses of various products
in different countries 38

Yankee bonds 104, 138
yield
and bond issuance 81
current 88
defined 9
and foreign-exchange markets 18
yield curve 68, 95–96, 97, 98, 260
inverted 96
"steepening" of 98
yield options 236–237
yield to maturity 88

Z tranche (planned amortisation class)
133
zero-coupon bonds 86, 87
Zhengzhou Commodity Exchange 213